BREAKTHROUGH ASTROLOGY

A19

Transform Yourself and Your World

JOYCE LEVINE

WEISER BOOKS

San Francisco • York Beach, ME

First published in 2006 by
Red Wheel/Weiser, LLC
York Beach, ME
With offices at:
500 Third Street, Suite 230
San Francisco, CA 94107
www.redwheelweiser.com

Library of Congress Cataloging-in-Publication Data

Levine, Joyce.
Breakthrough astrology : transform yourself and your world / Joyce Levine.
p. cm.
ISBN 1-57863-357-5 (alk. paper)
1. Astrology. 2. Horoscopes. I. Title.
BF1708.1.L4642 2006
133.5--dc22   2006004298

Typeset in Minion by Sky Peck Design

Printed in Canada
TCP

10 9 8 7 6 5 4 3 2 1

CONTENTS

*Special thanks to my colleague Michael Lutin
who wrote the foreword, for his support
and encouragement as I wrote this book.*

FOREWORD

From the moment you find out that life is no picnic, you do yourself a big favor by trying to figure out where you're strong, where you're weak, what you need more of and what, if you know what's good for you, you'll get rid of as soon as you can. There are many paths to awareness, and astrology is just one of them.

When you embark on such a journey, you have to understand one thing: Whatever therapist you go to, whatever book you read, you're getting somebody else's spin on what's best for you. Nobody steps off a cloud to help you unravel your mystery. Everybody you talk to, everybody you read, has a point of view. For that reason you need to be as detached and as critical as you can be when turning to anybody for help. There are wonderful astrological practitioners all over this world, so it behooves you to find the one or ones best suited to your ideas, beliefs, and way of thinking. In fact, just walk into an astrology bookstore and you'll see a myriad of philosophies, attitudes, and approaches toward this mystical path toward awareness.

Of course, one could say that the world *doesn't* need another astrology book saying the same old thing rehashed for the millionth time. If you're going to read a book on astrology, it should have a fresh perspective with clear insights. It should be a little edgy so you can have some fun with it. It should be dark when it needs to be dark and hopeful when hope is appropriate. It's got to cut to the chase and give you the real skinny on the what, where, how, when, and why of your horoscope, with no holds barred because these days, who's got time, money, or patience for fluffy, puffed up euphemism?

Breakthrough Astrology is the hot-ticket item for astrology in the twenty-first century. Joyce Levine's work is alive and keenly to the point. She's a no-nonsense writer who knows her stuff and communicates with a direct approach that is as practical as it is spiritually sound. In short, she's definitely one of the cool people you'll find on this path.

—MICHAEL LUTIN

INTRODUCTION

This book is dedicated to you, the reader. I have been involved in astrology for over thirty years and believe it is the best tool for human understanding available. My intent is to make that tool available to you.

For each of us, based upon our date, time, and place of birth, the astrological chart provides a picture of our life potential—what we do easily, where we have problems, and what our motivations are. In essence, it reflects why we are the way we are and why we make the choices that we do.

Once we deeply understand ourselves, it becomes easier to maximize our strengths and work through the personal obstacles that we all have. In all my years of working with people, I have never met a person without internal obstacles. No matter how rich, successful, beautiful, or handsome a person may be, within that person there are internal conflicts. This is human nature. Yet internal conflicts do not negate incredible possibilities.

Where astrology significantly differs from psychology is that in psychology there is a norm, and deviating from that norm is considered "abnormal." In astrology, we recognize that what is normal for one person is not normal for another, whether we are referring to talents or hang-ups. We all have both. The chart is inconsistent. We have wants and needs that conflict with one another. Again, I have never met a person that this was not true of. A happy, successful life comes from balancing these inconsistencies rather than choosing among them.

Sometimes we just need permission to be what we are like. One of the first things I tell new clients is, "The good news is that you were meant to be this way, or you wouldn't have been born at this time." The second thing I tell them is "the bad news is that this is what you have to live with. While we are meant to be the way we are, being human, we all need to be 'tweaked.'" The chart is akin to our genetic makeup. While we can't change our genes, we can express the best or worst of our capabilities. Generally, most of us fall somewhere in between. While it is easy to blame our parents, our boss, or our fate for problems in our lives, that changes nothing. Transformation comes from looking inside. The better we understand ourselves, the better able we are to make changes that bring out the best of our capabilities. To that end, a good portion of this book contains the challenges associated with planetary positions and insights into how to work through these challenges.

To use this book as a transformational tool, it is best to have a copy of your chart in hand and look up the descriptions that apply to you. If you have an internet connection, you can get a free copy of your chart at my web site. It's easy. Just go to *www.joycelevine.com*. On the home page, click on the "Calculate Your Chart" button. This will take you to a page entitled "Your Astrological Chart." Enter your date, time, and place of birth where indicated and hit the "submit" button. This will take you to a page that gives you a picture of your chart and indicates where your planets fall.

Then as you go through and read each section, spend some time considering how each planetary placement affects your life. Clearly, there will be areas of life that you are totally happy with. There is great value in recognizing and appreciating these areas. There will also be areas that you want to transform. Spend some time reviewing the circumstances in your life that reflect the more difficult planetary placements. As you read the suggestions for change, think about what you can do to implement these ideas. You may want to make notes to yourself about specific actions to take that will foster these changes. Remember that transformation takes place one step at a time but is possible for all of us. And as you read each section, try to avoid negative judgments. Be compassionate with yourself and celebrate your strengths.

This book is also meant to be a teaching tool if you are interested in learning astrology in a deep and meaningful way. I also hope this book will help astrology gain its rightful place in the universe. If schoolteachers, guidance counselors, therapists, and all others in helping professions incorporated astrology into the work they already do, they would be better able to guide those they help.

My own journey into astrology started when I was in college studying psychology and a friend "did my chart." She told me things about myself that I not only had never told her but never would. Astrology conveyed information about my character traits and my life with specificity that I had never seen in psychological theories of personality. After college, the same friend and I moved to Boston. I had been working full time and going to school full time and intended to take a year off before going to graduate school to become a social worker or clinical psychologist. But the astrology bug caught me, and I never looked back.

The 1970s were an idealistic time. Social causes were in. Protests against the Vietnam War were ongoing. We baby boomers wanted to save the world. My mantra was, "I don't want to save the world, only the people I reach in it."

Boston in the early 1970s was a center for astrological learning. Famous teachers abounded on every corner. My friend took me to an astrology class with Isabel Hickey, and that one class changed my life. Right then and there, I decided I would be an astrologer. Being young and idealistic, I had no idea that being proficient at something and making a living were very different. I was fortunate. Another well-known astrologer in the area, Oscar Weber, took me under his wing. Oscar had been president of the American Federation of Astrologers. He wrote a column for the *Boston Herald* that actually taught astrology rather than the more typical sun sign column and had a call-in radio show where he answered people's questions. Once I had sufficient knowledge, he referred opportunities to me, such as clients who could not pay his fees and guest spots on radio shows. It took me six years (it was like a kind of graduate training) to learn astrology and how to support myself as a consultant, and I have been working at it ever since.

My study of astrology has led me into many other realms—from the studies of Tarot, Kabbalah, and meditation, to the studies of financial markets and historical events, to working on radio and being interviewed on the radio and television and in newspapers countless times (including having had my picture, along with articles, on the front pages of the *Boston Globe* and its Living/Arts Section), to writing articles for astrology magazines such as *Dell Horoscope* and a monthly advice column in *Horoscope Guide*, to writing a computerized astrology report, AstroAnalysis, and my first book, *A Beginner's Guide to Astrological Interpretation*.

Along the way, in addition to teaching astrology and lecturing to astrological organizations all over the world, I developed a motivational course called Creating the Life You Desire. The course helps people I work with integrate change into their lives by using meditation and visualization techniques. This led me to recording meditation tapes, initially to give to participants in the course and later for wider distribution. The two meditation tape series are: Astrology Series: Pluto, The Shadow or the Light; Neptune, Spirituality or Escapism; Uranus, Erratic Conditions and Upheaval or Freedom to Be Ourselves; Saturn, Handling Your Responsibilities; and Jupiter, Good Luck, Opportunity, Expansion, Abundance; Self-Help Series: Meditation, Creative Visualization, Releasing Anger and Resentment, and Contacting Your Guardian Angel.

For me, my involvement in astrology has been a never-ending search for answers and truth in the universe, a means of personal self-expression, and a way of helping other people find themselves.

I have worked with numerous clients from all walks of life, ranging from welfare moms to venture capitalists. When I first became an astrologer, the image of people who consulted astrologers was something like ditzy females wanting to know about their love lives. In 1988, the press crucified Nancy Reagan for having an ongoing relationship with an astrologer. Yet it had been had rumored for years in the astrological community that the Reagans, both Nancy and Ronald, consulted astrologers. Many other prominent people are working with astrologers behind the scenes, not all of whom are as forthright as J. P. Morgan who was quoted as saying, "Millionaires don't consult astrologers, billionaires do."

In reality, typically, the first time a person comes to see me, he is at a turning point—experiencing a roadblock or feeling dissatisfied with life as it is. Making an appointment is a step toward change. My intent has always been to provide the people who consult me with a better understanding of themselves, why they are the way they are, and ultimately what they can do about it. This is the same intent I have for readers of this book. I wish you the best on your journey.

—JOYCE LEVINE

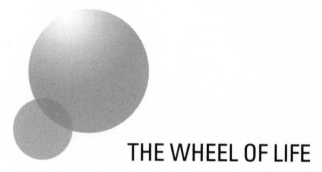

Chapter 1

THE WHEEL OF LIFE

The astrological chart is based on the date, time, and place of birth. It is a map of the planetary positions in the heavens as seen from the earth at that exact moment. You may wonder how it is possible for the planets to affect us. This truly is a mystery. The famous psychiatrist Carl Jung is said to have drawn up charts for all his patients. Jung believed in synchronicity—that simultaneous occurrences reflect one another. Synchronicity tells us that we reflect the characteristics of the planetary placements at our moment of birth. Some scientific explanations assert that the planets exert vibratory pulls that affect us. An increase in arrests and accidents during the time of the full moon is often presented as proof for this line of thinking. Perhaps physics will ultimately provide the answer.

What we do know by observation is that the planetary positions on the date, time, and place of our birth reflect our temperament and therefore our fate. The horoscope, in essence, is like our genetic makeup. What we do with the traits that we are born with is where fate and free will intersect.

The language of astrology is made up of four factors: planets, signs, houses, and aspects. The planets represent the energies of life. They are the major driving forces of our nature. The signs show how these energies or driving forces manifest. The houses show where the action takes place, and the aspects identify the interrelationships among the planets. Using the metaphor of a play, the planets are like the actors, the signs represent the roles they play, the houses are the stage setting, and the aspects show how the actors get along with one another.

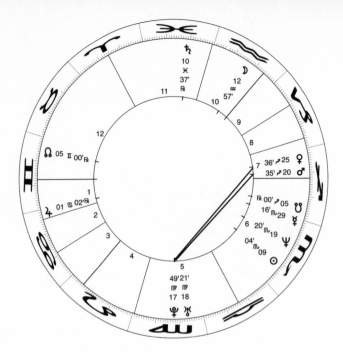

There are ten planets.* Briefly speaking, the Sun represents the sense of identity; the Moon, our emotions; Mercury, the way we think; Venus, our love nature; Mars, how we assert ourselves; Jupiter, values and abundance; Saturn, duty and responsibility; Uranus, freedom urges and independence; Neptune, spirituality and creativity; Pluto, internal drive.

The Moon, Mercury, Venus, and Mars move through the Zodiac relatively quickly. These, along with the Sun, are called the personal planets, and the signs they fall in describe our personal traits. Jupiter, Saturn, Uranus, Neptune, and Pluto take longer to move through the Zodiac (from 12 to 248 years). They are called the outer planets and have to do with social order. Uranus, Neptune, and Pluto, the planets farthest from the Sun, remain in one sign for 7, 14, and 12 to 32 years respectively, and define generational differences and the social and political trends of a timeframe.

Each planet is associated with a particular sign, which it is considered to "rule." When a planet is in its own sign, the planet's functioning is most consistent with its basic nature. The chapter on planets contains a more complete discussion of this. What is important to note is that in our particular charts, planets are not necessarily found in the signs that they are associated with, and this will change the manner in which the planet functions. Traditional astrology uses terms such as exaltations, debilities, and falls to describe the best

---

*While the Sun and Moon are technically not planets but celestial bodies, for purposes of discussion, they will be referred to as planets.

or worst places for each planet. This book refers only to the ruling planet, as the descriptions of the planets in signs speak for themselves.

The entire Zodiac has 360 degrees that are divided in 12 signs of 30 degrees each. The signs are Aries, Taurus, Gemini, Cancer, Leo, Virgo, Libra, Scorpio, Sagittarius, Capricorn, Aquarius, and Pisces. The sign in which a planet falls depicts the expression of that planetary energy. Planets in Aries express independence, directness, and self-sufficiency. Planets in Taurus display patience and stability. Planets in Gemini show versatility and curiosity. Planets in Cancer reflect nurturing and domesticity. So, while the Sun is always a person's sense of identity, if it falls in Aries, a person is direct, independent, and self-sufficient. He sees compromise as giving in. On the other hand, a person with the Sun in Taurus is patient and stable. These are not characteristics we choose to have but rather the ones that we are.

Planets in Leo express magnetism and drama. Planets in Virgo show practicality and discrimination. Planets in Libra seek harmony and cooperation. Planets in Scorpio reflect intensity and are deeply penetrating. So, if a person has Mercury in Libra, she seeks harmony in relationships and in conversation. She considers all sides of an issue before making up her mind. If a person has Mercury in Scorpio, she seeks the bottom-line truth regardless of its political correctness. Again, these are not traits we choose to have, but those we are born with.

Planets in Sagittarius are freedom-loving and optimistic. Planets in Capricorn show ambition and traditionalism. Planets in Aquarius value friendship and individualism. Planets in Pisces display compassion and sympathy. So, if a person has Venus in Capricorn, she is attracted to a conservative mate. On the other hand, if a person has Venus in Aquarius, he equally befriends men and women, does not make distinctions between the sexes, and values friendship as much as love.

The third factor in the horoscope is houses. The houses bring the chart down to earth. Being directly based upon the time and place of birth, a few minutes of time or a change of latitude and longitude produces different placements. A person born at noon in Chicago does not have the same chart, or the same fate, as a person born on the same day at noon in Boston or in Los Angeles. Differences within the same time zone also exist, and a person born in Boston does not have the same house placements as one born in Florida or even New York.

The twelve houses relate to differing departments of life. Each is associated with a particular sign and planet in the natural Zodiac, i.e., the first house with Aries and Mars, the second house with Taurus and Venus, and so forth. But they are not necessarily associated with one another in individual charts. In our charts, the sign on the cusp of each house determines the association, which then reflects our personal attitude in these domains.

Simply speaking, the first house reflects the outer layer of our personality. The second house shows how we make and spend money; the third house, communication. The fourth house reflects home and family; the fifth house, creativity, love affairs, and children; and the sixth house, work and health. The seventh house represents marriage and partnership; the eighth house, what we derive from relationships; the ninth house, philosophy and travel. The tenth house represents career and, along with the fourth house, family; the eleventh house, friendships and associations; and the twelfth house, the subconscious mind.

The fourth factor is aspects. Aspects represent the angular relationships among the planets. Aspects may be favorable or difficult. When aspects are favorable, the areas of life represented by the signs, planets, and houses in which the aspects fall combine easily. When aspects are difficult, problems occur in blending planetary energies. The domains represented by the planets, signs, and houses they fall in are at odds with one another. This creates internal conflict, conflict with others, or both. The chapters on aspects explain this in much more detail, but it is important to keep in mind that easy aspects do not necessarily mean a person does what is right, only that what he does what is easy for him.

The varying combination of all these factors makes us unique individuals. So it takes two people born at the same time and the same place to share the same fate.

The chart as a whole reflects our talents, abilities, and potential problem areas. Just like some gene pools seem more favorable, some horoscopes appear easier to live with than others do. Yet being born rich and beautiful does not guarantee a happy life, and having more favorable planetary positions does not equate with success. In fact, those with few difficult tension aspects typically have less capability to deal with hardship, even though they may have less of it. Those with more difficult charts have more problems but are generally better equipped to handle them, provided they do not give up in their struggles. While it may sound old-fashioned, difficulties build character in ways that ease never does. Ultimately, fate and free will intersect based upon what we do with what we have.

Chapter 2

ELEMENTS OR TRIPLICITIES —YOUR TEMPERAMENT

The twelve signs of the Zodiac are divided into the four elements of fire, earth, air, and water. Fire signs are Aries, Leo, and Sagittarius. Earth signs are Taurus, Virgo, and Capricorn. Air signs are Gemini, Libra, and Aquarius. Water signs are Cancer, Scorpio, and Pisces. The three signs in each element share common temperaments and distinct ways of perceiving the world. Each element has inherent strengths and weaknesses.

The notion of Sun sign compatibility arises from the elements. Fire and air signs, which have outgoing temperaments, are seen as compatible with one another. Water and earth signs, which have more introverted temperaments, are seen as compatible with one another. In reality, life is never so simple. All the planets and the Rising Sign (the cusp of the first house) in the chart must be counted in looking for elemental balance. Our individual charts are a combination of elements, and our worldview reflects this combination.

The fire signs, Aries, Leo, and Sagittarius, are the most positive, or yang, of the elements. They represent the spark, or spirit, of life. They are internally motivated and have their own sense of truth. Fire signs want life to be an exciting adventure. Spontaneous and enthusiastic to the core, they crave activity and directly pursue whatever inspires them. Their dreams focus on the possibilities of what can be and they have difficulty understanding when others do not do the same.

Fire signs like to see themselves as logical but make decisions based more upon intuition than reason. A stirring from within, rather than society's conventions, calls fire signs to pursue a particular goal. In fact, fire signs (with the exception of Leo) care little for what others think. This at times can make them appear insensitive.

Fire signs are more emotional than they care to admit, but are more comfortable with outgoing emotions like enthusiasm or anger. They find the more introverted emotions like sadness or grief difficult to express, and can even be ashamed of having them. Because of this, fire signs find it easier to throw a temper tantrum or make fun of their problems than to show vulnerability. This may make them appear to be unfeeling.

The earth signs, Taurus, Virgo, and Capricorn, are just what the word earth implies—down-to-earth. Their approach to life is practical. They relate to the world through their senses. To earth signs, whatever they can see, feel, taste, or touch is what is real. They possess commonsense reasoning. They are not interested in abstract theories but want tangible evidence. Logic to earth signs is what is provable.

Earth signs have strong needs for financial security. They seek stability. Their approach to life is patient, disciplined, and conservative. Because of this, they excel at handling money, responsibilities, and the day-to-day demands of the material world. Hard work presents no problem, as it is what earth signs expect to do—and what they expect to be rewarded for.

While earth signs are conservative, being earthy, they are the most physical of the elements. They have a strongly sensuous side, whether it has to do with sex or creature comforts. Taurus, particularly, loves a good meal, a fine perfume, and well-made clothes.

It is possible for earth signs to become overly conservative and narrow-minded. Sticking to tradition may be a positive solution to a problem or it may represent a failure to recognize how the world has changed.

The air signs, Gemini, Libra, and Aquarius, are intellectually oriented. These signs are stimulated by ideas. They want the facts. They seek information and knowledge and never tire of learning. Air signs are logical, rational, objective, and clear-thinking. They excel at abstract reasoning and have the ability to stand back and view almost any situation with detached perspective.

Air signs are outgoing and positive like fire signs, but not as spontaneous. They think before they act. They are the communicators of the Zodiac and excel at writing, speaking, planning, and organizing ideas. (They enjoy conversation.) Unlike earth signs, air signs are not concerned with the workability of their ideas, only whether or not the ideas are interesting.

Air is the most socially oriented element. After all, communication can only be interesting if one has interesting people to communicate with. However, air signs relate mind to mind, not heart to heart. Being more comfortable thinking than with feelings, it is hard for air signs to deal with illogical emotions—their own or those of others. Because of this, air has a cold side.

The water signs, Cancer, Scorpio, and Pisces, like fire signs, are internally motivated; but unlike fire, they are motivated by feelings. For water signs, what they feel is what is real. They are sensitive, intuitive, and emotional. They are naturally empathic and compassionate, and possess emotional depth.

Water signs rely on their instincts to make decisions. They easily perceive undercurrents of moods, feelings, and vibrations in whatever environment they find themselves in. This can be a double-edged sword, as it means these same undercurrents influence their own moods. When water signs are in the company of uplifting people, they feel uplifted. When in the company of depressed people, the depressive energy brings them down. Because water signs are so sensitive to what goes on around them, they can be overly sensitive and take things personally that are not meant that way.

Water signs are the natural nurturers. They know what others feel without having to be told and are likely to go out of their way to help those they care about. Rational communication, however, is not their forte and they can expect others to be able to anticipate their needs without being told, and can feel rejected when these needs are not met. In essence, water signs have to be careful of expecting others to be mind readers just because they are.

Chapter 3

QUADRUPLICITIES —YOUR MODE OF ACTIVITY

The signs of the Zodiac are divided into quadruplicities, which are three categories—cardinal, fixed, and mutable—containing the four signs that share similar qualities. The quadruplicities define modes of activity and reflect how signs adapt to circumstances. Each quadruplicity shares certain commonalties even though each one is made up of a fire, earth, air, and water sign. The cardinal signs are Aries, Cancer, Libra, and Capricorn. The fixed signs are Taurus, Leo, Scorpio, and Aquarius. The mutable signs are Gemini, Virgo, Sagittarius, and Pisces. No actual horoscope contains only one quadruplicity, so our individual modes of activity are determined by their combination in our individual charts. Like the elements, each quadruplicity has inherent strengths and weaknesses. The notion of Sun sign incompatibility is based on signs in the same quadruplicity.

The cardinal signs, Aries, Cancer, Libra, and Capricorn, are oriented toward initiation. They act upon present circumstances. Their action or leadership brings forth something new. The type of action is defined by the element in which the sign falls. Aries represents the beginning of spring, Cancer of summer, Libra of autumn, and Capricorn of winter.

Aries, a fire sign, initiates anywhere. Cancer, a water sign, takes action where her feelings direct her; feeling comfortable and secure is a must. Libra, an air sign, displays initiative most easily when it comes to communication, particularly in the relationship arena, while Capricorn, an earth sign, is most likely to initiate in business or practical matters. What these signs have in common is a willingness to take the lead, a need for activity, and a low tolerance for boredom.

People with a cardinal sign emphasis are at their best in start-up situations. They like to get things going. Whether or not they finish anything depends upon the combination of other quadruplicities.

The word "fixed" conveys a perfect image of the fixed signs, Taurus, Leo, Scorpio, and Aquarius. These signs are strong-willed, persistent, and motivated by their own sense of principles. They are goal oriented and complete what they start. Fixed signs do not like change; they preserve what they are familiar with. Taurus, an earth sign, is the most preservation-oriented, particularly when it comes to money and possessions. Leo, a fire sign, preserves whatever sparks his interest. For Leo, it is what his heart is set on that counts. Scorpio, a water sign, preserves whatever she becomes emotionally attached to. Aquarius, an air sign, is most concerned with preservation of his ideas. All of these signs have a stubborn streak.

The mutable signs, Gemini, Virgo, Sagittarius, and Pisces, are flexible. They are versatile and adaptable and easy to get along with. Being idea oriented, they willingly listen to new information and change their minds based on that information. Having a somewhat chameleon-like nature, they can fit into changing environments, which can bring their loyalties into question.

Gemini, an air sign, is concerned with rational ideas and people. Virgo, an earth sign, is most concerned with how to put information to use. Sagittarius, a fire sign, tends toward a more philosophical plane. Pisces, a water sign, focuses on spiritual ideals.

A mutable emphasis conveys adaptability and flexibility. Mutable people (except for Virgo) perform best in situations where they come up with the ideas and someone else carries them out. They may leave projects unfinished or to give in to others when they should stick to their principles.

Chapter 4

THE HOUSES—HERE ON EARTH

The twelve houses represent various departments of life. There is a correlation among planets, signs, and houses, but they do not represent the same things. Going back to the metaphor of a play, the planets represent the energies or life forces. The signs represent the roles that the life forces play, and the houses represent the stage setting, or where the action takes place.

The following descriptions of houses correspond to what is called the natural Zodiac, where Aries is associated with the first house, Taurus, the second, and so forth. The lines that separate one house from another are called cusps.

Our individual charts, calculated for the date, time, and place of our births, do not necessarily follow in this order. This makes the houses the most personal part of the chart. Anyone born on the same day as we were will have the planets in the same signs (unless a planet changes signs during the day). This means that our internal natures are very much alike. However, the rotation of the earth on its axis causes all the signs and planets to pass through each house once every day. Because of this, the house positions of planets and signs and the degrees on house cusps change significantly depending upon the time and place of our births. Since even twins are not born at the same minute, these placements differentiate our fate from that of others born on the same day.

In an actual horoscope, houses may contain a number of planets, one planet, or no planets. Many planets in a house emphasize that department

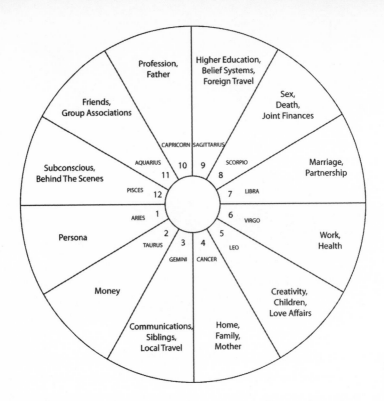

of life. By contrast, empty houses do not mean that nothing happens in that area of life. There are twelve houses and only ten planets, so it is impossible for each house to contain a planet. The sign on the cusp of the house and the placement of the ruler of the sign, as well as planets in a particular house, indicate a person's attitude toward that department of life.

FIRST HOUSE

The cusp of the first house is also known as the Ascendant or Rising Sign. In an individual chart it reflects the exact degree of the sign on the eastern horizon at the moment of birth.

The first house represents the outer layer of the personality, or the face one presents to the outer world, as well as the lens through which one looks at the world. In addition, it affects the physical body, appearance, and health.

The first house has an association with the sign of Aries and the planet Mars and is therefore is associated with new beginnings. Planets found here take on an Aries overtone, but that overtone is manifested through the sign the planets fall in. For instance, planets in the sign of Cancer do not become Arian in nature, but are more likely to take over the immediate environment in Cancer's way of mothering and nurturing. The Rising Sign and any planets in the first house in our individual charts reflect what we are like in new situations and the behavior we are likely to revert to when we feel threatened. A person with a first-house emphasis takes charge of his immediate environment.

The Ascendant is one of the three major personality indicators in the chart, the others being the Sun and Moon. The following descriptions show the outer personality as depicted as each sign rises.

Aries Rising

In new situations, you jump in and are direct and straightforward. Being self-motivated, you place more importance on what you want or what you think is right rather than on the opinions of others. Competitive drive to be number one pushes you but you aspire to positions of leadership more so that you can do what you want than to tell others what to do. You get things done faster than others do. Hence, patience is not one of your strong points, which makes it important not to give up if results do not come as quickly as you would like. You can lose your temper quickly, but you get over it just as quickly and do not hold a grudge. Since the Rising Sign is the way you appear to be, the rest of the chart determines if you are as assertive as you appear to be.

Taurus Rising

You approach unfamiliar situations cautiously. In new circumstances you draw people to you by charm and grace, but are not directly outgoing. You make commitments and take action slowly, thoroughly thinking situations through, not allowing yourself to be pushed. Comfort, money, and security are priorities. You enjoy physical delights of eating a good meal, smelling a fine perfume, or lying back on a comfy couch. You want luxuries now and investments for later. You provide comfort and security for loved ones and expect the same in return. You are easygoing in most situations and dislike disagreements, but underneath your calm exterior lies a resolute, indomitable person. You are loyal and steadfast. You finish what you start.

Gemini Rising

You have a friendly, outgoing manner in new situations. Intellectual curiosity, a sharp mind, and a quick wit give you the ability to talk with almost anyone about almost anything. You enjoy socializing with different types of people, and being adaptable and flexible makes it easy for you to fit into diverse social settings. You excel in communication fields and convincing people of your ideas. Enjoyment comes from learning; once you believe there is nothing left to learn in a situation, boredom sets in and you can become restless. Others see you as fun, intelligent, and easy to get along with. The rest of the chart indicates whether or not you are as easygoing as you appear to be.

Cancer Rising

In unfamiliar situations, you hesitate. You want to feel secure before venturing forth. There is a desire to know how situations will turn out before you enter into them (even when this is not possible). In a room full of strangers you may appear aloof, but more likely you are shy. Yet when comfortable, you make sure everyone feels at home. You are mothering, nurturing, and protective of those you care about. You are sensitive to the emotional needs of others and expect them to be sensitive to yours. Security, emotional and financial, is of the utmost importance. You are sensitive to criticism, even the most constructive. A dislike of disagreements makes it likely for you to sidestep conflict.

Leo Rising

In new situations, you are charming, friendly, and outgoing. Your appearance is typically impeccable. You meet people easily; and no matter how you feel inside, you project self-assuredness and confidence. Initially, you step into leadership roles easily. Love of the limelight and flair for dramatics make it possible to overdo your bid for attention. You appreciate compliments, yet you want admiration and respect for being yourself. You will risk disapproval by standing up for what you believe in. You are direct, honest, loyal, and trustworthy. When it comes to keeping commitments, you finish what you start.

Virgo Rising

You are reserved in new situations with the exception of learning environments, where you want to make sure you gain as much information as possible. You approach the unfamiliar practically and methodically, carefully taking in the details of your surroundings. There is a desire for life to be neat and orderly. A perfectionist at heart, no matter what you do, you want to do it the right way. You are good at seeing details that others miss but must be careful of getting so caught up in details that you miss the bigger picture. However, you are flexible, and if someone shows you a more efficient way of producing results, you gladly make changes.

Libra Rising

In new situations, you are friendly, outgoing, and socially appropriate. What people think of you is important, so you go out of your way to look your best, get along with people, and make a good impression. Seeking harmony and being diplomatic makes you easy to get along with. Typically people see you as charming and nice and having good taste. While you are relationally oriented, you work equally as well with ideas as you do with people. Relationally, you prefer associating with people who are your intellectual and social equals. In romance, you seek an attractive person who shares your interests and becomes your life partner.

Scorpio Rising

In new situations, you prefer the background to the foreground. With astute powers of observation, you notice what goes on around you. You intuitively analyze situations and recognize people's underlying motivations. You make decisions based upon how you feel about things, and your instincts are usually right on. Passion makes you feel alive, and you have an all-or-nothing attitude toward whatever you care about. While you may see yourself as quiet and self-effacing, you exude a sense of power that either attracts or repels others.

Sagittarius Rising

In new situations, you are friendly and outgoing. Faith in the future and the belief that life is primarily good make it easy for you to be open and optimistic. You have a charming exterior and typically get along well with people easily. Yet you are independent and individualistic and refuse to be fenced in. You wish to come and go as you please, and ideally life is an adventure. You have curiosity about what is around the next corner. The desire for travel and excitement are driving forces.

Capricorn Rising

In new situations, you are cautious and reserved. It takes time to warm up to people. This can make you appear cold, but more likely you are somewhat

shy. You have been mature and responsible from an early age, are hard working, and take duty and responsibility seriously. Situations are approached
conservatively. There is respect for older people, tradition, and authority
figures. Being looked up to and respected are important as you aspire to
positions of authority. Once authority has been conferred upon you, leadership is easily assumed.

Aquarius Rising

In new situations, you are friendly and outgoing. You take pleasure in meeting and exchanging ideas with all sorts of people. People find you easy to be
around. Yet you are independent and individualistic. Intellectually, you are
inventive and believe in breaking with the past and moving into new territory.
Though you are social, your ideas and ideals mean more to you than anything else. You are stubborn intellectually, and once you adopt a belief, you
can be so convinced of its truth that you want everyone else to believe it too.

Pisces Rising

You are sympathetic and compassionate, creative and imaginative. In new
situations, you are somewhat reserved as it takes you a while to feel comfortable. You are so sensitive to the moods and vibrations of your immediate
environment that they affect your own moods. Your soul is poetic, and
beauty in your life is a necessity. An idealist, you look for the best in people
and situations. This may cause somewhat of a rose-colored-glasses way of
looking at life. Your imagination can be creative or escapist, and a part of
you may look to rescue others or to be rescued by them.

SECOND HOUSE

The second house represents earned income, money, and movable possessions (not real estate). This house represents earning capacity, gain or loss
through one's own efforts, and how one handles one's personal finances.
This is differentiated from family money, inheritance, or spousal income.

The second house has an association with Taurus and Venus. Planets
found here take on Taurus' concern with money, possessions, and security,
but what is valued depends upon the sign on the cusp of the house and the
planets and signs that fall within the house. A second house emphasis reflects
strong needs for money and security.

THIRD HOUSE

The third house represents communication, early education, writing, and speaking. It also represents siblings, neighbors, one's geographic neighborhood, short trips, and driving.

The third house has an association with Gemini and Mercury. Planets here take on Gemini's attributes of intelligence and curiosity, but what the mind focuses on in an individual's chart depends upon the sign on the cusp and the planets and the signs they fall in within the house. A third house emphasis heightens one's intellect, regardless of sign.

FOURTH HOUSE

The fourth house represents the home and family and either the father or the mother. It includes heritage, ancestry, and psychological roots. Along with the tenth house, which represents the opposite parent, the fourth house reflects how one was brought up and the effects of early conditioning. On a tangible level, the fourth house represents real estate.

The fourth house is associated with Cancer and the Moon. Planets here reflect Cancer's emotionality and concern for security. A planetary emphasis here heightens the influence of the early environment, making it difficult to leave home psychologically regardless of one's age or the ease or difficulty of familial relationships. The influence of family in an individual's chart depends upon the sign on the cusp of the fourth house and the planets and the signs they fall in within the house.

FIFTH HOUSE

The fifth house rules self-expression, creativity, children, and love affairs. It also rules entertainment, dramatics, theater, and parties.

The fifth house is associated with Leo and the Sun. Planets here take on the Leonine quality of self-expression, a desire to be center stage, and an inclination toward the dramatic. Love affairs of the fifth house are distinguished from marriage or living together which are seventh-house phenomena. Fifth-house relationships are more like play, with each person expressing his or her own identity. Compromise comes with the seventh house. "I need to be me" is the theme for those with a fifth-house emphasis.

The fifth house indicates not only what a person is like romantically, but also the type of person with whom one enters into a relationship. In the same way, this house describes not only one's relationship with children, particularly the oldest, but what the children are actually like from the parent's perspective.

In an individual chart, self-expression, children, and love affairs are specifically defined by planets in the fifth house, the signs they fall in, and the sign on the cusp of the house.

SIXTH HOUSE

The sixth house rules work and health. It shows one's work ethic, day-to-day performance, and service to others. The sixth house reflects the daily work environment, while the tenth house represents the career path. It also reflects the work or service one receives from others. As can readily be seen, astrologically there is a direct correlation between work and health.

The sixth house is associated with Virgo and Mercury. Planets here take on Virgo overtones of health consciousness, perfectionism, meticulousness, and detail orientation, regardless of what sign they are found in. An emphasis here heightens workaholic tendencies and the possibility of stress-related health problems. The sign on the cusp of the sixth house and the planets and the signs they fall in within the house show the specific way an individual manifests these qualities.

SEVENTH HOUSE

The seventh house rules marriage and partnerships. Beyond this typical definition, the seventh house also rules all significant one-to-one relationships. This includes close friends, coworkers of equal status, and professionals that one hires for advice. In addition, the seventh house rules "open enemies," i.e., enemies that one knows about, such as a spouse in a divorce proceeding or a colleague who is sabotaging one's work efforts.

The seventh house is associated with Libra and Venus. Planets here take on the Libra qualities, particularly the importance of relationships. Other qualities include cooperation, the willingness to compromise, and caring what others think.

The cusp of the seventh house is called the Descendant. In an individual's chart the qualities associated with the sign on the Descendant and the planets and the signs they fall in within the seventh house describe marriage or business partners. Qualities described are frequently projected onto the marriage partner or other people, rather than seen as part of oneself. The seventh house describes what a person gets relationally, no matter what he may think he wants.

EIGHTH HOUSE

The eighth house represents what one derives from relationships or shared resources. This ranges from sex to joint finances, loans, inheritances, insurance, and taxes. It also rules death, occult interests, and the astral plane. This house also represents how one's marriage or business partner handles money or resources.

The eighth house is associated with Scorpio and Pluto. Planets here take on the Scorpio overtones of depth, intensity, emotionality, and the piercing ability to get to the bottom of situations. They influence one's attitude toward sex as well as sexual desires. A planetary emphasis can bring about such divergent traits as interests in reincarnation and the desire to know the meaning of life, to sexual intensity, to financial acumen. In an individual's chart, the sign on the cusp of the eighth house and the planets and the signs they fall in within the house show the specific way these qualities are manifested.

NINTH HOUSE

The ninth house represents higher education, philosophy, religion, belief systems, legal systems, and long-distance travel. It has to do with all institutions that embody social concepts ranging from colleges to churches to courts. It is also the house of publishing.

The ninth house is associated with Sagittarius and Jupiter. Planets here reflect Sagittarius overtones. This includes a desire for travel and adventure, whether it is the travel of mind or body. A ninth-house planetary emphasis typically conveys a highly developed intellect. Higher education becomes a must for self-esteem. In an individual's chart, the sign on the cusp of the ninth house and the planets and the signs they fall in within the house show the specific way these qualities are manifested.

TENTH HOUSE

The cusp of the tenth house is called the Midheaven. This house represents profession, reputation, prestige, and public standing. It represents one's boss. Along with the fourth house, the tenth house represents family and upbringing and describes either the mother or father.

The tenth house is associated with Capricorn and Saturn. Planets here reflect Capricorn overtones of duty and responsibility, as well as the desire to be looked up to and respected. They show the aspiration to be in a position of authority and how one gets along with authority figures. A planetary emphasis here makes it easy for a person to stand out. This can be a double-edged sword. Standing out makes it is easier to get recognition, which helps in achieving status and authority, but it can also lead to notoriety, depending upon what one is recognized for. In an individual's chart, the sign on the cusp of the Midheaven and the planets and the signs they fall in within the house show the specific way these attributes are manifested.

ELEVENTH HOUSE

The eleventh house represents friendships, social relationships, groups, and organizations. It has to do with creative group expression. It is associated with hopes, ambitions, and the willingness to work on ideas of universal or humanitarian concern.

The eleventh house is associated with Aquarius and Uranus. Planets here take on Aquarian overtones, which heighten intellectual acuity. A planetary emphasis here is associated with social ideals, friendship, and the wish to belong to groups of like-minded people. In an individual's chart, friends, social ideals, and groups to which one may belong are specifically described by the sign on the cusp of the eleventh house and the planets and the signs they fall in within the house.

TWELFTH HOUSE

The twelfth house rules the subconscious mind, spirituality, and psychic ability. It is the depository of unconscious habit patterns. It rules hospitals, prisons, confinement, and secret enemies. It has to do with confinement and what is unseen or unrecognized by oneself. This gives the twelfth house a bad reputation and it is frequently referred to as the house of one's self-undoing. Yet, it conveys the ability for one-pointed concentration.

The twelfth house is associated with Pisces and Neptune. Planets found here have Pisces overtones of compassion, spirituality, and naïve idealism.

They also reflect the manner in which one's unconscious habit patterns affect life. A planetary emphasis heightens one's spirituality and idealism as well as one's naiveté. An emphasis here makes one more comfortable working behind the scenes, unless one's work, such as acting, in some way disguises his nature. In an individual's chart, the sign on the cusp of the house and the planets and the signs they fall in within the house show the specific way these attributes are manifested.

THE HOUSES AS TRINITIES

The houses, like the signs, correlate to the elements. Houses one, five, and nine are associated with fire signs. These houses emphasize get-up-and-go and self-expression. Houses two, six, and ten are associated with the earth signs. These houses emphasize practical concerns and are associated with work and wealth. Houses three, seven, and eleven correlate to the air signs and emphasize intellect and relationships. Houses four, eight, and twelve are associated with water signs and are associated with feelings and emotional connections.

THE HOUSES AS QUADRUPLICITIES

The houses, like the signs, correlate to the quadruplicities. Houses one, four, seven, and ten are called angular houses and correlate with the cardinal signs of Aries, Cancer, Libra, and Capricorn. These houses are the most readily visible and play a role in the initiation of situations.

Houses two, five, eight, and eleven are called succedent houses and correlate with the fixed signs Taurus, Leo, Scorpio, and Aquarius. Succedent houses reflect stability and the completion of circumstances.

Houses three, six, nine, and twelve are called cadent houses and correlate with the mutable signs of Gemini, Virgo, Sagittarius, and Pisces. Cadent houses are associated with the dispersal of ideas.

Chapter 5

THE SUN—YOUR SENSE OF IDENTITY

Key Words: *Identity, Vitality*
Rules: *Leo, Fifth House*
Cycle: *Approximately 30 days in each sign,*
1 year for entire Zodiac
Somatic Influences: *Heart and Spine*

The Sun is the center of the solar system. It gives off the light and warmth without which we could not live on earth. Likewise, the Sun in our birth charts is our light, our consciousness, and the celestial body around which all others revolve. The Sun represents our self-expression. It rules drive, vitality, will, and ego, as well as constitutional strength. The Sun is a yang or masculine planetary influence, which means its energy is positive or outgoing. It represents authority figures and men in general.

Each celestial body rules a particular a sign, which in turn reflects the truest expression of the planetary energy. The Sun rules the sign of Leo and the fifth house. The Sun and Leo are associated with dignity, self-reliance, leadership, strength of character, and an appreciation of one's personal value.

A person with a strong Sun seeks to express himself and to be at the forefront of the endeavors that he participates in. He likes to make things happen and wants recognition for doing so.

Positively expressed, the Sun endows personal strength, power, courage, confidence, and leadership. Negatively expressed, these same traits turn into willfulness, arrogance, boastfulness, or egocentricity.

As the earth revolves around the Sun, it spends approximately thirty days in each sign. In our individual charts, the Sun may be in any of the twelve signs and twelve houses. While the Sun always represents our basic sense of identity, the sign it falls in reflects how that sense of identity is expressed in terms of personality, drive, and instinctual patterns. The house the Sun occupies shows the department of life where our ego and drive get expressed and where we want to shine.

SUN IN THE SIGNS

Sun in Aries ☉ ♈

I Act, Initiative, Activity

Dynamic, independent, and self-sufficient best describe you.
You're a self-starter and competitive by nature;
you want to be number one in whatever you do.

Aries is the first sign of the Zodiac and, as such, symbolizes beginnings. You are a self-starter. Being a cardinal fire sign, ruled by Mars, you take initiative easily. Waiting for things to come to you is not your style. You are straightforward, direct, and independent. You make decisions quickly and go after what you want. A competitive drive pushes you forward. First is exactly where you want to be, and you compete not only with others but also with yourself. There is a desire to be the best you can be at whatever you do. You aspire to be in positions of leadership, not so that you can tell others what to do but so that you can do precisely as you please.

This placement provides tremendous energy and vitality. You enjoy constant activity and accomplish tasks faster than any other sign. Because of this, patience is not one of your strong points. Everyone else can seem slow by comparison. In essence, there is Aries time and everyone else's time; so unless another person has planets in Aries, he is not likely to keep up with you.

While you are great at initiating projects, finishing may be a problem. If you are working on a project that does not come to fruition quickly, you may easily become discouraged, believing it is not going to work out. Practicing patience would help you greatly. Also, once you have accomplished a challenge, you can lose interest. Unless the rest of your chart has significant planetary placements in fixed signs, management is not for you. It is better to allow someone else to take over once the project has been initiated.

You have a keen intellect as well as a propensity for action. You enjoy a good debate—which others may see as being argumentative. And when it comes to arguments, you lose your temper quickly but get over your anger just as quickly. You do not hold a grudge. This makes it difficult for you to understand when others do not get over your outbursts quite as easily.

Being internally rather than externally motivated, you care little for the opinion of others. What you think and believe is more important than anything else. This reinforces self-sufficiency and competitiveness, but may create relational problems. You are so independent that it is hard to fathom that others may not be, or that they may find your directness off-putting. Your attitude is "I do what I want and you should do what you want. Why should I care what you think and why should you care what I think?" The positive side of this is that you are true to yourself and extremely honest. You say what you mean and you mean what you say. The negative side of this is that you do not necessarily take other people's feelings into account. You would say, "Why ask for my opinion if you don't want it?" But no one has to necessarily ask for it to get it. Diplomacy feels more like lying than being socially appropriate. Yet, this is precisely how you offend others without meaning to. Recognizing the line between being honest and being hurtful would help your relationships immensely.

JOYCE SAYS:
Traits to treasure: The honest, direct way you go after what you want.
To transform: Avoid acting impulsively and take other people's feelings into account.

Sun in Taurus ☉ ♉

I Have, Possessions, Practicality
You are stable, security-oriented, and practical; yet sensuous. You enjoy the good life. Comfort and luxury are priorities. You appreciate fine dining, expensive wine, well-made clothes.

Taurus is a fixed earth sign, ruled by Venus. You possess grace, charm, and an easygoing manner. You combine practicality and stability with an appreciation of the finer things in life.

You are slow to start projects and make up your mind, wanting to make sure that whatever you put effort into has the intended return. Once you get started on a project, you are totally committed. You have determination, perseverance, and staying power. You work long and hard to achieve desired goals, no matter how much time they take. This makes you both stable and stubborn. In fact, Taurus is the most stubborn sign of the Zodiac, but your graciousness masks this trait.

You dislike conflict, but do not allow others to push or pressure you. This may be a positive or negative quality. It demonstrates strength of character, but also stubbornness. You avoid disagreement whenever possible, and yet you do not give in easily. Because of this, you are quite capable of letting others believe you will go along with them despite intentions to the contrary. Later this may become a sore point in relationships. You are very slow to anger but once you lose your temper, it is difficult for you to get over it.

Taurus represents the earthy side of Venus; you appreciate comfort and sensual delights. You enjoy the taste of fine wine or a good meal, the scent of flowers or fine perfume, or the touch of soft fabric next to your skin. The touch of another person is also appreciated, whether that touch is by massage or the sensuality associated with sex. The Taurus-Scorpio axis of the Zodiac is associated with sensuality and sexuality. Pure physical pleasure is a Taurus delight.

Stability and security are very important. With regard to finances, there is a need for money in the bank for later, just in case. Possessions equate with security. You are a collector, holding onto things. These collections may have dollar value or purely emotional value. It is important not to let the desire for possessions or the finer side of life interfere with much-needed financial security.

Domestic happiness is a priority. You are loyal mate. Regardless of your sex, you are very likely a nurturing and protective spouse and parent and also probably an excellent cook and skillful gardener. The desire to provide "the good life" for yourself and your family clearly motivates you. In return, you expect the same loyalty that you give. This may become a problem if protectiveness is carried too far and you become overprotective and possessive. At worst, there is the possibility of treating other people like possessions or defining loyalty as agreement and differences of opinion as disloyalty. Recognizing significant others as unique individuals rather than seeing them as an extension of you is of the utmost importance.

JOYCE SAYS:
Traits to treasure: Your graciousness, perseverance, and quiet determination.

To transform: Avoid letting determination turn into stubbornness by recognizing that change is not your enemy.

Sun in Gemini ☉ ♊

I Think, Versatility, Intelligence

Quick-witted, intelligent, and versatile best describe you. Variety is the spice of life, and you want plenty of it. You appreciate good conversation and smart company.

Gemini is a mutable air sign ruled by Mercury. True to your Mercury ruler, you have a keen intellect, an inquisitive mind, and a quick wit. You love to learn and you question everything. As a child, very likely you followed your mother around asking for explanations, questioning why things are the way they are. As an adult, you still want explanations and find it hard to trust anything that cannot be explained logically. Intellectual stimulation is a lifelong necessity. This stimulation may come from advanced degrees, adult education classes, reading, or just talking to people.

You excel in all fields that involve communication and persuasiveness. This includes speaking, writing, teaching, reporting, selling, public relations, and inventing. You may also have the ability to work with your hands. In whatever you do, variety is a must. You dislike routine and are better at multitasking than you are at finishing one project at a time. Once you have learned enough about what you are doing to satisfy your curiosity, you may become bored and want to do something else. Because of this, you work much better in positions where you come up with the ideas and others carry them out, thereby leaving you free to move on to the next project.

Intellectual companionship is important. On a casual level, you get along with people easily. Your sharp mind and terrific sense of humor make you an enjoyable companion, and you are attentive to anyone whose conversation you find interesting. You put others at ease and truly enjoy collecting the bits of information learned through conversation. These traits contribute to your persuasiveness, which you have fun with. You may argue a position, whether or not you believe in it, just to see if you can convince people. You question others for your own edification and willingly change your mind if you discover evidence contrary to your beliefs. These traits can lead to misunderstandings. To you, ideas are not personal. Because of this, it is hard to understand that others may perceive your probing as an indication of a lack of trust or as an attack, and that changing your mind may be perceived as unreliability.

Unless Saturn is strong in your chart, your changeability may in fact be unreliability. In all situations, you hate to be fenced in. You do not want to be questioned. You want to come and go as you please, including in romance. Given that freedom, you may not go far, but you need to believe that you have it. You also want the freedom to change your mind—even if it means reneging on commitments. And while you enjoy debate, you dislike actual conflict, so you tend to sidestep issues rather than deal with them truthfully. And your arguments are so persuasive that you may even convince yourself. It is important to recognize the line between adaptability and unreliability.

JOYCE SAYS:

Traits to treasure: The ease in which you come up with ideas and communicate with people.

To transform: Avoid letting adaptability turn into unreliability and honestly say what you mean instead of talking your way out of uncomfortable situations.

Sun in Cancer ☉ ♋

I Feel, Mothering, Nurturing

Mothering, nurturing, and caring, you enjoy taking care of those you love. Family bonds are important, and once you have children, they tend to come first.

Cancer is a cardinal water sign ruled by the Moon. You are sensitive, emotional, and nurturing and have a strong sense of intuition. You perceive the undercurrents of what goes on around you. In a sense, you "feel the vibes." This may make it difficult to explain how you know what you know. A person does not have to tell you that he is sad or upset. You feel it and do your best to lend a helping hand if it is someone you care about.

Cancer represents the mother of the Zodiac and is the sign associated with home and family. This makes early family life exceedingly important. A vivid memory for the past makes you the family historian. It also makes it unlikely that you forget a kindness or a hurt. As an adult, you retain strong family ties, regardless of the ease or difficulty of early relationships.

Whether you are male or female, you are the family protector and nurturer. You love your home and are in all likelihood a good cook, particularly of comfort food.

Providing for those you care about is of prime importance to you. You have a strong need for emotional and financial security. In relationships, it is important to feel emotionally safe and cared for. That is the way you treat others and is therefore the way you expect to be treated in return. Financially, there is a need to have money put away for a rainy day in order to feel secure. You may worry unnecessarily and conjure up "what ifs?" about what could go wrong, which does not contribute to a sense of security. Fears may cause you to be overprotective of loved ones, particularly your children; and you may overeat for comfort.

The symbol for Cancer is the crab, and like the crab, you can have a hard outer shell while being soft inside. When you are hurt, a wall of protection goes up, and even constructive criticism is taken personally. Dislike of conflict creates the tendency to sidestep disagreements. However, you do not give in easily. You are more likely to resort to passive resistance and attempt to manipulate others into doing what you want. Normally you are sensitive and intuitive, but when hurt, you can self-centeredly ignore other people's feelings and are not above making them feel guilty in order to get your way. Learning how to voice concerns and to honestly deal with differences is a must. Viewing differences as rejection and withdrawing cuts you off from the emotional support you so desire.

JOYCE SAYS:

Traits to treasure: The way you mother and nurture family members and those you love.

To transform: Avoid being overly sensitive to perceived slights by developing a thicker skin in sensitive situations.

Sun in Leo ☉ ♌

I Will, Vitality, Leadership

Naturally self-expressive, you have zest and enthusiasm for whatever you care about. There is a love of the limelight, and appreciation means everything.

Leo is a fixed fire sign. You have zest, enthusiasm, spontaneity, and tremendous energy, and you approach life optimistically. You are self-expressive, true to yourself, and possess leadership capabilities. Like your ruler, the Sun, there is a desire to shine and share your light.

You know what you want and you go after it. Being persistent and well organized, once you make commitments, you follow through. This gives you the distinction of being the only fire sign that finishes what you start. You function well in positions of leadership, inspiring others through magnanimity and natural exuberance. But you do not function well in subservient roles. You bristle at being told what to do, and it is possible for even the most constructive criticism to offend your pride. While you will always remain true to yourself, it is important for you to recognize the rights of those in authority, and the difference between helpful suggestions and insults.

You love the limelight. No matter what you do for a living, there is an actor inside of you. Like a star, you beam at being the center of attention. The need to be recognized and appreciated makes you subject to flattery. Yet you really want to be appreciated for being yourself and are capable of taking unpopular stands because of moral convictions. At heart, you are honest and direct and will not pretend to be something other than what you are.

A flair for drama shows in your appearance. It is important to you to look your best—even if you are only going to the corner store to get a newspaper. Self-expression shows in your attraction to flamboyant clothes and jewelry, flashy cars, and the way you throw lavish parties.

Leo is the fire sign most concerned with people. The image of a lioness protecting her cubs best symbolizes you as a parent. Loyal and faithful in all significant relationships, you are at heart a romantic. When in love, you are demonstrative and affectionate, and there is nothing that you will not do for another. What you want in return is appreciation; relational problems are mostly likely to arise when you do not feel appreciated.

Working through personal differences is not easy. You are stubborn, and tend to see yourself as the one who is "right," which ultimately means that others are "wrong." Also, despite your self-confident manner, the importance you place on looking good might lead you to walk away rather than risk rejection. Relational health depends upon working through what may be issues of misplaced pride.

JOYCE SAYS:

Traits to treasure: Your self-expressiveness, leadership abilities, persistence, and honor.

To transform: Avoid boasting and acting based on misplaced pride, and develop a modicum of humility.

Sun in Virgo ☉ ♍

I Analyze, Discrimination, Industriousness
A perfectionist at heart, you are practical and hard working. Learning and self-improvement are lifelong quests, and you excel at keeping order.

Virgo combines the intellect of Mercury with the commonsense practicality of Earth. Intelligent and industrious, you value learning. There is a lifelong seeking of knowledge, whether that knowledge comes through higher education, on-the-job training, or self-education. You are interested in facts and useful information. You seek ideas that may be put to work, and have little sympathy for airy-fairy ideals. Your approach to work is methodical, analytical, and detail-oriented. Always seeking the most efficient ways to accomplish tasks, you are flexible and open to new and better methods of producing demonstrable results.

An analytical intellect helps you excel at breaking things down into their component parts. You naturally think in terms of "this is step one, this is step two, etc." Because of this, it is easy for you to learn from how-to manuals and to excel at writing them, as well as in teaching and training others. You also excel at detail-oriented work such as accounting, editing, or proofreading.

You are interested in health-related matters, and your orientation toward being of service makes you a good doctor, nurse, or dietician. Regardless of what you do for a living, you are very likely knowledgeable about vitamins and alternative health remedies. Your interest in health extends to hygiene and cleanliness. Ideally, your surroundings are neat and orderly. You function best when everything is in its own place, but need to take care not to become fanatical in this regard.

You see order and self-improvement as the norm and strive toward an ideal of perfection. Perfection may be in the form of a balanced checkbook, a clean home, an efficient workspace, or a healthy body. You offer others "helpful suggestions" so that they may also improve. It may not occur to you that not everyone shares this urge or that what you consider helpful might be considered critical. And when you are upset but not ready to confront a situation directly, this criticalness turns into nagging. It is important to distinguish between your standards of being helpful and the standards of others, and to learn the difference between being helpful versus just plain critical.

Being a perfectionist may also engender another set of problems. Expecting perfection can lead to a lack of self-confidence and low self-worth, as perfection does not exist. Worrying about little things may cause unnecessary anxiety and the tendency to miss the bigger picture. At work you can spend time on details that only you value, which makes you appear inefficient despite hard work. In positions of authority, you may be even more overworked. You have trouble delegating due to difficulty trusting anyone to do the job well enough, or upon delegating, you may micromanage. All of this increases the pressure. Perfection may also cause reluctance to apply for promotions because you tend to underrate your actual know-how. It is important to use external criteria for accomplishment, as your own are likely to be overly stringent. It is also important that you insist on adequate compensation for your services. Perfectionism may lead to feelings of inferiority, which may in turn allow you to remain in circumstances where you are overworked and underpaid.

JOYCE SAYS:
Traits to treasure: Your analytical and discriminatory abilities and attention to detail.
To transform: Avoid getting caught up in details by developing discrimination between what is important and what is not.

Sun in Libra   ☉ ♎

I Balance, Harmony, Relationships
Relationships are of primary importance, as Libra is the sign of partnership. You seek harmony and cooperation and dislike being around crass behavior.

Libra is a cardinal air sign ruled by Venus. You have charm, grace, and an eye for beauty. As Libra is the sign of marriage, relationships, and partnership, one-to-one relationships are highly valued, and harmony and cooperation are priorities. You seek balance and moderation and carefully weigh all sides of an issue in making decisions. As an air sign, you require mental stimulation and work equally well with systems and ideas as with people.

You dislike arguments and crude behavior and are committed to getting along well with others, yet you are no pushover. Excelling in diplomacy, you get people to do what you want believing it was their idea. This ability makes you a good lawyer, executive, diplomat, or counselor, or helps you to excel in the fields of sales, advertising, or public relations. A commitment to fair play enhances abilities as a judge, arbitrator, or mediator. Libra is the sign associated with war as well as with peace, but as military commanders who strategize battles, not as foot soldiers who fight them.

In addition to being intellectually oriented, being ruled by Venus conveys an aesthetic sense. You appreciate culture and enjoy art, theater, and music. You dress well, like to be noticed, and compliments go a long way toward winning your heart. The desire to personally look your best and live in an aesthetically pleasing environment coincides with talent in fields of fashion, beauty, and interior design.

On the more personal side, you are a master of social appropriateness and believe that people should be nice. Avoiding arguments makes you appear indecisive, but the avoidance stems from the wish for harmony and from the desire to be liked. This may cause you to tell others what they want to hear regardless of what you really think. Carried too far, tact turns into dishonesty and affects people's ability to trust you.

For Libra, relationships are of prime importance, and life without a significant other, whether a spouse, lover, or best friend, is unimaginable. There is a desire for an equal partner to share your life with, a companion who shares your interests. Yet as an air sign, not a water sign, you relate mind to mind and are more comfortable thinking than feeling. This may lead to avoiding dealing with your own emotions or those of others. You may avoid confrontations but behave coldly toward your mate, or rationalize staying in unsuitable relationships so as to avoid being alone. Staying true to yourself while honoring others, accepting feelings, and being honest are necessities to achieve the harmonious relationships you so desire.

JOYCE SAYS:

Traits to treasure: Your charm, diplomacy, and the ability to get along with people.

To transform: Avoid letting diplomacy turn into dishonesty by being truthful (including with yourself) as well as socially appropriate.

Sun in Scorpio   ☉ ♏

I Desire, Passion, Intensity.
You have an all-or-nothing nature. You are either in love or not interested, whether it's with regard to a person, place, job, or ideal.

Scorpio is a fixed water sign ruled by Pluto. Scorpio is the only sign that has three symbols, exhibiting the heights and the depths possible for Scorpio consciousness. At the highest level, you are represented by the phoenix, the mythical bird rising out of the ashes that symbolizes resurrection and transformation. You have the desire to transcend, to become better. At the lowest level, you display the qualities of the scorpion, the arachnid with the poisonous sting. When hurt, you brood and wait for the opportunity to gain revenge; or when in a bad mood, your piercing tongue deliciously cuts others to the quick. The symbol of the eagle represents the middle ground, where most Scorpios lie. The eagle flies higher than any other bird but can still descend to the depths. As a Scorpio, the challenge is to choose among the qualities of these symbols.

Despite an outward appearance of calm, you are an intensely emotional person who lives by passion. With an all-or-nothing approach to life, you make no distinction between moderation and apathy. Your passion is frequently misunderstood as purely sexual, but it is a passion for life. You are in love or not interested, whether it is with a person, a job, or an idea.

Deep and determined, shrewd and secretive, fearless and brave, you seek truth and defend justice, no matter what the consequences. Good instincts about people and situations give you the ability to pierce through appearances. Depth perception gets you to the core of the matter, whether you are analyzing a person, a procedure, or an ideal. These traits make you an excellent psychologist, doctor, scientist, researcher, detective, financier, banker, troubleshooter, or occultist.

While outwardly you appear pragmatic, you base your decisions upon how you feel. Once you make a choice, tremendous willpower goes into achieving the aim. Problems can arise because you are so sure that you have made the right decision that you do not stop to examine choices. If you are headed in the right direction, determination and will help you produce incredible results. If headed in the wrong direction, the refusal to examine evidence contrary to your thinking produces results that are far from what you bargained for.

In all relationships, you are vehemently loyal and trustworthy. You give a lot and expect a lot. You have little tolerance for weakness in yourself or in others. Yet you may stay in unhappy romantic situations for too long, trying to "fix up" your lover so that both of you can be happy (particularly if you are a woman). Passion and sexual attraction can cloud judgment. And while there is never too much sex with the "right person," you are not likely to let the "wrong one" hold your hand.

Intense passion can lead to being possessive and controlling. You try to control the environment because you cannot, or will not, control yourself. Whatever the case, it is important that you do not make your desires more important than you are. Also, it is important to recognize that it is possible to make a mistake; just because you desire something does not automatically make it a wise choice.

JOYCE SAYS:

Traits to treasure: Your passion and intensity, depth perception, and good instincts.

To transform: Avoid letting passion devolve into obsessive behavior by being willing to reevaluate situations.

Sun in Sagittarius   ☉ ♐

I Perceive, Freedom, Straightforward
You want life to be an adventure, chock full of travel and excitement. Freedom and independence are valued, and you won't allow yourself to be fenced in.

Sagittarius is a mutable fire sign ruled by Jupiter. The mutable-fire combination gives you a strong need for freedom and independence. You seek adventure and truth, and want to be the master of your own fate. Your approach to life is cheerful and optimistic; you think positively, and expect the best from people and situations. Friendly and outgoing, the faith that you have in yourself inspires others to have faith in you. You speak your mind in no uncertain terms, sometimes to the chagrin of those around you.

Sagittarius is the most intellectually oriented fire sign and, regardless of educational background, you understand abstract concepts. You are interested in ideas and ideals ranging from philosophy and religion to beliefs about how people should live. Seeing the big picture, you have little interest in details. Depending upon your beliefs, you may stand up for social reform or the prevailing social order. Your interest is more in theoretical concepts than how ideas actually work out in the real world. Because of this, it is important to gather all information necessary to make decisions rather than to optimistically jump to conclusions about what is possible. However, while you may fervently argue for a particular ideal, you are not afraid to publicly change your mind based on additional information.

There are two types of Sagittarius, and it is possible for one person to embody both types. The first is philosophical and scholarly, concerned with learning and gaining wisdom, and improving the social order. If you are this type, you make a good minister, humanitarian worker, politician, teacher, or college professor. However, you may have difficulty distinguishing between the truth and your personal opinion. It is important not to become narrow-minded and prejudiced against those with different views. As much as you value being honest and forthright, becoming a hypocrite is possible if you fail to live up to your principles and pretend otherwise. Staying honest and being respectful of other people's opinions is a must.

The second type has more personal concerns. A sense of freedom takes precedence above all else. If you are this type, you desire travel and excitement, and are unwilling to be fenced in. Life is an adventure, which may be found in professions such as journalism, photojournalism, the military, sports, or even business. Or adventure may take the form of running away from the responsibilities of everyday life. In this case, even the most reasonable expectations are interpreted as unreasonable demands. Though you may have the best intentions, you have a tendency to promise more than you actually deliver. Being optimistic, you may believe that you will come through, but can easily rationalize your behavior if you do not.

Whichever type you are, you enjoy the outdoors. Camping, hiking, biking, horseback riding, and communing with nature provide much needed tranquility.

JOYCE SAYS:

Traits to treasure: Your optimism, independence, and positive approach to situations.

To transform: Make sure that optimism does not cause you to promise more than you can deliver by realistically assessing possibilities.

Sun in Capricorn ☉ ♑

I Use, Conservative, Conscientious
You are hardworking, practical, and conservative. Aspiring to positions of authority, you want to be the boss and run the show. Status and respect are important.

Capricorn is a cardinal earth sign ruled by Saturn. You are serious, sensible, self-disciplined, and dedicated to duty. Skeptical by nature, you approach life from a pragmatic point of view. Before you believe anything, you want tangible proof. You have no interest in abstract ideas, but judge ideas by their workability. This trait makes you an astute businessperson. Talents may also lie in physical sciences, medicine, and law.

True to your ruler Saturn, you have been mature and responsible, accepting societal rules of right and wrong from an early age. This, coupled with the tendency to be somber and reserved, may not have made childhood much fun. Frequently young Capricorn people get along better with adults than with children. Life tends gets easier as you get older, as at some point age catches up with maturity. In fact, you may enjoy yourself more as you get older after having satisfied a quest for success. Capricorn is the only sign that becomes more youthful with age.

You are patient, persistent, and good organizer. These qualities, along with discipline and a strong sense of purpose, endow you with the capacity for hard work. You play by the rules of whatever environment you are in and put in the time and effort it takes to get ahead. In performing tasks, you look to tradition to see how they were handled and then improve upon standard methods. You respect authority because ultimately you want to be the authority figure. Status and position, power and money, and being looked up to and respected mean a great deal to you. Not every Capricorn becomes a CEO, but in order to have a sense of achievement, you must be in charge of whatever you are doing, no matter how large or small.

An unlikely naiveté stems from the belief that those who follow the rules and do what is right will be rewarded for their effort. If life does not turn out so fairly, you may become melancholy or self-pitying.

Your social and political views are conservative and your lifestyle prudent. This, combined with your fondness for tradition and belief that people should get what they earn, can lead to being dogmatic. It is important not to let a law-and-order point of view turn into cruelty and intolerance.

In the quest for success, there is a tendency to forego relationships early or put them on the back burner,. In relationships, emotional expression does not come easily, as you are uncomfortable with feelings. This discomfort can make you appear cold no matter how you feel inside. It is easier for you to do something for loved ones than it is to express feelings for them. The one area where you are quite comfortable romantically is sexually. While you believe public demonstrations of affection vulgar, being a sensual earth sign you feel that what happens in private is a completely different matter.

In relationships, it is possible to feel rejected and withdraw if significant others do not appreciate your efforts to take care of them or if they fail to respond in a reciprocal manner. Yet your outward lack of warmth, outside of sex, can make it difficult for loved ones to recognize your caring.

JOYCE SAYS:

Traits to treasure: Your reliability and responsibility combined with pragmatism and capacity for hard work.

To transform: Avoid letting conservatism turn into dogmatism by being tolerant of other people's values.

Sun in Aquarius   ☉ ♒

I Know, Originality, Humanitarianism
Intelligent and forward thinking, you are an intellectual pioneer who can be ahead of your time. Intellectual companionship is a must, and friendship a considerable value.

Aquarius is a fixed air sign. You are independent, individualistic, and freedom-loving, as well as intellectually oriented and mentally curious. With Uranus as your ruler, your thinking is original and inventive. No fan of the past or of tradition, you are attracted to people, places, ideas, and entertainment that are out of the ordinary. You enjoy breaking down barriers and pioneering new fields. You can excel in scientific, intellectual, or humanitarian pursuits, or anything just a little bit weird.

You are friendly and outgoing and enjoy meeting people, making it easy for you to fit into new social surroundings. You value companionship, thrive on exchanging ideas, and have many friends who, in all likelihood, would not have much in common with each other. In general, you accept people for themselves, not where they come from or their social status. In fact, the people you consider the most interesting might be considered eccentric by others. The people you find the most difficult to accept are conservative thinkers who stand up for the status quo.

You yourself are not easy to get to know. Because the symbol for Aquarius is the water bearer, many mistake you for a water sign. What the water bearer is disseminating is life force or knowledge, not emotions. As an Aquarius, you relate to people through intellect, not feelings (unless the rest of your chart has a stronger water emphasis). You probably have trouble admitting—even to yourself—that you have feelings. Instead, you view people, places, and situations through a detached perspective.

It is easier to have relationships with groups of people than to relate to one particular person. In romance, you do not want to be fenced in. Friendship and intellectual companionship are necessary components for a lasting romantic relationship. In fact, friends can become lovers and lovers can become friends. Meeting mind to mind is your forte. Relating emotionally is much more difficult for you. While you have great sympathy on an impersonal level, an overabundance of emotions makes you want to run. This makes it difficult to deal with the feeling side of a relationship. Also, your friends mean so much to you that even in the best of romantic relationships, if forced to make a choice, you are more likely to choose a friend over a lover. This is because you do not believe you should be put in the position of having to make the choice.

Also, while your liberal ideas make you appear open-minded, you are actually quite stubborn. Once you make up your mind, you resist change. Though you believe in individual liberty, once you adopt an idea or belief system, you are so convinced of its truth that you expect everyone else to believe it too. Loyalty to a group or a way of thinking can be so strong that you dismiss everyone who disagrees. This may cause difficulties in your personal and professional life. You are highly intelligent, but no one is always right. It is important to respect the intellect of others or at a minimum to appear to do so.

JOYCE SAYS:

Traits to treasure: Your intelligence, originality, and inventiveness.
To transform: Avoid becoming stubbornly attached to your views by developing the intellectual tolerance that allows you to live up to your own ideals.

Sun in Pisces ☉ ♓

I Empathize, Compassion, Spirituality

Sensitive and compassionate, you are a romantic idealist. You have a poetic soul, strong imagination, and seek beauty in life. You feel sympathy for those less fortunate, and are willing to lend a helping hand.

Pisces is a mutable water sign ruled by Neptune. You are kind, tolerant, and loving, a bit of a dreamer, intuitive, and creative. You have faith but are more in tune with the mystical or the spiritual realms than with organized religion. Water signs live in their feelings, and Pisces is the most sensitive of the water signs. Not just sensitive about yourself or those close to you, your sensitivity extends to everyone and everything.

Like your ruler Neptune, you have a lack of boundaries. Because of this, you are easily influenced by your environment, absorbing its moods and vibrations. If you are upset and your environment is uplifting, your mood improves. If you are happy and the environment is depressing, your spirits decline. Spending time alone helps you rejuvenate. Meditation can help you distinguish between what stems from your own psyche and what stems from the environment. Meditation also helps to get in touch with the strong inner voice that nudges toward destiny.

An idealist, you long to see life the way it should be. Positively, this idealism is coupled with imagination and creative vision. You seek beauty. Creative abilities may lie in art, music, writing, dance, or theater, or these areas may serve as pleasurable escapes. You may have talent in interior decorating or design and have the ability to create beauty in any setting. Creative imagination, combined with intuition, may also help in business ventures. However, like your symbol, two fishes, one swimming upstream, the other downstream, it may be difficult to decide which direction to go in, and this indecision can cause you to drift.

You believe your behavior should be that of a "good" person. There is sympathy for the underdog and a desire to help those in need. Regardless of your profession, there is something of a social worker in you. You look for the good in people, intuitively see their potential, and do your best to help them achieve that potential. While these traits express kindness and concern for fellow human beings, they are not always realistic. You may be a poor judge of character, being so taken with what you see as potential that your ignore actual behavior. At some point, you wake up and recognize the difference between what is supposed to be and what is. Then you go from being an optimist to being a pessimist. While to begin with you see everything as being wonderful, later you may see everything as being terrible. You can feel crushed at being deceived, but it is questionable whether the deception stems from another person or your own images. To avoid disappointment, it is necessary from the start to pay attention to people and situations and deal with them as they are rather than the way you would like them to be.

When disappointed, you seek to escape. This makes it important to avoid drugs and alcohol, which can have a deleterious effect. If you have been hurt over and over, the danger of sensitivities turning inward exists. It is possible to become so immersed in your own feelings that you lose concern for anyone else. In this case, you go from the extreme of being overly giving to the extreme of being overly self-absorbed or demanding.

JOYCE SAYS:

Traits to treasure: Your creativity, compassion, kindness, and intuition. To transform: Avoid being naïve and overly idealistic by developing discrimination so that compassion and sympathy do not end up in disappointments.

SUN IN THE HOUSES

Sun in the First House

Identifies with Self
You are easily noticed and significantly influence your immediate environment.

You exert an influence on your immediate environment. The sign the Sun falls in shows how you exert this influence, but regardless of sign you are easily noticed, and others are see you as self-confident. This may or may not be the way you see yourself, as your self-image depends upon your Sun sign and the aspects among your Sun and other planets.

Since planets in the first house have an Aries overtone, you are strong-willed, independent, and self-motivated. The manner in which you take the lead depends upon your Sun sign. If your Sun is in Aries, you are completely self-directed. If your Sun is in Pisces, you take the lead in a more sympathetic fashion.

Traits to treasure: Your ability to influence your immediate surrounding.
To transform: Avoid becoming self-absorbed.

Sun in the Second House

Identifies with Money

Your self-worth is tied to your financial worth. This makes money-making a priority.

The second house has Taurus overtones. There is a strong need for financial stability and security. Having a good income and money to put away for a rainy day are essential for your sense of self-worth and well-being. This gives you a drive to make money. You are possession oriented and likely to be a collector of "things." These things may be valuable collector's items or may just be an indication of a tendency to overconsume.

The sign in which your Sun falls indicates the way you make money, what you actually value, and the type of possessions that you are attracted to. If your Sun has favorable aspects in this house, you are lucky in moneymaking endeavors. Difficult aspects to the Sun do not mean that you cannot make money, only that you have obstacles to overcome in doing so. If your Sun is in Taurus, the desire for money and possessions is greatest. If your Sun is in Aries, money is more likely to be seen as a means to support your independence.

Traits to treasure: Your ability to engender financial security.
To transform: Avoid equating possessions with self-worth.

Sun in the Third House

Identifies with Intellect

You are intellectually curious. Learning is a lifelong priority.

The third house has Gemini overtones. You have an impressive intellect and see learning as a lifetime adventure. Communication skills in both writing and speaking are excellent. Your mind is quick, and being curious, you do not hesitate to ask questions. You enjoy a friendly debate with others. You dislike actual conflict, but may be more forceful in asking questions or debating than you realize.

The third house also indicates siblings, the neighborhood in which you live, and short-distance travel. Having the Sun here places an importance on these areas in your life. You may prefer traveling by car and visiting areas close to your home to getting on a plane for a trip. Your relationships with siblings and neighbors affect your sense of identity.

Your Sun sign and the aspects to your Sun indicate the manner in which you communicate as well how you handle your relationships with siblings and neighbors. If the Sun is in Gemini, curiosity and intellectual capacity are at their height. If the Sun is in Cancer, you are still intellectually curious, but your intellect will function through intuition and feelings.

JOYCE SAYS:
Traits to treasure: Your intelligence and curious mind.
To transform: Recognize the impact your words can have on others.

Sun in the Fourth House

Identifies with Family
Family relationships significantly impact your identity, and you exert influence on family members.

The fourth house has Cancer overtones. Families of origin influence all of us, but with the Sun in this house, parental influence is even stronger. No matter how old you are, how good or bad your family relationships have been, or how far away from home you move, leaving home psychologically is difficult. Strong bonds exist both with your biological family and with the family you create as an adult. Whether you are a man or a woman, you are mothering and nurturing and are instinctively protective of loved ones. Providing security for yourself and your family is of the utmost importance, and when feeling bad or threatened, you want to be able to retreat to a supportive home environment. Your feelings are hurt easily by those close to you, and you should take care not to be overly sensitive to seeming slights.

The way in which you mother and nurture and provide security depends upon the sign that the Sun falls in and the aspects to it. If in Cancer, you are the mother par excellence. If Sun is in Leo, you are like a tigress defending her cubs. The aspects to the Sun indicate the ease or difficulty of family relationships.

JOYCE SAYS:

JOYCE SAYS:

Traits to treasure: Your dedication to family.
To transform: Make sure that you fully understand the past and early family influence.

Sun in the Fifth House

Identifies with Self-expression

The need to express yourself is primary. Relationships with romantic partners and your children affect your self-esteem.

The fifth house has Leo overtones. This makes self-expression primary. You love life and have dramatic flair. Being enthusiastic, you throw yourself into chosen endeavors. You have a great deal of loyalty and expect loyalty in return. Being recognized and appreciated is of the utmost importance. In this vein, you have to be somewhat careful of trying to be at center stage too often and expecting more than your share of the attention.

In addition to creativity and self-expression, the fifth house rules love affairs and children. You throw yourself into love affairs, and even though strong willed, your identity may become submerged with that of a paramour. You maintain a childlike spontaneity throughout life while at the same time being protective of your own children.

The sign the Sun falls in and the aspects to it reflect the ways in which self-expression is manifested. If in Leo, drama is the name of the game. If in Virgo, self-expression comes through practical endeavors.

JOYCE SAYS:

Traits to treasure: Your self-expression.
To transform: Avoid trying to grab more than your share of the limelight.

Sun in the Sixth House

Identifies with Work

Your identity is tied to your work or day-to-day activities. You are a perfectionist at heart.

The sixth house has Virgo overtones. You are orderly, meticulous, and discriminating and have perfectionist tendencies no matter what your Sun sign. Your identity is tied to your job or daily activities. Unless there are contraindications in the chart, you are an excellent worker and take pride in a job well done. But you have to be careful of being overly critical of yourself, always expecting to accomplish more and more. Spending too much time on details may interfere with work efficiency. Your sense of self-worth may fluctuate with the ups and downs of daily activities. In positions of authority, it is difficult to delegate, being fearful that no one else will do the work as well as you do.

The sixth house also rules health. With your Sun here, it is important that you get enough time off from work to rejuvenate.

The Sun's sign and planetary aspects indicate the ways in which you handle daily activities and physical vitality. If in Virgo, all the above traits describe you in triplicate. If in Libra, your work life includes a greater need for cooperation.

JOYCE SAYS:

Traits to treasure: Your commitment to work.
To transform: Avoid getting caught up in details at the expense of the big picture.

Sun in the Seventh House

Identifies with Mate

You want to be well thought of. One-to-one relationships affect your self-esteem.

The seventh house has Libra overtones. As this is the house of partnerships, the Sun here describes attributes of your spouse or partner as well as your own sense of identity. In all likelihood, you attract people who are more like you than unlike you. As seventh house attributes are frequently projected onto others, you may recognize your own qualities or you may see them as those of significant others without seeing them in yourself. Marriage, partnerships, and significant one-to-one relationships are priorities. You value cooperation, which is fortunate since you typically end up in situations where cooperation is essential in order to get ahead.

You deeply care what other people think of you. This helps you to get along with most people, but there is a danger of losing yourself by allowing the opinions of others, particularly those of your mate or partner, to overly influence you.

The Sun sign and aspects to the Sun indicate the manner in which you relate in marriage and partnership. If the Sun is in Libra and has favorable aspects from other planets, you get along well with others and prosper in significant relationships. If the Sun is in a more independent sign such as Aries or Sagittarius, an internal conflict exists between the desire to cooperate and the wish to do precisely as you please.

JOYCE SAYS:

Traits to treasure: Your wish to get along with other people.
To transform: Avoid losing your own identity by allowing other people to overly influence you.

Sun in the Eighth House

Identifies with Mysteries of Life

You have a drive to understand the meaning of life. In joint finances, you prefer to control the money.

The eighth house has Scorpio overtones. It also rules a variety of seemingly unrelated matters. You possess depth, intensity, and a strong sex drive. You want to understand the meaning of life—why we are here and why we do the things we do. You have an uncanny ability to size up people and situations and ferret out underlying motivations. This may lead to interests in the occult, reincarnation, or psychology.

The eighth house Sun also conveys involvement in matters surrounding joint resources. This includes investments, insurance, inheritance, and sex. You have the same uncanny knack of ferreting out information from a stock prospectus or corporate balance sheet as you do in understanding human beings. In a marriage or partnership, you want control of the money. If the Sun has favorable planetary aspects, you make money from investments and benefit from partnerships. If the Sun has unfavorable aspects, money may be a source of conflict in marriage or partnerships. Sex plays a prominent part of any relationship, and sexual compatibility in a marriage is paramount.

The Sun sign and aspects to it indicate the manner in which you express the above attributes. If the Sun is in Scorpio, the emotionality of this house is strengthened and depth and intensity rule. If the Sun is in one of the air signs, Gemini, Libra, or Aquarius, you seek logical explanations for your intuitive insights.

JOYCE SAYS:

Traits to treasure: Your uncanny ability to perceive beneath the surface of situations.

To transform: Avoid letting intensity become obsessive when it comes to sex or money.

Sun in the Ninth House

Identifies with Beliefs

Your beliefs are intrinsic to your sense of identity. The search for knowledge is lifelong.

The ninth house has Sagittarius overtones. You want life to be an adventure of the mind, body, or spirit. There is a love of travel and learning about foreign cultures and an attraction to people from distant places. You are intellectually oriented, and learning is a priority, regardless of your socioeconomic background. You are interested in law, politics, philosophy, and religion. Your beliefs are intrinsic to your identity, and your self-esteem depends upon living up to personal ideals. The tendency to judge yourself by degrees and intellectual achievements makes higher education highly desirable.

The Sun sign and aspects to the Sun indicate the manner in which you express the above attributes. If the Sun is in Sagittarius, your intellectual capacity and wanderlust are heightened. If the Sun is in a more conservative sign like Capricorn, your worldviews are more practical than idealistic.

JOYCE SAYS:

Traits to treasure: Your love of knowledge.

To transform: Avoid wandering from one idea to another or one place to another.

Sun in the Tenth House

Identifies with Career

You aspire to positions of leadership. Your identity is tied to professional success.

The tenth house has Capricorn overtones. The Sun here conveys ambition and drive for professional success. You are serious and disciplined in career pursuits and work long and hard in order to attain your aims, as self-worth is tied to being in positions of authority. You stand out easily, whether or not you are trying to do so. This makes it easier for you than for others to end up in the public eye or in leadership positions in your particular circle, although standing out can be a double-edged sword. It helps you to get ahead, but also means that you are more closely scrutinized than others are.

The tenth house, along with the fourth house, also indicates family influence. Close ties, for better or worse, exist with your family of origin. The Sun sign and aspects to the Sun indicate career aspirations and how you get along with authority figures. If the Sun is in Capricorn, you aspire to be a CEO of a large company. If the Sun is in Aries, running your own business is preferable.

JOYCE SAYS:

Traits to treasure: Your capacity for sustained effort in pursuing career goals. To transform: Avoid confusing status with self-worth.

Sun in the Eleventh House

Identifies with Friends

Friendships and group activities are priorities. You influence people around you, and in return they influence your self-esteem.

The eleventh house has Aquarius overtones. You get along casually with all sorts of people. Friendship is important. A romantic partner must be a best friend in order for the romance to last, and you do not allow romance to supersede other friendships. You have an attraction to groups or organizations of like-minded people. You might say you want to be just like everyone else, but somehow you end up taking the lead in organizations and excel at inspiring others around specific causes or ideals.

The Sun sign and aspects to the Sun indicate the type of people you are attracted to, the kinds of causes that call you, and how you get along with friends and associates. If the Sun is in Aquarius, very likely you are liberal and attracted to humanistic endeavors. If the Sun is in Capricorn, the organizations you join are more likely to be conservatively oriented.

JOYCE SAYS:

Traits to treasure: Your loyalty to friends.
To transform: Avoid prejudice against those who think differently than you do.

Sun in the Twelfth House

Identifies with Subconscious

You are very aware on a psychic or subliminal level. You feel what goes on around you, which then influences your well-being.

The twelfth house has Pisces overtones. You are sensitive, compassionate, idealistic, and strongly intuitive. Whether you are conscious of it or not, you have a spiritual approach to life. When you pay attention to your instincts, you can be highly psychic and rely on intuitive insights. There is capacity for focused concentration on whatever you put your mind to, but it is also possible to spend time in daydreams or fantasies instead of constructive action.

Being idealistic, you want to see the best in others and have strong sympathies for the underdog. If in a helping profession, you can assist people in becoming what they are capable of. In other relationships, this trait is more naïve, and focusing on potential rather than actual behavior can put you in the position of being taken advantage of.

The Sun in the twelfth house is the repository of the unconscious. This makes it difficult to see yourself as others see you. Being very sensitive to environment, there is need for time alone every day where you can close off the world. Meditation helps with maintaining a sense of equilibrium as the moods and vibrations around you influence your own moods.

The Sun sign and aspects to the Sun indicate how you handle these energies. If in Pisces or another water sign, you accept sensitivity as being natural. If in one of the fire signs, Aries, Leo, or Sagittarius, it is more difficult to identify with being vulnerable.

JOYCE SAYS:

Traits to treasure: Your extraordinary imagination.
To transform: Pay attention to the way people and situations are instead of focusing only on their potential.

Chapter 6

THE MOON — YOUR EMOTIONS AND FEELINGS

Key Words: Emotions, Feelings, Domesticity
Rules: Cancer, Fourth House
Cycle: 2 ½ days in each sign. 28 days to revolve around the Zodiac
Somatic Influences: Stomach, Breasts, Female Organs,
Containers in Body, Fluids

The planets revolve around the Sun, and the Moon revolves around the Earth. It is the fastest moving celestial body and the one closest to the earth. The Moon and the Sun are the most important celestial bodies in the horoscope. The Moon represents emotions and feelings as well as the ways in which we mother, nurture, or take care of others and ourselves.

The Moon also represents the memory, which affects how we take in information. Mercury rules the conscious mind and what we think, but responses to present situations do not occur purely based on reason. Instinctive responses come from the Moon's repository of memories, while the chart as a whole determines how we look at the world.

The Moon is associated with mothering. The sign it posits more specifically represents emotional messages that we received from our families while growing up and the emotional impact of those messages. The Moon also reflects the emotional impact of past and present experiences and how these experiences subconsciously affect the present.

The Moon is a yin, or feminine, element. As such, it represents women in general. The Moon is associated with the fluids in the body, the tides in the oceans, and the moods of our feelings, which like the tides, go up and down. It is also associated with fertility, and along with Venus, rules the female organs.

The Moon rules the sign Cancer and the fourth house. All are associated with mothering, nurturing, sensitivity, and protectiveness. Sensitivity is in relation to others and not just to oneself. Negative expression of the Moon ranges from emotional instability and wide mood swings to being totally out of touch with feelings or being insensitive to the needs of others.

MOON IN THE SIGNS

Moon in Aries ☽ ♈

Emotionally Assertive

Emotional responses are quick and decisive. You know precisely what you feel and have no difficulty expressing it.

With the Moon under Mars' domain, the emotional message you received from your family was to be independent and self-sufficient and to express yourself honestly regardless of what anyone else thinks. You may have received this message by the example of an independent mother, or by being forced to be independent early in a family environment that lacked support, or by watching dependent family members and making a possibly unconscious decision not to be that way. As a parent or nurturer, you encourage others to be independent and to stand up for themselves. Whatever the case, you possess tremendous vitality and zest for life. You make your own decisions and enjoy challenges. You are honest, direct, and straightforward. Emotional responses are quick and spontaneous, and you do not question them or censor yourself. You are comfortable with extroverted feelings like joy or excitement or even anger but find it hard to accept introverted feelings like sadness or grief. You want to skip over these feelings, seeing them as signs of weakness, and the last thing that you want to be is weak.

Since your feelings are direct and immediate, you make emotional decisions quickly. People do not grow on you. Either you like them or not. This makes romantic situations difficult if another is not as spontaneous as you are. You can perceive lack of immediacy from a prospective paramour as rejection, whether it is meant that way or not. It is important to remember that unless another person has planets in Aries, he or she will not make decisions as quickly as you do. Impatience also exists in other areas. You hate waiting for an answer and have to be careful of almost preferring, or pushing for, an immediate "no" rather than waiting for a long-delayed "yes." In this way, you may unconsciously sabotage situations.

Losing your temper too quickly can also create problems. Though you anger quickly, you also get over it quickly, so it is difficult understand why others do not forgive your behavior as quickly as you calm down. Anger may be seen as self-expression with little recognition of the way in which it impacts others. Aries is the "me" sign. This makes it important to become conscious of other people's feelings so as not to ride roughshod over them and create relational difficulties.

JOYCE SAYS:

Traits to treasure: Your emotional self-sufficiency and the way you encourage others to find their own voice.

To transform: Learn not to push too hard for what you want and allow situations to take their own course.

Moon in Taurus ☽ ♉

Emotionally Stable

Emotions combine with common sense. You seek stability and security while appreciating the finer things in life.

With the Moon under Venus' domain, the emotional message you received from your family is to be stable, secure, and have money. You may have received this message by example, for instance, coming from an affluent family or one that made sure its bills were paid on time and that everyone was safe. Or you may have come from a family where either stability or money, or both, were lacking and unconsciously decided that you would not live that way. Whatever the case, money, stability, and security are of prime importance to your emotional well-being

Money is somewhat of a double-edged sword because you want investments for later and also want to enjoy luxuries now. You have good taste and prefer to purchase quality items. Being sensually oriented, you enjoy a good meal, a fine wine, and soft fabric next to your skin. Physical pleasures are of prime importance. This includes the sensuousness of sex, where great enjoyment is derived from touching and being touched.

The Moon here conveys common sense. You are slow in making emotional commitments, but loyal and steadfast once you do. A healthy sexual relationship with a stable partner means a great deal. Family is of prime importance, and you are protective of them, possibly overly so. There is a desire to shield those you love, particularly children, from any mistakes they could possibly make. Even though you are security conscious, you can be more generous with family members than makes financial sense.

Being security conscious, you tend to be a collector. You may save items that have actual dollar value. In this regard, you can be adept at ferreting out antiques at yard sales, or you may save items that have emotional meaning, or you may just collect junk.

You value harmony and dislike conflict. In most situations, you are easygoing and avoid disagreements. However, you are much more stubborn than you appear to be, and once you make up your mind you are unlikely to change it—even when you should. In the midst of any disagreement, you generally see yourself as the "nice one." The obvious implication is that whoever disagrees with you is "not nice." This is particularly true when your protectiveness has crossed the line into possessiveness, and you see yourself as only trying to help. Giving others the freedom to make their own choices and learning to compromise are essential for maintaining the peace and harmony you so desire.

JOYCE SAYS:
Traits to treasure: The way you provide comfort and security for those you love. To transform: Avoid letting protectiveness turn into possessiveness by allowing family members to make their own choices.

Moon in Gemini ☽ ♊

Emotionally Versatile
Feelings are filtered through your intellect. Mental stimulation and variety are necessary for emotional satisfaction.

With the Moon under Mercury's domain, the mind and the emotions mix. The emotional message you received from your family was to filter emotions through the intellect. You may have received this message from rational, intellectually oriented parents, or ones who were so emotional that you unconsciously decided never to let your emotions hold sway. In either case, emotions are subject to reasonable analysis. You question whether it is okay to feel what you do, and when there is conflict between feelings and thinking, thinking wins. This heightens your intellect and objectivity, but it may cause you to deny emotional needs, which can make it difficult for you to be present for the emotional needs of others. You nurture by encouraging loved ones to be objective rather than to feel. This may help them in coming to terms with feelings, or it may get in the way of intimacy. Wanting to run from emotional neediness can make you cold and unfeeling. Recognizing the difference between rational assessment and intellectual denial is essential.

This placement conveys a high degree of intelligence. You are resourceful and quick-witted. A craving for intellectual stimulation exists, and learning is lifelong. You are interested in a variety of topics and enjoy working on many projects simultaneously. Because of this, it is possible to spread yourself too thin.

You socialize easily with all sorts of people and on a casual level can get along with just about anyone, but emotionally you are changeable. What you feel today may not be what you feel tomorrow. You do not want to be hemmed in or have emotional demands placed on you. A part of you does not want to commit for fear that a better opportunity will show up or that you will get bored. This may make emotional relationships difficult if others expect more than you want to give. As you dislike conflict, there is a tendency to talk around issues rather than deal with them honestly. A silver tongue may get you out of immediate hot water momentarily, but only being honest changes situations long term.

JOYCE SAYS:
Traits to treasure: Your ability to be emotionally objective.
To transform: Avoid letting objectivity get in the way of what you actually feel by recognizing the difference between rational assessment and intellectual denial.

Moon in Cancer   ☽ ♋

Emotionally Mothering
Emotionally sensitive, you are mothering and nurturing to loved ones. Family loyalties run deep.

The Moon rules Cancer, so this is a strong placement. With the Moon here, the emotional message you received from your family was to put family first. You may have learned to be sensitive, emotional, and nurturing from a caring family, or you may have come to recognize the importance of nurturing because it was lacking in your upbringing. In either case, the Moon in Cancer represents the most mothering placement of the Zodiac, regardless of whether you are a man or woman. There is a love of home and family and protectiveness toward those you care for. You have strong loyalties to your family of origin, regardless of the ease or difficulty of the relationships, and strong loyalties to your spouse and children as an adult. This makes it difficult to say no to loved ones, particularly to your children, and may lead to being overprotective.

With the Moon in a water sign, you are comfortable with feelings. They do not have to be logical or explainable. You are naturally intuitive and trust your instincts. There is an awareness of undercurrents in the environment and perception of how others feel. Yet your perceptions are difficult to explain. The conclusions are so obvious that it is hard to comprehend that others cannot see exactly what you do. This may cause problems in two ways. One, you may expect those close to you to be just as aware of your needs as you are of theirs. When someone you care about is sad or hurt or upset, you go out of your way to do something for that person and you expect the same in return. If you have to ask for something, you may feel hurt and rejected, as if another deliberately ignored your needs rather than being unaware of them.

The second source of misunderstanding may occur when someone asks you how you know what you know. Since the insights are so obvious to you, when questioned, you can feel as if you are not trusted, rather than realizing that perhaps the person is simply seeking additional information. Your sensitivity is a double-edged sword. It helps you to mother, nurture, and to take care of others, but it can also make you overly sensitive to seeming slights. And you have a long memory for what hurts you. While it is wonderful to be at home with your feelings, it is also important to develop some emotional objectivity and learn not to get carried away by momentary feelings.

JOYCE SAYS:
Traits to treasure: The way you take care of and nurture your family.
To transform: Avoid emotional suffering by recognizing that your own sensitivity, more than other people's actions, is often the source of your hurt feelings.

Moon in Leo ☽ ♌

Emotionally Proud

Emotionally, being appreciated means everything. You are loyal and steadfast in commitments and want to be loved for being yourself.

With the Moon under the Sun's domain, the emotional message you received from your family was to be recognized and appreciated. You may have received this message by example, for instance, coming from a prominent family or one that adored you. Or this message may stem from precisely opposite causes, such as a desire to make up for a family that paid little attention to you or your needs. Whatever the case, feeling appreciated is a must.

As an adult, you love romance, parties, entertainment, and extravagance in general. Your extroversion, social magnanimity, and sexual magnetism are coupled with a generous spirit and a strong sense of pride. You have tremendous loyalty to loved ones. You readily shower your mate and children with affection, and you will do anything in your power to benefit them. All that you require in return is appreciation. Compliments will get others everywhere with you, provided the compliments are sincere. You want to be loved for being yourself.

Your pride and love of attention heighten your strength of purpose. These qualities can propel you toward success, but they can also be the source of problems if you do not feel recognized or appreciated enough. The operative word is "feel" because being appreciated and feeling appreciated are not the same thing. Your need may be so great that others may either find it hard to fulfill or tire of having to fulfill it. As an adult, it is important to recognize that feeling important must come from inside rather than outside, or you are forever dependent upon others for self-esteem.

You seldom lose your fiery temper but are hurt much more easily than is apparent. Loyalty means everything to you, but blind spots in your emotional nature can cause you to expect unquestioned loyalty. This may lead to perceiving disagreement as disloyalty. Pride may prevent you from admitting emotional needs, making it easier to withdraw than to attempt to resolve differences. It is important to be as honest and expressive when you are hurt as you are when feeling good.

JOYCE SAYS:

Traits to treasure: Your generous spirit, loyalty, and sexual magnetism.
To transform: Admit that you actually have emotional needs so that they can more easily be fulfilled.

Moon in Virgo ☽ ♍

Emotionally Analytical

Emotions combine with pragmatism. You analyze your feelings and show affection by being helpful to loved ones.

With the Moon under Mercury's domain, the emotional message that you received from your family was to keep your feelings under wrap and that it is better to be practical than emotional. This message may have been received from a family that was stoic in its emotional expression or from one that was so overly emotional that you unconsciously vowed never to behave that way. Either way, you instinctively subject your feelings to practical analysis.

You are emotionally conservative and do not express feelings easily. Being emotionally analytical allows you to examine feelings, but it is important not to become so logical that you rationalize what you actually feel. It may be difficult to understand, or be sympathetic to, the feelings of others.

Believing that caring shows more by action than romantic gestures, you nurture by taking care of, or helping, loved ones. On the home front, you seek neatness and order. Very likely, you are a good cook, more concerned with healthy diet and nutrition than with rich gourmet meals.

You are always seeking ways to improve and want to help loved ones do the same. This gives you perfectionist tendencies. Carried too far, constantly seeking self-improvement gets in the way of self-acceptance. And suggestions meant to help others improve may be considered critical rather than helpful. Perfectionism also causes worry about little things, and when worried, you are likely to nag. The key to your emotional well-being is distinguishing between what is important and what is not and letting others decide the same for themselves. Loved ones need sympathy and compassion as well as clean socks and fresh sheets.

JOYCE SAYS:

Traits to treasure: The tangible way you take care of those you love.
To transform: Avoid letting perfectionism get in the way of accepting yourself or family members.

Moon in Libra   ☽ ♎

Emotionally Genteel
Emotionally you seek balance and harmony. You dislike conflict, and you go out of your way to avoid it.

With the Moon under Venus' domain, the emotional message you received from your family was to be nice, to please others, and to seek harmony. You may have received this message by example, such as coming from a genteel, well-mannered family. Or this message may stem from precisely opposite causes, such as coming from a crass or conflict-oriented family, which caused you to make an unconscious decision never to behave that way. In either case, there is emphasis on refinement and value placed on harmony and cooperation. You do your best to behave socially appropriately and are more likely to compliment than to criticize others.

You naturally possess grace and refinement and dislike crude behavior. You appreciate the arts and beauty, want your home to be aesthetically pleasing, and enjoy hosting social gatherings.

Libra is the sign of relationships, so you get along with others easily. Significant one-to-one relationships are important for emotional well-being. You want to share experiences but not with just anyone. In order to be content, relationships must be with intellectual and social equals who share your interests.

You relate to people mentally more than emotionally and subject your feelings to intellectual scrutiny. You believe that thinking is better than feeling and that you should always remain rational, well poised, and gracious. These beliefs help you detach and see all sides of a situation. However, it may be easier for you to think about feelings than let yourself actually feel them.

Objectivity works well as long as it does not turn into rationalizations that discount your original feelings. A desire for social approval may make you emotionally dependent. This, coupled with your dislike of conflict, makes it safer to feel what you believe others expect than what you truly feel. In relationships, you are susceptible to flattery, and you may flatter in return. You may tend to tell others what you think they want to hear or to behave the way you perceive they want you to behave in order to gain approval. A little white lie about someone's appearance hurts no one and saves feelings. However, if carried too far, little white lies turn into dishonesty, whether it is with yourself, others, or both. Emotional fulfillment requires appropriately balancing your needs with the needs of others.

JOYCE SAYS:

Traits to treasure: Your willingness to consider others.
To transform: Avoid letting your wish to please others get in the way of
honest interactions by balancing their emotional needs with your own.

Moon in Scorpio ☽ ♏

Emotionally Intense

Emotions and feelings are intense with regard to whatever you find
meaningful. Life, to feel worth living, must be full of passion.

With the Moon under Pluto's domain, the emotional message you received
from your family was to be strong, keep your powerful emotions close, and
not to let anyone know too much. You may have learned this by example
from a family that was intensely emotional and secretive. Or you may have
come from a family with two extremely opposite scenarios. Family members may have been completely alienated from feelings, making it impossible to express your own. Or the family may have been so emotionally
volatile that you unconsciously decided never to behave that way. Whatever
the case, your feelings are powerful and not easily expressed.

Motivated by deep emotional desires, you make no distinction between
moderation and apathy. Life, to be worth living, must include passion. This
passion may be expressed sexually, but it may also be displayed in a fervent
commitment to a person, job, or ideal. You are loyal and steadfast, and no
sacrifice is too great once you make a commitment.

You are a natural psychologist or detective. Innately in tune with undercurrents, you have the ability to pierce through facades. You instinctively
grasp the core meaning of situations and recognize the underlying motivations of people. You have no need to rationally define where your insights
come from; you just know they are true.

Your natural abilities may be the source of emotional or relational problems. Since you perceive undercurrents so easily, it is hard for you to believe
that other people cannot perceive in exactly the same way. Your feelings are
strong and deep but not easily expressed; because of their intensity, you
think they are obvious. This does not provide much incentive to communicate how you feel. It is possible for strong emotional attachments to lead
to jealousy and possessiveness and to perceive disagreement as disloyalty.

Being far more sensitive than you appear to be, you are easily hurt, particularly when those you love are not aware of your needs. And pride may

prevent you from admitting needs, which you see as signs of weakness. Secretive by nature, it is far easier for you to try to subtly dominate a situation than to actually talk about what is bothering you. When you are hurt, you may overreact emotionally and obsess about being wronged. This is when the famous Scorpio sting rears its head and you become vengeful. Cutting remarks may make you feel better for the moment but do nothing to resolve relational differences. You may never be able to completely avoid emotional highs and lows, but learning to communicate about emotional differences and recognizing that others have a right to their thoughts and feelings, even when they disagree with yours, goes a long way.

JOYCE SAYS:

Traits to treasure: The depth of your feelings and the strength of your commitments.

To transform: Avoid letting hurts fester into resentment by acknowledging how you feel and talking about differences as they arise.

Moon in Sagittarius ☽ ♐

Emotionally Independent
Emotionally, you are independent and wish to feel free. You have a lust for adventure and excitement.

With the Moon under Jupiter's rule, the emotional message you received from your family was to be free and independent. This may have been learned by positive example, such as growing up in a family whose freedom came through success or self-sufficiency. Or it may have been learned by growing up in an unreliable family where you had to fend for yourself at an early age, or the complete opposite scenario of being brought up in an overbearing environment, leading you to make an unconscious decision never to be hemmed in again. Whatever the scenario, you want to live life spontaneously and come and go as you please, and you encourage loved ones to do the same.

It is possible that your family held strong religious or philosophical beliefs. Sagittarius is the most intellectual of the fire signs, which gives you a restless, searching intellect. You are eager to learn and desire to find truth. Your interests lie in the big picture, and not in the details. Enjoying the role of the teacher, when you believe in something, you eagerly and easily persuade others to agree.

The desire to tell the truth as you see it has the potential to get you into trouble. While you would not purposely hurt someone's feelings, you may speak without considering how your words will affect others and then be amazed when others are offended at your bluntness.

Your basic nature is cheerful and optimistic. If situations are bad today, you tend to believe that tomorrow will be better. Positive thinking may actually be positive, or it may be a way of denying that situations are as they are. It is important not to overestimate your abilities or to let optimism get in the way of critical analysis.

As a fire sign Moon, you do not question feelings. You thoroughly enjoy positive feelings like joy and excitement but may run away from, or rationalize, less positive feelings, such as sadness or grief. It is hard for you to accept that no one is positive all the time.

You express feelings of love and affection easily and enjoy being generous to loved ones, so long as loved ones do not make demands on you. Feeling demanded of is a hot button. The combination of the need for freedom and a refusal to be fenced in may make you balk at even the most reasonable requests. It can be hard to fathom that all relationships include expectations and that if you want others to be there for you, you must satisfy their needs in return.

JOYCE SAYS:
Traits to treasure: The freedom that you allow those you care for.
To transform: Avoid letting your freedom needs get in the way of intimacy by respecting the emotional needs of loved ones.

Moon in Capricorn ☽ ♑

Emotionally Cautious
Emotions and duty go together. A conservative nature makes you more likely to do things for loved ones than to talk about your feelings.

With the Moon under Saturn's domain, the emotional message you received from your family was to keep your emotions to yourself. You may have been brought up in a family that was emotionally stoic, where feelings were not allowed. Or your family may have been overly emotional, causing you to unconsciously decide never to make a spectacle of yourself. Whatever the case, your conservative nature does not allow for easy expression of feelings.

Feelings are subject to practical analysis and a questioning of whether or not it is okay to feel a particular way.

You place emphasis on achievement, status, and prestige. These ambitions are also part of the emotional messages from your family, whether by example or lack of it. Money and material possessions mean a great deal because they symbolize success.

You were born with a strong sense of duty, have always been mature, and in youth may have related better to adults than people your own age. You work hard, are responsible, and aspire to positions of leadership.

Dealing with the feeling side of life is not easy. You are cautious emotionally and it takes you time to get to know and trust people. Being fearful of rejection can cause you to keep feelings bottled up. An outer reserve may make you appear cold and indifferent rather than shy. Even when comfortable, you are more likely to show that you care by what you do for others than by emotionally expressing yourself. Yet those you get close to know that you are reliable and that they can count on you.

There is a tendency to look to tradition for how things are done. Especially if your family of origin was conservative or authoritarian, you have to be careful of developing an overly righteous sense of right and wrong. As Saturn's combination with the Moon is not an easy one, you may become a taskmaster, turning nurturing into getting others to do "what is right" in your definition. This is the same definition that you try to live up to yourself.

Your feelings may be hurt more easily than is apparent, as you seem too practical to let things bother you. Yet at home, you are hurt if those you love do not appreciate your efforts on their behalf. At work, you may be sensitive to what you deem slights that offend your dignity. These feelings, which you keep under wraps, can become brooding or melancholic and may cause excessive self-protectiveness. In close relationships, this self-protectiveness can be expressed by turning cold and unconsciously pushing others away. Healthy emotional ties depend upon allowing yourself to feel whatever you do, communicating those feelings, and replacing strict judgment with acceptance of loved ones (assuming they deserve it).

JOYCE SAYS:
Traits to treasure: The way your family can count on you.
To transform: Work on becoming more comfortable expressing your feelings to loved ones.

Moon in Aquarius ☽ ♒

Emotionally Detached

You seek emotional detachment and objectivity and you prefer to relate to people intellectually rather than emotionally.

With the Moon under Uranus' domain, the emotional message you received from your family was to be intelligent, original, and independent. You may have received this message by example from intelligent, original, free-thinking family members. Or you may have deciphered this message by growing up in a restrictive, conservative family and making an unconscious vow to break free of limitations. Whatever the case, you are attracted to what is new and out of the ordinary. Intuitive insights frequently put you ahead of your time.

You are friendly and outgoing in an impersonal way. Friendship means a great deal to you, and intellectual companionship is a must. You are idea-oriented, with particular interest in politics, humanitarian or social concerns, and metaphysical truths. Your home may be a meeting place of friends, and a spouse or lover does not take the place of other companions. Even your children, from an early age, get treated like friends and equals.

Freedom and independence are of prime importance. It may be difficult for you to make long-lasting relational commitments unless you are free to come and go as you please. You may not actually go anywhere; you just want to know that you can.

It is easier to relate mind-to-mind than emotionally. A second message received in childhood was that it is better to think than to feel. As an adult, your mind and emotions tend to react together. Instinctively, you detach and analyze so that you do not get emotionally carried away. Yet it is important to recognize and stay true to what you actually feel. When conflicts arise between thinking and feeling, you prefer that feelings conform to logic. Talking about what you think is much more comfortable than honestly addressing what you feel. This disparity can send mixed messages to loved ones. Also, it may be difficult to understand others or be sympathetic to their needs when they behave emotionally rather than rationally. This can cause disconnect in relationships. Your all-so-sensible judgments do not alter how you really feel, despite your best efforts at rationalization. And the tendency to want to run when others express messy emotions makes you appear cold and erratic.

Traits to treasure: The way you embrace friends like family members.
To transform: Avoid letting the intellect completely override feelings.
Admitting that you have feelings is a good start.

Moon in Pisces   ☽ ♓

Emotionally Intuitive

Emotionally you are sensitive, compassionate, and empathetic. On an intuitive level, you are very aware of other people's needs.

With the Moon under Neptune's domain, the emotional message received from your family was to be kind and compassionate, and to ignore what is unpleasant. You may have received this message by example from caring, nurturing parents, or from a home environment where, due to necessity, you took care of others and ignored unpleasant circumstances. Or you may have come from a family that was cruel and intolerant and therefore you made an unconscious decision never to be that way.

You have a creative, imaginative, and artistic soul and a true appreciation for beauty. Talent may lie in art, music, theater, writing, or decorating and design. Beautiful surroundings make your spirit soar. Listening to music, going to a movie, the theater, or a museum lift you out of the doldrums.

Pisces is the most sensitive, compassionate, and psychic of the water signs. Your sensitivity and compassion are for all people and living creatures, not just those who are close to you. Facing life through your feelings and instincts makes you sensitive to the moods and vibrations of your environment. If you are consciously aware of these vibrations, you readily perceive undercurrents that others cannot see. If you are not consciously aware, you are unconsciously affected. This sensitivity creates the need for time alone every day to detach from outside influences. Practices such as meditation and yoga help you to distinguish between feelings that are yours and those that come from outside vibes. They also help fulfill spiritual longings to connect with something greater than yourself.

Because of your kindness and emotional sensitivity, seeing another person in need acts like a call for your help, regardless of whether your help has actually been requested. You readily provide nurturing and caring. Your preference for seeing the good in all people allows you to help others get in touch with their potential. You hold yourself up to the criteria of what a "good" person would do for another. This gives you the tendency to play rescuer with all people, but particularly with a mate or child.

Seeing only the admirable characteristics of another may lead to disappointment when you discover his or her negative qualities—which everyone has. And because you feel loved when you are needed, there is a tendency to attract people who need to be taken care of. At the beginning you do this willingly. The unspoken and perhaps unconscious expectation is that you will be taken care of in return. In essence, you want to rescue and be rescued. Being sensitive to the unspoken needs of others, it is hard to believe that not everyone can perceive in the same way. You may be deeply hurt when those you love are not mind-readers responding to your unspoken wishes. When hurt, you may withdraw inward, and it is possible to go to the extreme of no longer doing anything for anyone. Developing discrimination is a must. It enables you choose whether or not you truly want to help another in a given situation.

JOYCE SAYS:

Traits to treasure: The way you show kindness to all those you come in contact with.

To transform: Avoid being hurt by expecting those you love to be mind-readers—that's your department.

MOON IN THE HOUSES

Moon in the First House

Sensitive About Surroundings

You are emotionally in tune with your immediate environment, and the environment affects your feelings.

You are sensitive and emotional and have a mothering nature, regardless of the Moon's sign. If you are not aware of your sensitivity to the environment's effects, you may experience what seem like inexplicable mood swings. Your moods and feelings are obvious to others whether or not you want them to be. You have a strong need for personal recognition even though you are emotionally independent. Also, very likely there are close family ties, particularly to females.

Traits to treasure: Your emotional awareness of your immediate environment.
To transform: Avoid letting the immediate environment affect your emotional well-being.

Moon in the Second House

Sensitive About Money
Financial security and emotional security go hand in hand.

Money and security are important to your emotional well-being. Your moods may fluctuate with your income, and money must be tucked away for a rainy day in order for you to feel safe. Yet there may be internal conflict between saving and spending, as you desire the best of physical comforts and material possessions. Your mood of the moment very likely determines spending. One moment you may spend freely, only to worry the next if you have overspent. You may be financially generous to family members, or you may feel put upon by their requests. Balancing the need for security with the desire for the finer things in life is essential to emotional well-being.

JOYCE SAYS:
Traits to treasure: Tucking away money for later for security.
To transform: Avoid letting your mood of the moment determine your spending.

Moon in the Third House

Sensitive About Ideas
Your emotions and your decision-making abilities are tied together.

Feelings influence your thinking and your decision-making abilities. When emotionally upset, communication is difficult. Yet, you have the intellectual capacity to examine your emotions and you excel at talking about feelings once you have examined them. You enjoy learning, yet in all likelihood, early education was influenced by how comfortable you felt at school. A strong bond exists between you and any siblings, and you may be mothering toward them. If the Moon is in a cardinal or mutable sign, you may tend to change your mind based upon your mood of the moment.

Traits to treasure: Your ability to intellectually examine your feelings.
To transform: Avoid letting emotions get in the way of making decisions.

Moon in the Fourth House

Sensitive About Family

You are particularly nurturing and have extraordinary emotional ties to your family.

The Moon is the natural ruler of the fourth house, so this is a strong placement. Irrespective of your sex, you have a strongly mothering nature. You are emotionally attached to your family of origin and the family that you create as an adult, and there is a desire for their approval, regardless of the ease or difficulty of these relationships. Very likely you are a good cook and enjoy hosting family gatherings. A happy home life equates with security. You are particularly protective of your children and spouse, but also protective of extended family members, roommates, or anyone who lives with you or who you consider family.

JOYCE SAYS:

Traits to treasure: The way you nurture family members or people you consider like family.
To transform: Avoid being overly sensitive to the approval or disapproval of family members.

Moon in the Fifth House

Sensitive About Self-expression

Your emotions are most invested in creative expression, your children, and any love affairs.

You are emotionally invested in creative expression, children, and love affairs. You exude charm and are fun to be with. You have vitality, zest for life, and the desire to express yourself creativity. Strong bonds exist between you and your offspring, and you are a protective parent. In romance, emotional attachments are powerful. You are loyal and expect loyalty in return. It may not be obvious, but you desire recognition, attention, and approval, and are easily upset if you do not feel appreciated by those you love.

Traits to treasure: Strong emotional bonds with the people you love.
To transform: Avoid going overboard on your need to be appreciated by loved ones.

Moon in the Sixth House

Sensitive About Work
Your health, work, and emotional well-being all influence one another.

Your emotions are tied to work and health, so feeling emotionally in tune with work is a must. Your daily performance can vary depending upon your mood, and your mood is affected by how you perceive your performance. Perception is the operable word, as you are a perfectionist and may be overly self-critical, which can lead to undervaluing your efforts. Oversensitivity to even constructive criticism in the workplace is possible. At the same time, you are a very hard worker and expect the same from others. Because of this, you may alternate between being a nurturing and considerate boss or coworker and one who is overly critical. Your health may go up and down with your emotions, and work difficulties can take a toll upon your physical well-being.

JOYCE SAYS:
Traits to treasure: The way you nurture coworkers.
To transform: Avoid being sensitive to even constructive criticism in the workplace.

Moon in the Seventh House

Sensitive About Relationships
Your emotions are tied to one-to-one relationships, and your emotional well-being depends upon having harmony.

Emotions are intertwined with all one-to-one relationships. You have a need for emotional security in marriage and partnership, as well as approval from your mate, best friends, and colleagues. A sixth sense about the feelings of others makes you sensitive to their needs. Your own feelings may go up and down depending upon the perceived state of significant relationships. Perceptions are important, as you may be so overly sensitive that differences of opinion seem like criticism and disapproval. This in turn creates a sense of insecurity.

The seventh house represents the marriage partner as well as you. It is possible that your spouse is the one with emotional ups and downs. It is also possible that rather than owning your own emotions, you project them onto your mate. If this is the case, you see your mate as the overly emotional one and yourself as being more rational.

JOYCE SAYS:

Traits to treasure: Your concern for other people's feelings.
To transform: Avoid being overly dependent on other people for your own emotional well-being.

Moon in the Eighth House

Sensitive About Sex

Your emotions are tied to whatever is shared in relationships, from sex to money.

Your emotions are intense and your feelings deep. You are very intuitive, and possibly psychic. There is an interest in the occult and reincarnation. You want to know the meaning of life. You have an instinctive understanding of other people and why they do what they do, and have a heartfelt desire to understand and get to the bottom of situations.

Your emotions are tied to whatever is shared in relationships. Sexual urges are powerful, but sex must be tied to emotional connection or it creates feelings of emptiness. Emotional ups and downs may occur relating to joint finances and inheritances. Money in long-term investments makes you feel secure.

JOYCE SAYS:

Traits to treasure: Your instinctive understanding of other people.
To transform: Avoid hinging your emotional well-being on momentary ups and downs relationally.

Moon in the Ninth House

Sensitive About Beliefs

Emotions are attached to your attitudes and beliefs about the world.

You feel emotionally comfortable any place in the world. You have a yearning to experience different cultures and a desire to know what is around the next corner. Travel represents an exciting adventure, and you may live far from where you were born. Your worldview, which includes religious, ethical, moral, and philosophical beliefs, is influenced by your travels. Yet this worldview is colored by your emotions and possibly influenced by your early childhood, no matter how far from home you end up.

Emotional well-being is also tied to educational and intellectual achievement. Education may come through universities or it may come through life experience.

JOYCE SAYS:

Traits to treasure: The ability to be emotionally comfortable any place in the world.

To transform: Avoid letting your worldview be colored by any family prejudices.

Moon in the Tenth House

Sensitive About Career

Emotions are invested in your professional reputation, success, and status.

Your emotions are tied to professional ambitions, public standing, and family relations. Prominence and professional recognition are priorities. There are strong emotional ties to family and a desire for their approval as well as the approval of other authority figures. How you feel greatly influences career potential, which makes it important that you do not react to people and situations in an overly sensitive manner. Women may help you get ahead.

You possess an intuitive sense about social, political, or business trends, and public charisma assists you in taking advantage of and influencing these trends.

JOYCE SAYS:

Traits to treasure: Your intuitive ability to sense trends.

To transform: Avoid tying your emotional well-being to praise from authority figures.

Moon in the Eleventh House

Sensitive About Friendships

Good friends are like family members, and these relationships contribute to your emotional well-being.

Your emotions are tied to friendships and group activities. Companionship is needed for a sense of emotional well-being, and it is important to you to be part of a group or organization with social or humanitarian goals.

You have close attachments to friends and treat friends like family members. You are nurturing and emotionally responsive to their needs, and expect the same in return. If overly sensitive, it is possible to feel slighted when no slight was intended.

JOYCE SAYS:

Traits to treasure: The way you treat friends like family members.
To transform: Avoid being overly sensitive in friendships.

Moon in the Twelfth House

Sensitive to Undercurrents

Intuition makes you sensitive to undercurrents in your environment that affect you emotionally.

You are extremely sensitive, both to yourself and to others. Very likely, you have psychic ability. You feel things before they happen. You feel the atmosphere around you, and whether you are conscious of it or not, the atmosphere has a direct effect on your emotions. You are also intuitively in touch with the needs of others. These unspoken needs appear to you as direct requests for help, which in your compassion, you find difficult to disregard.

This sensitivity may cause you to feel overwhelmed and possibly depressed. There is a need to retreat from people and situations. Spending time alone in meditation or contemplation, particularly when you are upset, helps keep you centered. But it is important to use this time alone to assess problems rather than to escape from them. Ultimately, too much time alone is isolating and depressing.

JOYCE SAYS:

Traits to treasure: Your kindness and compassion.
To transform: Avoid getting so pulled in by other people's problems that you can only escape them by isolating yourself.

Chapter 7

MERCURY — HOW YOU THINK AND COMMUNICATE

Key Words: Thinking, Reasoning, Intelligence
Rules: Gemini and Virgo, Third and Sixth Houses
Cycle: 88 days to revolve around the Sun,
never more than 28 degrees from Sun
Somatic Influences: Respiratory System, Intestines

Mercury is the planet that rules the conscious mind and intellect. It represents how we think, communicate, write, speak, and learn. Logic, reasoning, and objective analysis fall under its domain. Mercury rules Gemini and Virgo, an air sign and an earth sign, and their respective third and sixth houses. The association with Gemini relates to abstract reasoning, A + B = C logic, and to intellectual curiosity—knowledge for the sake of knowing. The association with Virgo relates to more practical intelligence and manual dexterity, the kind of knowledge it takes to accomplish tasks. Gemini is associated with books or magazines; Virgo, how-to manuals.

Mercury is the planet closest to the Sun. In our individual charts, it is never more than 28 degrees away, which means that Mercury is either found in the same sign as the Sun, the sign before it, or the sign after it. Typically speaking, the closer in degree that Mercury is to the Sun, the more difficult it is to be objective about ourselves. If Mercury is in the same sign as the Sun, it may be difficult to listen to other points of view.

Mercury is considered neither a masculine nor a feminine planet but takes on the characteristics of the sign in which it falls. In individual charts, the sign Mercury posits reflects the manner in which we think and communicate and what information we pay attention to. If Mercury falls in an air sign, thinking is logical. If Mercury falls in an earth sign, thinking is pragmatic. If Mercury falls in a water sign or a fire sign, thinking is more intuitive. These differences reflect the way the mind works, not the accuracy or inaccuracy of the conclusions formed. Because air signs communicate more clearly than water signs, it does not necessarily follow that air signs have the right answer, only that they express it in more easily understandable ways. Mercury's house position shows where we place our mental energy.

Positive expressions of Mercury are mental agility and good communication skills. Negative expression can be indecisiveness, overemphasis of the intellect at the expense of emotions, and verbosity.

MERCURY IN THE SIGNS

Mercury in Aries ☿ ♈

Quick Mind

You think rapidly, learn quickly, and do not mince words. You say exactly what is on your mind and appreciate forthrightness from others.

You have a quick mind, learn rapidly, and are intellectually competitive. You thrive on mental challenges, whether those challenges come from learning something new, debates, or arguments. You make up your mind quickly and communicate in a direct, honest, and straightforward fashion. Others know they can count on you to tell the truth; you say what you mean and mean what you say. You excel in debates and when quick decision-making is a must. However, being impatient, it is important for you to remember to get all the facts and not jump to conclusions.

You place such high value on straightforward honesty that any type of social diplomacy seems like a lie. This may be problematic, as you tend to think and speak at the same time, without censoring your thoughts, and may see arguments as self-expression rather than as conflict. Because of this, you are surprised when another person sees your honest assessment as insulting or aggressive. Paying attention to social cues and recognizing the perspectives of others is important if you want them to listen to your views.

Traits to treasure: Your ability to think on your feet and make quick decisions.
To transform: Listen to others and avoid jumping to conclusions.

Mercury in Taurus ☿ ♉

Commonsense Thinking
Your thinking is slow and deliberate. You take a commonsense approach to situations and value practical ideas, not grandiose schemes.

Mercury in Taurus conveys common sense. The mind focuses on practical considerations rather than abstract ideas. You are most interested in learning what is useful and prefer on-the-job training to book learning. It takes time to assimilate information, but once you do, you remember it forever. Being materially oriented and having good business sense, you excel at business management, moneymaking ideas, or in finding practical solutions to problems.

When it comes to decision-making, you take your time, assessing all available information before coming to conclusions. Once you make up your mind, you are reluctant to change it, and can be quite stubborn about your opinions. This is a positive attribute when you are standing up for principles and not allowing others to shake you out of deeply held beliefs. This attribute becomes negative if you refuse to look at information simply because it contradicts your attitudes and beliefs. Keeping an open mind is essential.

JOYCE SAYS:
Traits to treasure: Your commonsense approach to problem solving.
To transform: Be willing to change your mind.

Mercury in Gemini ☿ ♊

Quick Witted
You have a sharp mind and quick wit. Born curious, you question everything. As a child, you most likely never tired of asking your mother "why?"

This is a strong placement, as Mercury rules Gemini. Intellectual stimulation is a must and learning a joy. You were born curious and you question everything. You want to know why things are the way they are and seek logical explanations. Thinking is logical, objective, and detached. Your wish to understand gives you the ability to impersonally analyze information.

Your mind is sharp and your wit is quick. You are intellectually versatile and have an interest in a wide variety of topics. Versatility can make it difficult to find one topic that is interesting enough to stick with, and you may jump from one idea to the next. This makes it best to work in the field of ideas. You are a persuasive communicator and excel at writing, teaching, reporting, selling, and public relations.

Varied interests make it possible for you to converse with just about anyone. You enjoy intellectual repartee. And when it comes to convincing people of your ideas, you present your case so logically that you can convince almost anyone of whatever you like, and you enjoy the challenge of doing so. However, while you enjoy debates, you dislike actual conflict. This may cause you to say whatever it takes to get yourself out of hot water or to talk around situations that need resolution rather than dealing with them head on.

JOYCE SAYS:

Traits to treasure: Your ability to talk people into your point of view.
To transform: Avoid talking around situations without actually facing them.

Mercury in Cancer ☿ ♋

Receptive Thinking
Your thinking is intuitive, which can make it difficult to explain how you know what you do. Somehow you just do.

Mercury in Cancer conveys a retentive mind and subliminal awareness of the environment. There is a strong sense of intuition, and thoughts and feelings are inextricably linked. In listening to others, you exhibit caring and compassion, and are empathetically in tune with not just their words but the underlying meaning attached to them.

You approach ideas by what they feel like. If they feel right, you trust their validity. If not, you distrust them. Since feelings rather than logic guide decision-making, this might be called emotional intelligence. While logic does not insure a correct answer, it does make the answer easily explainable. Since your insights come through feelings and intuition, it is difficult for you to stand back and objectively view information or to explain how you know what you do. This can lead to being overly sensitive and feeling threatened when asked even the simplest questions about your conclusions. It is also possible for emotional attachments to obscure facts and get in the way of intuition when you are personally involved in situations. While you will never be completely analytical or detached, cultivating objectivity helps stop emotions from compromising better judgment.

JOYCE SAYS:

Traits to treasure: The way you know what people mean no matter what they say.

To transform: Avoid letting emotions get in the way of good judgment.

Mercury in Leo ☿ ♌

Dramatic Communication

You are verbally self-expressive and can communicate dramatically. This gives you persuasive abilities in conveying ideas.

Mercury in Leo conveys the ability to communicate in a self-expressive and articulate manner, with the warmth of your heart showing through. A sense of humor and a flair for dramatics make you an entertaining storyteller. These qualities provide talent in teaching and training. They also give you the ability to persuasively to sell personal or professional ideas. Your communications exude self-confidence and show executive ability. You enjoy being the boss or the authority figure and being in the limelight. You also very much enjoy intellectual entertainment—good books, movies, and plays all delight you.

As Leo is a fixed sign, you form opinions slowly, and once your mind is made up, you are reluctant to change it. Ego attachments to opinions can cause you to disregard contrary information. While you yourself are strong-minded, you may perceive those who disagree with you as disloyal. Keeping an open mind is ultimately essential to good decision-making. In business, an open mind helps you to change strategies when necessary. In personal relationships, it allows for the resolution of differences.

JOYCE SAYS:

Traits to treasure: The creative way you dress up a story and make it more interesting.

To transform: Avoid letting your ego get in the way of better judgment.

Mercury in Virgo ☿ ♍

Discriminating Analysis

Your thinking is analytical and practical. Your attention to detail and ability to think in a sequential manner helps you excel in teaching or training positions.

This is a strong placement, as Mercury rules Virgo. You possess common sense and are interested in useful ideas. This position combines analytical thinking with the ability to actually put ideas to work. Value is placed on education and on developing specialized skills. Having the right tools and the ability to use them properly is a must, whether the tools are a computer or a hammer and nails.

Attention to detail and the ability to think in a sequential manner (i.e., this is step 1, this is step 2) help you to excel in teaching or training positions, in writing how-to manuals, or in presenting information. You excel at detail work such as accounting and any work that requires precision. However, if perfectionism is carried to too far, you may spend too much time on unimportant tasks or emphasize minutiae that only you deem important.

When learning, you ask questions that no one else thinks of. Instructors may believe that you do not understand the subject, when in fact you are seeking greater clarity on the material presented. You look for ways to improve, and if someone can show you a better, more efficient way to perform a task, you are happy to learn about it. Because of this, you believe that others also seek to improve, and you offer others suggestions to help them to do so. However, it is possible for others to view your suggestions as critical rather than helpful.

JOYCE SAYS:

Traits to treasure: Your ability to analyze facts and information.
To transform: Avoid getting lost in minutiae.

Mercury in Libra ☿ ♎

Diplomatic Communication

You have a logical, intellectual mind and place importance on human relationships. You present ideas diplomatically, but convincingly.

Mercury in Libra conveys a logical and intellectual mind. You are concerned with making fair and balanced judgments. Focus on relationships makes you charming and diplomatic. Value is placed on harmony, cooperation, and getting along with others. You enjoy sharing ideas, and avoid heated conflict or disagreements. In essence, you behave civilly and want to associate with others who do the same.

You possess excellent communication skills and analytical abilities. Before making a decision, you weigh and balance all sides of an issue. This makes you a natural for law, mediation, arbitration, or diplomacy. Weighing all sides may lead to indecisiveness, but once you make up your mind, you excel at winning people over to your ideas. And like a diplomat, you excel at not only winning them over but also convincing them that your thoughts were their own.

You are also diplomatic because you want to be liked. Being diplomatic by telling a white lie to save a person's feelings, such as saying they look nice rather than expressing a harsh truth, is good social behavior. However, diplomacy carried to a greater extreme, even to avoid conflict, is less than honest.

JOYCE SAYS:
Traits to treasure: The way you weigh and balance information to come to a fair conclusion.
To transform: Be truthful as well as diplomatic.

Mercury in Scorpio   ☿ ♏

Delving Mind
You say exactly what you mean or nothing at all. Your thinking is deep and profound, and you are attracted to the mysteries of life.

Mercury in Scorpio conveys a deep and profound mind. You delve into, research, and have to know all about any topic that interests you. Being instinctively discerning, you look directly into situations and ideas and get to the heart of matters, or "the bottom line." This can be characterized as shrewd or suspicious.

This perceptiveness extends to human nature. You intuitively psychoanalyze yourself and others. It is difficult to explain or justify how you know what you do, as your insights are not based upon logic or observable behavior. You instinctively recognize your own underlying motivations and those of others, see hidden motives, and perceive the truth behind whatever is spoken. Your judgments are usually accurate, but not always kind, and you need to be careful of being overly judgmental.

It is possible to be overly secretive or self-protective. You either say exactly what you think or nothing at all. Your biting humor can be witty or sarcastic. When angry or upset, your default mechanism is to be sarcastic and hurtful, particularly when you do not want to acknowledge or deal with what is actually bothering you. Since good instincts show you just where to strike, your harsh words are not easy to forgive. Learning to deal openly and honestly with upsetting situations as they happen, rather than storing up hurts, is a must.

JOYCE SAYS:

Traits to treasure: Your ability to zero in on the heart of any matter.
To transform: Avoid sarcasm and communicate directly about what's on your mind.

Mercury in Sagittarius   ☿ ♐

Grandiose Ideas

Your extraordinarily curious mind focuses on ideas and ideals. Blunt and to the point, you say precisely what you think.

Sagittarius is the most intellectual of the fire signs. Mercury here conveys an extraordinarily curious mind that focuses on ideas, ideals, and religious or philosophical concepts. You highly value education and perceive learning as an adventure. You concentrate on the big picture and excel in idea-oriented areas, such as teaching, political causes, and propagandizing. Yet your lack of interest in facts or details may cause you to overlook information, and the tendency to have too many irons in the fire may scatter your energy. Staying focused is a must.

Mercury here provides a good sense of humor, optimistic thinking, a quick mind, and direct speech. The desire to speak what you perceive as the truth helps you excel at debates and possibly at sermonizing a point of view. Naturally blunt, you do not necessarily take the impact of your words on others into consideration. Since you value honesty and have no malicious intent, it can be hard to recognize that your words may be hurtful.

Being optimistic helps you get through what others may see as the worst of times, but being optimistic may also exaggerate possibilities. It is possible to promise more than you can deliver and, despite the best of intentions, end up being unreliable.

Traits to treasure: The way you see learning as an adventure.
To transform: Avoid scattering your energy by having too many irons in the fire.

Mercury in Capricorn ☿ ♑

Practical Thinking
Your thinking is down-to-earth and practical. A methodical mind gives you outstanding organization skills, and you focus on what is useful.

Mercury in Capricorn conveys practical, methodical, and businesslike thinking. You are a realist, not an idealist. In commonsense fashion, you are interested in what is useful, what it takes to accomplish tasks. Airy-fairy ideas are not for you. The focus is on success. Good organizational skills, attention to detail, and a memory for facts and figures help in the quest for executive positions. Education and learning are undertaken with an eye toward furthering career, income, and social status.

Even at an early age, your thinking was mature. As an adult, your approach to ideas, people, and situations is conservative, and you look to tradition to see how things were done. If carried too far, this may make you adverse to innovation and resistant to change. It is possible to be stern about what you consider right and intolerant of differing opinions, particularly if you perceive them as threats to your authority. Overly realistic thinking can turn into negative thinking that makes it difficult, if not impossible, to see new opportunities. Keeping an open mind is important, as is distinguishing between realism and pessimism.

JOYCE SAYS:
Traits to treasure: Your ability to focus on useful information.
To transform: Avoid letting conservative thinking get in the way of progress.

Mercury in Aquarius ☿ ♒

Liberated Ideas
You have an inventive mind and are attracted to ideas that are out of the ordinary. Once you make up your mind, you are reluctant to change it.

Mercury in Aquarius conveys an inventive mind and thinking that is original, free, and liberated. You see traditional views as entrapping and you aspire to a worldview that is objective and unbiased. You believe in values of friendship, social justice, and equal opportunity for all. Truth-seeking may lead to ideas that are far afield from mainstream thought.

Your thinking is intellectual, even if a bit quirky. You excel at abstract thought, mental organization, and scientific inquiry, and at communicating ideas in writing or speaking. You are witty and sociable and happiest when associating with intelligent people or with groups or organizations of those who are like-minded.

You view people as individuals and listen to their ideas accordingly. The one arena where you might be prejudiced is in judging another's intellect—intellect as distinct from education or background. You cannot stand to be around those you consider "stupid," and there is a tendency toward intellectual arrogance. And while you are very objective in making up your mind, once you do so, you are not likely to change it. Aquarius is a fixed sign and, as such, it is possible to become stubborn and opinionated. Being rigidly attached to your ideas may lead to prejudice against those who disagree with you, despite your search for truth.

JOYCE SAYS:

Traits to treasure: Your unique and quirky way of thinking.
To transform: Learn to change your mind when it's appropriate.

Mercury in Pisces ☿ ♓

Creative Imagination

Your intellect combines with intuition and instincts, giving you a rich, fertile imagination. Decisions are made by how you feel about situations.

With Mercury in Pisces, intellect, intuition, and instincts all work together. Your thinking is sensitive, empathetic, and possibly psychic. You absorb subliminal cues from your environment. Decisions about people and situations stem from how you instinctively feel about them, not from logical deduction. This in no way implies that your decisions are wrong, but it can make them difficult to explain or defend. This, combined with your dislike of conflict, may cause you to keep your ideas to yourself. Yet, having a photographic memory, you can quote chapter and verse where an idea from another originates.

Your vivid imagination is both creative and poetic. There is a love of arts and possibly talent in writing, music, or entertaining. You excel in the domains where beauty and ideals prevail, but have more of a problem when cold intellect is needed for discernment. Yet, as unlikely as it may seem, such notable scientists as Galileo and Copernicus had both the Sun and Mercury in Pisces. This suggests that breakthroughs and genius may come as much from intuition as intellect.

Tremendous powers of concentration make it possible to get lost in whatever interests you, but when uninterested, you are more likely to daydream than to pay attention, and therefore may possibly overlook important information. Optimism in starting new ventures may turn to pessimism or despondency if circumstances do not turn out to be as ideal as originally envisioned. Recognizing the difference between the world as it is and as you would like it to be is essential.

JOYCE SAYS:

Traits to treasure: Your poetic way with words.
To transform: Recognize the difference between fantasies and ideals.

MERCURY IN THE HOUSES

Mercury in the First House

Thinking About Self

You have a quick mind that is attuned to your surroundings, and you speak your mind easily.

You pay attention to your immediate environment and very likely do not miss much that goes on it in. Your mind is curious and restless, your intellect strong, and your wit quick. Seeing situations from your own point of view, it is important for you to remember to listen to others.

You enjoy being recognized for your ideas. The sign Mercury falls in shows how you express yourself. If it is in the positive signs, Aries, Gemini, Leo, Libra, Sagittarius, or Aquarius, you directly express your opinions and will not take a back seat to anyone in conversation. If your Mercury is in the receptive signs of Taurus, Cancer, Virgo, Scorpio, Capricorn, or Pisces, you express yourself well but are not as likely to express your opinions forcefully in new situations.

JOYCE SAYS:

Traits to treasure: How you pay attention to your immediate environment.
To transform: Listen to other people.

Mercury in the Second House

Thinking About Money

Your commonsense thinking focuses on business and money. You communicate well on financial matters.

Your mind is oriented toward money and business, and you possess good old-fashioned common sense. You value ideas that have practical applications. Important decisions are based upon pragmatic considerations, not hopes, dreams, or wishes (unless Mercury is in Pisces or in aspect to Neptune).

You pursue education to enhance moneymaking abilities and are able to make money through ideas. No matter what your profession, you possess good business sense. It is possible for you to excel as an economist, accountant, financial manager, businessperson or business adviser, or a corporate person who decides where the money will go. It is also possible to make money through writing, speaking, teaching, or communicating in general.

JOYCE SAYS:

Traits to treasure: Your ability to turn ideas into money.
To transform: Avoid unnecessary worry about finances.

Mercury in the Third House

Thinking About Ideas

You are intellectually curious, have a wide variety of interests, and express yourself easily.

The association of the third house with Gemini gives superior intellectual abilities, regardless of the sign Mercury falls in. You are curious, enjoy learning, and crave intellectual stimulation. This leads you to question just about everything. As a child, you were probably always asking "why," and this tendency has not changed much as an adult. When someone makes a statement, you want to know where the information came from. Your probing may lead people to wonder whether you trust them when clarity is all you seek.

Regardless of your educational background, you are a lifetime learner. You learn through books, magazines, the media, and conversations with others. You excel in all types of communication including writing, speaking, and speechmaking.

Since the third house is also associated with short-distance travel, you may spend a lot of time in your car and prefer short trips to neighboring areas to long-distance vacations.

JOYCE SAYS:

Traits to treasure: Your insatiable curiosity.

To transform: Avoid jumping from one study to the next.

Mercury in the Fourth House

Thinking About Family

Your thinking is greatly influenced by early family life, and as an adult you influence your family.

Early home and family life affect everyone. With Mercury in the fourth house, family influence colors your thinking even more strongly than it does most people's. Mercury's aspects tell whether family relationships were favorable or difficult; but either way, you are greatly influenced by what was said in your early environment. As an adult, you greatly influence the mental outlook of your own family. If early familial relationships were difficult, coming to terms with their unconscious remnants is important in order to avoid repeating the same patterns within your own family.

There is a need for emotional and financial security, and your mind focuses on how you can provide that security for your loved ones. Mercury here may also give you an interest in genealogy, ecology, archeology, or real estate.

JOYCE SAYS:

Traits to treasure: Your concern for your family.

To transform: Don't hold onto family transgressions.

Mercury in the Fifth House

Thinking About Romance

Intellectual interests lie in creative endeavors. Your mind focuses on romantic affairs and children.

You have an intellectual interest in artistic or creative endeavors. You love to be entertained—you enjoy movies, plays, books, and concerts. Your own thinking is creative, and you express yourself dramatically.

Regardless of your profession, you are a natural entertainer and love to dress up a story to make it more interesting. You appreciate being admired for your intellect.

Your thinking is independent. Yet in the early stages of romance, a new paramour may become so much the focus of your attention that he or she is all you think about. It is possible for this to interfere with creative drive. However, communication between you and your lover should be positive unless Mercury is afflicted.

You exert a strong influence on your children's thinking and they in turn influence you. There is an ability to be honest and open with one another, unless Mercury has unfavorable aspects.

JOYCE SAYS:

Traits to treasure: The entertaining way you express yourself.
To transform: Avoid obsessing about romance.

Mercury in the Sixth House

Thinking About Work

Your methodical, work-oriented mind helps you notice details that others overlook.

The association of the sixth house with Virgo heightens your intellect and focuses your mind on practical considerations, particularly those surrounding work. You are an efficiency expert, always looking for ways to do a better job. You are methodical and detail-oriented and an excellent planner. Knowledge is sought to increase professional expertise. Having the right tools to do a good job is important, whether the tools are a computer, a wrench, or a vacuum cleaner. Problems may arise from being too meticulous. It is possible to overwork or to spend too much time on minutiae. Being too detail-oriented may hamper efficiency. In positions of authority, it is important to delegate. This is difficult, as you fear that no one else will do the job as well as you do.

Since the sixth house also rules health, you are interested in hygiene, healing, and possibly alternative medicine. Clean and orderly surroundings are important to you, as you find it difficult to work in a disorderly environment. If Mercury has difficult aspects, you may worry about ill health or work pressure, or other worries may adversely affect your health.

Traits to treasure: Your efficiency expertise in the workplace.
To transform: Avoid being overly critical about the small stuff.

Mercury in the Seventh House

Thinking About Relationships

Your mind is centered on relationships, and saying what it takes to get along with people is a priority.

You spend a lot of time thinking about relationships, whether marriage, business partnership, or close friendships. Getting along with people generally, and with significant others specifically, is a priority. Luckily, you have the ability to see other people's points of view, which makes this easier. You have excellent negotiating skills and are both influenced by others and have the ability to influence them. It is important for your self-esteem that other people see you as intelligent. This is a good placement for law, counseling, or dealing with the public.

In marriage, intellectual compatibility is of the utmost importance. You are attracted to an intelligent and quick-witted mate, one who significantly influences your thinking. If Mercury forms favorable aspects, you get along with your mate and most people easily. If Mercury forms more difficult aspects, you and your mate are unlikely to see eye-to-eye, and you may blame your mate for being the source of conflict rather than recognizing how you contribute to sparring.

Traits to treasure: Your ability to listen to other people's views.
To transform: Avoid being overly influenced by other people's opinions.

Mercury in the Eighth House

Thinking About Sex

Your deep, penetrating mind pays attention to joint resources ranging from money to sex to the mysteries of life and death.

Mercury in the eighth house conveys intuition, penetrating insights, and the wish to know the meaning of life. From early childhood, you have wanted to know why we are here on earth and have questioned the underlying meaning of circumstances. Your mind is delving and researching, and you take little for face value. This may lead to interests in the occult or reincarnation. Sex is also one of the mysteries of life, and you have plenty of curiosity in this area. You may enjoy reading books about sex, learning about unusual techniques, and want sexual relations to have an intellectual, playful component.

While your mind is delving, you do not share your thoughts with others easily. No matter what your sign, there is a part of you that is secretive and hidden and hard to get to know. In an argument, you know just where to strike to get your point across.

As the eighth house rules joint finances and other people's money, if Mercury receives favorable aspects, you and your mate agree upon finances. If Mercury receives unfavorable aspects, conflict over how to spend or manage money is likely.

Mercury in this house gives a variety of talents. You could be a good psychologist, astrologer, medium, banker, accountant, or tax lawyer.

JOYCE SAYS:
Traits to treasure: Your ability to perceive beneath the surface of situations.
To transform: Avoid obsessing about sex or partnership finances.

Mercury in the Ninth House

Thinking About Beliefs
Mentally curious, you have an interest in philosophy, religion, foreign cultures, and belief systems.

The ninth house is considered the "higher mind." You are interested in philosophy, religion, ethical or moral systems, and higher education. No matter what your socioeconomic background, there is concern with world issues.

You enjoy learning, whether in pursuit of advanced degrees or simply for personal edification. You have a curiosity about other cultures and a bit of wanderlust. If there are other planets in the ninth house, this wanderlust is fulfilled by foreign travel. If Mercury is the only planet in this house, you may satisfy this quest by reading about foreign places.

Debates about politics or ideas get your juices flowing. You have definite worldviews and may be a proselytizer. At your best, you excel in teaching, advertising, and foreign relations. At your worst, it may be difficult to give credence to points of view other than your own—as you are convinced that you are smarter or see more clearly than everyone else.

JOYCE SAYS:

Traits to treasure: Your intellectual curiosity and enjoyment of learning.
To transform: Listen to those with whom you disagree.

Mercury in the Tenth House

Thinking About Ambitions
Your thinking is pragmatic and focuses on career advancement and how to get along with people in authority.

Your life work involves using your intellect, and education is a means to enhance career and public standing. Prestige and professional success are priorities for you. You have good organizational abilities, a pragmatic approach to achievement, and readily attain recognition for your intellect. Even in the early stages of your career, when you speak, others listen. This makes it easy for you to exert influence. If you are an employee, you influence those in authority. If you are the boss, you inspire subordinates. If you are in the public eye, your words are often quoted.

If Mercury receives positive aspects, for the most part, you get along well with those in authority, and communicate easily when you are the authority figure. If Mercury receives difficult aspects, you still stand out, but your ideas may be controversial and your relationships with those in authority combative.

JOYCE SAYS:

Traits to treasure: Your intellectually pragmatic approach to achieving success.
To transform: Use influence honorably.

Mercury in the Eleventh House

Thinking About Friendship
Your thinking is innovative, and you enjoy the company of like-minded people.

Intellectual stimulation in friendship is a must. You are intellectually attracted to new ideas and enjoy the company of a variety of different types of people, learning from friends or associates, and sharing knowledge with them. At an early age, friends exert great influence on your thinking, but as you get older, you are the one who exerts the influence.

As an adult, being involved with groups of like-minded people is important to you. You are at your best when working with others who have common goals.

If Mercury receives favorable aspects, you communicate well and get along easily with friends or associates. If Mercury receives unfavorable aspects, getting along is not so easy. Differences of opinion may result in arguments or separations in friendship. Respecting the opinions of others, even when they disagree with you, is important. This is particularly true if Mercury is in one of the fixed signs of Taurus, Leo, Scorpio, or Aquarius.

JOYCE SAYS:
Traits to treasure: Your delight in sharing ideas with friends and associates. To transform: Avoid getting trapped in group thinking.

Mercury in the Twelfth House

Thinking About the Subconscious
You have strong intuition and the ability to make your subconscious thoughts conscious.

The twelfth house rules the subconscious mind and Mercury rules the conscious mind. This combination has the dual effect of making it easier to make the subconscious conscious and having subconscious memories affect seemingly conscious decisions. Your thinking is deeply influenced by past experiences, whether or not you remember these experiences. This affects your ability to be objective in the present. This is particularly true since you prefer to see the best in people and situations, giving you the tendency to tune out the unpleasant. If overly idealistic, situations may become painful when reality sets in.

At the same time, this placement helps you to consciously get in touch with your unconscious. Talk therapy or even just talking with friends helps to bring past experiences to the surface so that they no longer influence you.

You may be extremely psychic or intuitive and your dreams prophetic. The ability to recognize subliminal cues gives you insights into people and situations. Explaining how you know any of this may prove difficult, as no logic is involved.

You have a richly creative imagination and excel in make-believe. Positively, this gives talent in writing fiction or fantasy. Negatively, there is a tendency to live in a dream world. It is important to deal with problems as they happen, rather than file them away, hoping the future will get better, or ignoring present difficulties. The closer Mercury is to your Ascendant, the easier it is to make subconscious thoughts conscious, to directly express yourself intellectually, and to come to terms with what is hidden.

JOYCE SAYS:

Traits to treasure: The insights you gain through intuition.

To transform: Push yourself to deal with unpleasant situations head on.

Chapter 8

VENUS — YOUR LOVE NATURE

Keywords: Love, Sociability, Beauty
Rules: Taurus and Libra, Second and Eighth Houses
Cycle: 224-½ days around the Sun, never more than 46 degrees
from the Sun (approximately a sign and one-half away)
Somatic Influences: Blood, Throat, Larynx, Kidneys, Female Organs

Venus rules two things we are most interested in—love and money. Venus is the planet of relationships, sociability, and the ideals of love, beauty, and sensuality. Venus also has to do with money, possessions, and creature comforts.

Venus is the principle of attraction. We typically think of attraction as passive. Yet attraction is an inviting energy that draws what we want to us. In the plant kingdom, flowers are the reproductive part of a plant. Their scent and beauty attract animals and insects that help the plant reproduce through pollination and spreading its seeds. In the same way, beauty and sociability draw people to us. Venus rules the female organs and thereby literally has to do with reproduction.

Venus rules Libra, an air sign, and Taurus, an earth sign, and their respective seventh and second houses. Libra and Venus are associated with sociability, marriage, and partnership. Venus' nature is to seek harmony and get along with others. Through Libra, Venus meets others as intellectual equals. Through Taurus, Venus is associated with the earthy sensuousness. Enjoyment of money, possessions, creature comforts, and sensuality comes under Taurus' domain. Both Libra and Taurus are associated with art and beauty. Both wish for harmony, but only Libra is associated with compromise.

Interestingly enough, Venus, the planet of love, does not rule any of the feeling water signs. In the twenty-first century, it is hard to remember that marriage for love, being only a few hundred years old, is a recent historical phenomenon. Before that, marriage was a union based upon treaties or alliances, such as one royal family marrying into another. Or marriage was for the merger of properties, such as marrying a child off to the farmer next door to join adjacent lands. These conventions reflect the signs of Libra and Taurus.

In addition to the female organs, Venus rules the throat, larynx, and kidneys. The Moon co-rules the female organs. Venus and the Moon are the feminine indicators in a chart and as such represent women in general.

Venus gives us the ability to share and get along with others. Ancient astrology calls Venus "the lesser benefic," Jupiter being "the greater benefic." This implies that Venus can do no wrong. However, Venus, like all planets, can convey qualities that are less than ideal. The first reflects Taurus—the tendency to overindulge in creature comforts such as eating and drinking. The second reflects Taurus and Libra and has to do with self-image, seeing oneself as the "nice" one. Carried to an extreme, this translates into, "I'm so nice that if we have a problem, it must be you." The third reflects Libra—social appropriateness carried too far becomes dishonesty.

The sign in which Venus falls shows our ideals of love and beauty. The qualities associated with this sign reflect the way we give and want to receive love, the type of person with whom we want to fall in love, and what behavior we consider socially appropriate. The house in which Venus falls gives further clues to the type of people we are attracted to and what we value.

VENUS IN THE SIGNS

Venus in Aries   ♀ ♈

Love at First Sight
You fall in love at first sight. You know what you want romantically and find independent, self-sufficient people attractive.

Your ideal lover is an Aries type of person. You like the macho type, a person who is independent, self-sufficient, can stand up for himself, and who directly goes after what he wants.

In romance, love at first sight describes your attractions. In essence, people do not grow on you. Even in friendship, you either like someone right away or you do not. Romantically, you are impatient. If the person you are attracted to makes decisions as quickly as you do, you both jump into the relationship, perhaps before you really know enough about each other to determine whether it is an appropriate choice. If the person you are attracted to does not make immediate decisions, a different set of problems ensue. Given your pride, you do not care to admit that the timing difference leads to feeling rejected. You respond in one of two ways. Either you get competitive and adamantly pursue the person, or you quickly give up and move on to someone else.

While you jump into relationships quickly, once you are in an ongoing relationship, you need freedom and independence. You may find the chase more interesting than the catch, but even if you decide to maintain the relationship, you want to do as you please. You want your lover to put you first, yet you do not believe that lovers should restrict one another. Your motto is more like, "You do what you want, and I'll do what I want, and when we want to do the same things, we'll get together." This attitude may lead you to disregard the feelings of your significant other. This is not your intention as much as it is the result of your refusal to have demands placed on you.

Fulfilling relationships require recognizing that you cannot always have what you want the moment you want it and realizing that sometimes compromise is necessary.

JOYCE SAYS:
For best results in love, choose a mate who respects your independence.
To transform: Distinguish between compromise and giving in.

Venus in Taurus   ♀ ♉

Luxury Please
Emotional and financial security are priorities in romance. You want a stable mate you can count on who also enjoys the sensual pleasures of life.

Venus in Taurus is a strong placement, as Venus rules Taurus. Your ideal lover is a Taurus type of person. She is loyal, dependable, sensuous, and has money. Stability and security are important. Because of this, you are slow to make commitments in love, friendship, or business. It takes time to get to know people, but once committed, you are exceedingly loyal. Significant others know that they can count on you, and you expect the same in return.

Venus in Taurus is the most sensual placement of the Zodiac, but you are not aggressive sexually. You attract people by your charm and grace rather than by directly pursuing them. However, sensual pleasures are an important part of any romantic relationship, and no long-term relationship is satisfying without sexual compatibility.

Money is important, as there is a love of luxury, beauty, and of being pampered. Thorough enjoyments of sensual pleasures include gourmet dining, good wine, fine fabric, and the scent of expensive perfume. Only the best is good enough. You also enjoy accumulating possessions. Relaxation includes services such as manicures, pedicures, facials, and massage. As Taurus represents the earth, there is also a love of non-materialistic earthly pleasures such as gardening.

Very likely, you are a good cook and enjoy nurturing your family. There is a desire to take care of those you love. Positively, you are protective and provide emotional and financial well-being. Negatively, protectiveness leads to being overly protective. Jealousy and possessiveness rear their heads when you feel insecure. Disagreement can be interpreted as disloyalty. While your intentions may be honorable, you can be stubborn about beliefs and expectations.

JOYCE SAYS:

For best results in love, choose a loyal, sensuous mate.
To transform: Remember that people are not possessions.

Venus in Gemini   ♀ ♊

Keep It Light

Your ideal mate is an intelligent person with whom you can have interesting conversations. You have no desire to be fenced in and want at least the illusion of freedom in romantic relationships.

You are a social person and have friendly relationships with a wide variety of people. Your ideal lover is a Gemini type of person, someone witty and intelligent with varied interests. You yourself are friendly and outgoing. You possess a sharp mind, a quick wit, and a smattering of knowledge on all sorts of topics. All of this makes you good company and an interesting conversationalist. Sharing ideas is an essential ingredient in friendship and romance. In socializing, you may be so interested in a person's ideas that it appears as if you are interested in the person himself. This can give the impression that you are flirting, when in your estimation you are just having a friendly conversation. When the conversation is no longer interesting, you move on to the next person, which gives you the reputation for fickleness.

You may be fickle when it comes to romance. You hate the thought of being fenced in. Relationships are more mental than emotional, and part of you may always wonder if someone more interesting will come along. There is a strong need for the illusion of freedom, the idea that you can come and go as you please. The belief that you can do what you want may be more important than actually doing it. You hate to feel demanded of, and if you feel boxed in, there is an urge to break free. Sexual infidelity is more likely to occur because of curiosity and the desire for varied experiences than because of a strong sex drive. If you feel boxed in or get bored, you may be unfaithful and rationalize your behavior. Interestingly enough, while you enjoy conversation and debates, you thoroughly dislike actual conflict and go out of your way to avoid it. You are more likely to talk around issues than to address them directly. This makes it difficult for you to resolve relational differences. When problems arise, your line of least resistance is to become slippery or to move on. This approach means that at some point you are always moving on.

JOYCE SAYS:
For best results in love, choose a versatile, intelligent mate who gives you space. To transform: Be honest and direct around relational issues.

Venus in Cancer   ♀ ♋

Family First
You want a sensitive, nurturing mate who appreciates family life. Emotional security is a necessity for you to feel loved.

You are attracted to a Cancer-type person, one who, like you, is nurturing and family oriented. Your relational values are traditional and conservative. You value the home and family and take care of those you love. Whether you are a man or woman, you are mothering and nurturing. Close friends are treated like family members. Very likely, you are a superb cook and enjoy family gatherings around the dinner table.

Security is of the utmost importance. Financial security means having more money than you will ever need tucked away for a rainy day. Emotional security involves not just a mate, but having friends and family to rely on. In all relationships, it takes time for you to develop trust. This is particularly true in romance. You have strong loyalties to those you care about and you expect loyalty in return. You are a protective mate and parent.

You are sensitive, feeling, and emotional. Sensitivity can be a double-edged sword. Nurturing and compassionate, you instinctively recognize other people's needs. Because of this, you take care of loved ones without their ever having to ask. You expect the same in return and find it hard to believe that not everyone knows what you feel. You are hurt when unspoken needs are not met. Differences of opinions with loved ones hurt, and disagreement can be associated with lack of caring. You can tend to be overly sensitive and take things personally that are not meant that way.

As Cancer is a water sign, you are comfortable with feeling whatever you do; but as you do not necessarily verbalize your feelings, problems resolving relational difficulties can occur. (And problems always occur at some point no matter how well people get along.) When something hurts, it is hard to let go. This makes it particularly important that you discuss your feelings and needs instead of building up a wall between of protection.

JOYCE SAYS:

For best results in love, choose a sensitive, nurturing mate.

To transform: Instead of building a wall around you, give loved ones a chance to fulfill your needs by letting them know what they are.

Venus in Leo   ♀ ♌

Dramatic Flair

Your ideal mate is charming, attractive and has dramatic flair. Feeling appreciated by loved ones is of paramount importance.

Your ideal lover is a Leo-type person—one who possesses charm, self-confidence, and dramatic flair. You yourself are ardent and romantic and want a mate who has these qualities.

You know how to enjoy life. You love lavish parties and entertainment, including theater, concerts, and art. Fashion and beauty are important to you, as is looking your best. Very likely, your clothes and jewelry display a distinctive style that combines dramatic flair with good taste. Dramatic flair is also demonstrated in your ability to make even the simplest social gathering look like a lavish event, and you delight in being admired for your efforts.

When it comes to love, you are loyal, generous, ardent, and steadfast, no matter how much you enjoy compliments from others. Romantically idealistic, you want love to forever include romance. Affection is a must, and hugging and kissing are at least as important as sex. You do whatever you can for loved ones, and all you want in return is appreciation.

Difficulties arise when you do not feel appreciated—the operative word being "feel." You are far more sensitive than you appear to be, and it is all too easy for you to feel slighted. You may be hurt and angry over not being treated as important enough when you do not get the attention you so crave. While you are generous and protective, particularly as a parent, it can be hard for you to accept that the lives of your loved ones do not always revolve around you and your wishes. And your loved ones do not necessarily even know what your wishes are. Pride can inhibit you from voicing hurt, as you do not want to appear needy. This makes it difficult to resolve relational differences. At your most extreme, you may walk away from what you want rather risk rejection.

JOYCE SAYS:
For best results in love, choose a demonstrative, loving mate.
To transform: Avoid letting pride get in the way of love.

Venus in Virgo   ♀ ♍

Discriminating Taste
You believe that love is shown by what you do for another and what another does for you. You appreciate a hard-working mate with common sense.

Your ideal lover is a Virgo-type person—one who is hard working and practical. You are analytical about relationships and want a mate you can count on. For you, love has tangible expression. It is what you do for another and what another does for you that count. Mowing the lawn or cooking dinner goes a lot further with you than candy and flowers. Very likely, you are fastidious in household chores, a good cook, and concerned with health and nutrition. Cleanliness and hygiene are of the utmost importance, as are a neat and orderly appearance. You get great joy in taking care of those you love. Your best relationships are with those with whom you can share intellectual interests or work pursuits.

You are adept in noticing details that others overlook. This may cause you to be overly critical of others as well as of yourself. You are choosy about who you associate with, which may make it difficult to find a romantic partner. The tendency to make little things overly important may mean ruling someone out for the wrong color shoes or some minor faux pas.

There is a desire to be of service to loved ones. You seek self-improvement and similarly try to help significant others on their road to self-improvement. This leads to offering "helpful suggestions." You may actually be the most critical of those you are the closest to. After all, who would you want to help improve more than those you care for? It comes as quite a surprise if your suggestions are seen as critical or nagging rather than as helpful. While self-improvement is admirable, perfection is unattainable. It is important to accept yourself as you are and others as they are.

JOYCE SAYS:
For best results in love, choose a fastidious, hard-working mate.
To transform: Give up expecting perfection—in yourself and others.

Venus in Libra   ♀ ♎

Equal Relationships
Equality in a relationship is of paramount importance. You want a mate who is easy to get along with and who shares your interests and ideals.

Venus rules Libra, so this is a favorable placement. Graciousness and ease of sociability make you attractive to the opposite sex. Being liked and getting along with others are priorities. Your social standards are high, and in social situations you go out of your way to make people feel comfortable. You want to be "nice" and want to be around "nice" people. Those who behave coarsely are a definite turn-off.

Venus here makes you a good host and a considerate spouse. You are not interested in money in and of itself, but have an appreciation for beauty, which makes expensive items attractive. When it comes to clothes, jewelry, artwork, or furniture, good taste rules.

Your ideal mate is charming, attractive, and intelligent—qualities that you likewise display. Life without a significant other would be unnatural for you, but not just any mate will do. You want an equal to share your life with, one who shares your interests and ideals, someone with whom you can share your thoughts. Intellectual stimulation and rapport are necessities.

Meeting heart-to-heart takes place only after meeting mind-to-mind. And mutual admiration within the relationship is a must—you want to be admired by your mate, and you can only love another whom you admire.

Valuing peace, harmony, and cooperation, and disliking conflict, you listen to, and fairly weigh, other people's points of view, irrespective of your personal beliefs. Yet you are the consummate diplomat who excels at bringing others over to your viewpoint.

Relational problems arise if behaving socially appropriately, exhibiting good manners, and avoiding conflict are carried to the extreme. This results in peace at any price, where you become dishonest or lose your sense of self in order to maintain harmony. Venus' placement here requires that diplomacy be balanced with truth.

JOYCE SAYS:

For best results in love, choose a charming, sociable mate who shares your interests and ideals.

To transform: Avoid maintaining harmony at the expense of your sense of self.

Venus in Scorpio ♀ ♏

Passion Please

Passion and intensity are relational priorities. You are in love or not interested, and you want a lover who responds with equal intensity.

Passion and intensity rule when the love goddess Venus is found in the all-or-nothing sign of Scorpio. Only deep and meaningful relationships will do. In romance, you are either in love or not interested. In friendship, you make a huge distinction between those few close friends for whom you will do anything and everyone else. Close reciprocal relationships last a lifetime (or end in acrimony).

Intensely emotional, you possess a powerful sex drive, and love and passion are inextricably linked. Ideally, sex is not just sex but a transformational experience bonding two human beings. Your ideal lover matches your depth and intensity. You are attracted to people who have not only a powerful sex drive but a powerful demeanor. Easygoing types are not for you. This does not always make love comfortable or relationships harmonious.

Early on in romance, the chemistry of attraction pulls you in. When you feel that special spark that occurs infrequently, you are sure that you have picked the perfect lover—long before you have gotten to know the person. You give a lot and expect a lot in return. You are extremely emotional, but find it hard to put feelings into words. You are sensitive and vulnerable, traits you would rather not admit to. Being self-protective makes it especially unlikely that you will talk about hurt feelings when things go wrong. Instead, you try to covertly manipulate situations rather than dealing with them head on. As astute and observant as you are, intense emotions make it difficult for you to see another's point of view. You can become jealous and possessive or resentful at the smallest slight. All of this can lead to love-hate relationships where love becomes like an addiction. This makes it difficult for you to examine romantic choices, to step back and ask if you are happy in the relationship or if you have chosen the appropriate person. While love must contain passion, passion and chemistry cannot keep a relationship together. Learning to get to know someone before you emotionally commit, to communicate about problems as they arise, and to recognize when you have made an inappropriate choice are essential. Otherwise you are in the mode of singing those old blues song lyrics, "I'd rather be blue over you than happy with somebody new."

JOYCE SAYS:
For best results in love, choose a loyal, intense, passionate mate.
To transform: Put your feelings on the table and be willing to end
unhealthy relationships.

Venus in Sagittarius   ♀ ♐

Freedom Comes First
You find independent, outgoing, outdoorsy people attractive. In order to settle down, you need a mate who gives you a lot of room.

Venus here conveys a love of travel, adventure, and excitement. There is fondness for nature, the outdoors, and sports. Your friendly, outgoing, fun-loving nature makes it easy for you to meet and socialize with a wide variety of people. At parties, you can flit from person to person and appear flirtatious even when it is only the conversation you are interested in. You particularly enjoy meeting people from foreign cultures, or whose religion, race, or background differ from your own.

Settling down romantically may be a problem because no matter how interested in a person you may be, a part of you wonders if someone better or more interesting is just around the corner. Your ideal mate is highly intelligent, free-spirited, and independent—like you are in relationships. Honesty and directness are also important qualities. You hate hidden agendas.

In many ways, friendship is easier for you than love affairs. Since friendship is not a monogamous relationship, friends more typically allow one another to breeze in and out of their lives. Freedom to come and go as one pleases is a given. In romance, stronger commitments typically go with the territory. You enjoy giving generously to loved ones, but want to do so on your own terms, when it feels right. You abhor expectations or being demanded of. The give and take based on the needs of each party in a relationship is difficult. Expectations make you feel trapped, and you avoid feeling trapped at all costs. Romantically you need a long leash. You function much better with a mate who understands your freedom needs. Yet no matter who you are with, it is important that you consider the needs of others.

JOYCE SAYS:

For best results in love, choose an adventurous, independent mate who is not possessive.

To transform: Learn to make and keep commitments—even if you are on a long leash.

Venus in Capricorn   ♀ ♑

Practical Romance

You are far more impressed with reliability than romance. You prefer a conservative, hard-working, dependable mate.

Venus in Capricorn provides an earnest approach toward relationships. In love and friendship, you display what might be considered old-fashioned virtues—loyalty, faithfulness, and dependability. In youth, you may get along better with adults than people your own age. As an adult, you prefer to associate with industrious, practical, and reliable people.

You may marry a person older than you or someone your own age who is mature beyond his years. Your ideal mate is mature, hardworking, and successful. Love and respect go hand in hand, and you respect success. Enjoyment comes from socializing with the "right people" and going to prestigious places. If you marry someone who is less successful than you would like, a great deal of energy may go into furthering your mate's career. If you are the one with the successful career, you want a spouse who helps further your ambitions. If you have an unscrupulous bent, it is possible that you will use people for what you can get. This could take the form of marrying for money or position or befriending people solely based upon what they can do for you.

In relationships, you are far more impressed by reliability than romance. You take relationships seriously, keep your commitments, and expect the same in return. Duty and love go hand in hand. Pride combined with fear of rejection make you self-protective. You are reserved in expressing feelings, typically keeping them well under control. This may make you appear far colder than you really are—although you are quite capable of turning cold if you are hurt or if your pride is offended. Yet while you disdain public shows of affection, Capricorn is a sensual earth sign, and you are far more sensual in private.

While practicality will always be a part of love, acceptance of others, as well as of yourself, is important. Venus in Capricorn can put you in the position of pushing loved ones to live up to your expectations, or conversely, pushing yourself to live up to theirs.

JOYCE SAYS:
For best results in love, choose a dependable, reliable, successful mate.
To transform: Practice acceptance—of yourself and others.

Venus in Aquarius ♀ ♒

Friendship First
You get along with a wide variety of people. Your ideal mate is intelligent and appreciates your smarts. Friendship is an essential part of love.

Venus in Aquarius places importance on casual relationships, friendship, and group activities. You may enjoy teamwork with a focus on humanitarian ideals or charitable endeavors. You get along easily, and enjoy socializing with a wide variety of people, and you enjoy many platonic relationships. A party with all your friends would find different groups in different corners of the room with little in common. You are particularly attracted to intelligent people who hold unusual ideas or those who might be considered eccentric.

For you, friendship is a necessary component of love. Friends may become lovers, and lovers may become friends, but a new lover will never replace a friend. Your ideal mate becomes your best friend. You seek a person who is freedom oriented, independent, and somewhat out of the ordinary.

This allows you the freedom you so covet. A heart-wrenching torrid affair with a passionate, jealous, possessive mate is not for you. Not emotionally oriented, you are most comfortable in relationships where you can remain detached and objective. You would rather discuss ideas and ideals than feelings, which you believe should be subject to reason.

Since it is easier for you to be friendly than to be intimate, romantic relationships go best when you choose a partner who shares your intellectual enthusiasm and lack of emotionality. Problems can arise if you choose a more sensitive mate, as you can be uncomfortable with, and feel trapped by, your mate's messy feelings. Crying or other emotional displays make you want to run. Disdain for emotions, accompanied by the belief that your mate should be logical and reasonable, may lead to your being callous and insensitive. It is important to respect people's feelings as well as their ideas.

JOYCE SAYS:
For best results in love, choose an intelligent, independent mate who is a best friend as well as a lover.
To transform: Give credence to other people's feelings as well as to their ideas.

Venus in Pisces   ♀ ♓

Idealized Love
You are a romantic at heart and very sensitive when it comes to relationships. Your ideal mate provides romance as well as love.

Venus in Pisces is the Zodiac's most idealistic, tenderhearted, and spiritual placement when it comes to love and relationships. You are kind, considerate, and compassionate not just to those you are close to, but to all with whom you come into contact. Yours is a dreamy romantic nature with a profound appreciation of beauty in art, music, or literature. Your imagination is creative.

Unselfishly wanting what is best for others, you look for the good in human beings and prefer to ignore the bad. Your intuition allows you to see potential in people that they may not see in themselves. When it comes to love, you long for a romantic ideal that is difficult for mere mortals to live up to. It is possible to either over idealize lovers or to avoid relationships altogether because no one meets your standards. Desiring to be helpful and feeling loved when you are needed can lead to attracting a needy mate or needy people. Or, alternatively, you may be the one seeking a lover to rescue you from life's travails. Either way, you do what you can to please others, and intuitively you know just what to do.

Early in relationships, you overlook people's flaws, no matter how visible they may be. When you finally recognize that a paramour is less than perfect, you try to help him overcome his problems—so that the potential you so readily see can be fulfilled. In all relationships, you believe that if it is possible to help another, it is wrong not to do so. This leads to giving much without thinking about reciprocity. Being intuitive, you know people's needs without their having to ask. Because of this, there is an expectation that a lover should be aware of your unspoken needs. If needs are not met, hurt and disappointment follow, and the disparity between the person and the ideal come to light. At this point, it can be difficult to forgive another for not living up to the idealized image.

A romantic at heart, it important for you to recognize that no one is perfect. Early on, you should actually look for faults and flaws so that you are not disappointed later when you discover them. Perfection is a great ideal, but ultimately, no one can live up to it.

JOYCE SAYS:
For best results in love, choose a kind, loving, romantic, and sensitive mate. To transform: Give up the quest for idealized love and accept people as they are.

VENUS IN THE HOUSES

Venus in the First House

Values Oneself
You exude charm and grace and attract people easily.

You are charming and gracious. You find it easy to be friendly in new situations, and you attract people readily. In essence, you believe in being nice (unless Venus has difficult aspects). Very likely, you are physically attractive, and looking your best is important to you. There is a fondness for beautiful clothes, and if you are a woman, your makeup is always impeccable. You enjoy being pampered and indulging yourself. In romantic situations, you may crave independence or want to be spoiled by your paramour, or fluctuate back and forth between the two extremes.

JOYCE SAYS:

Traits to treasure: Your charm and sociability.
To transform: Avoid being self-absorbed.

Venus in the Second House

Values Material Resources

You love luxury, enjoy being pampered, and have good financial instincts.

Venus in the second house is a strong position, as it is the house that Venus rules. You value money and all it can provide. There is a love of luxury that includes beautiful possessions, expensive clothes, good meals, and being pampered. It is easy to be self-indulgent and to overspend. Luckily, you have good instincts in financial matters and the ability to attract money. Careers where you may easily make money range from beauty and the arts to banking and business.

A highly sensual nature makes sensual and sexual compatibility essential in romance. A mate who can provide well is appreciated.

JOYCE SAYS:

Traits to treasure: Your excellent taste and good financial instincts.
To transform: Avoid overspending on luxury items.

Venus in the Third House

Values Learning

You enjoy intellectual stimulation and have the ability to communicate with ease.

You love learning and enjoy intellectual stimulation, ranging from literature, poetry, and artistic pursuits to good conversation. You communicate with ease in speaking and writing and may excel in these areas professionally. You dislike disagreements and seek common ground when disagreements occur. Unless Venus is afflicted, you have close, harmonious relationships with siblings, extended family, and neighbors. You enjoy short trips as getaways from the routine of day-to-day life.

When it comes to romance, you want a mate you can talk to. Good intellectual rapport is of prime importance, as is the freedom to come and go as you please.

JOYCE SAYS:

Traits to treasure: Your love of learning.
To transform: Avoid sugarcoating disagreements.

Venus in the Fourth House

Values Family

You enjoy home and hearth and familial relationships.

Loving family relationships and a mate who shares your familial dedica-tion are priorities. You enjoy taking care of family, domesticity, entertain-ing at home, and visiting family members. Close friends become like family members. Early home life greatly influences your marital choices, and the tendency to recreate early family patterns exists. If Venus receives favorable aspects, you grew up in, and as an adult create, a loving household. If Venus receives difficult aspects, discipline and awareness are required for you to avoid recreating early hurtful family patterns.

JOYCE SAYS:

Traits to treasure: Your love of home and family.
To transform: Work through relational issues in the family.

Venus in the Fifth House

Values Spark

You adore life, appreciate good entertainment, and demonstrate ardor in love.

You have zest and enthusiasm for life. There is a strong pleasure orienta-tion and a love of entertainment. You may be artistically talented, but at minimum there is appreciation for music, theater, art, fashion, and jew-elry. You treasure beauty. Your clothes are likely to make fashion statements. You enjoy lavish parties, and when you entertain, you go all out.

You easily attract the opposite sex, but may not notice if the attraction is not mutual. When you fall in love, you have ardor and are extremely loyal. Being appreciated means everything to you. Pride makes it difficult for you to be forgiving when you do not feel appreciated.

You are very generous and loving to children, and it is difficult not to overindulge your offspring.

Traits to treasure: Your zest for life.
To transform: Don't let pride get in the way of love.

Venus in the Sixth House

Values Work
You enjoy working and having social relationships with coworkers.

You have a fondness for work and being of service to others. It is your nature to lend a helping hand when needed. Friends are easily made in the workplace (unless Venus is afflicted), and it is possible to meet romantic partners at work or through coworkers. Work must be both enjoyable and harmonious. Artistic ability or talent in working with your hands is possible.

In romance, you are sensible and analytical. Relationships encompass what people do for one another, not just how they feel. The sincere desire to help those you care for causes you to offer helpful suggestions as to how they can "improve." It is possible for your motives to be misunderstood and for you to be perceived as critical rather than helpful.

JOYCE SAYS:
Traits to treasure: Your creativity in specialized skills.
To transform: Recognize that not everyone wants to be critiqued.

Venus in the Seventh House

Values Relationships
Harmony and cooperation are primary, as you place a high value on one-to-one relationships.

Venus in the seventh house is a strong placement, as Venus is the ruler of the seventh house. A high value is placed on harmonious relationships. You possess charm and social grace and are very likely popular. It is easy for you to get along with most people (unless Venus receives difficult aspects). The desire to be liked motivates being pleasing to others.

Mutual respect and equality are important factors in all one-to-one relationships. Equality is especially important in marriage, and you seek a mate who will treat you like an equal. The seventh house also represents the type of partner you attract or what you project onto a mate. You see your mate as charming and desirable. Once married, your identity merges with that of your spouse. Keeping your spouse happy becomes of prime importance despite your need for equality. It is extremely important for long-term marital happiness that you balance your spouse's needs with your own.

JOYCE SAYS:

Traits to treasure: Your concern for other people.

To transform: Avoid pleasing others without pleasing yourself.

Venus in the Eighth House

Values Passion

Your love nature is intense, and your romantic relationships must include passion.

Love, sex, and passion are all intertwined. Your emotional nature is intense. When you fall in love, it is deeply and completely. Sexual desires are strong, and sexual compatibility is a necessity for you to have lasting love and marriage. It is possible for intense emotions to turn into jealousy and possessiveness, to the detriment of matrimonial harmony. Being self-protective, you are more likely to keep your feelings in and covertly try to manipulate and control your mate than to admit hurt or vulnerability.

Learning to talk about feelings is a must to work through any relational issues and to avoid power struggles. Since the eighth house also represents joint finances, with Venus here it is possible to benefit financially from marriage and partnerships (unless Venus receives difficult aspects).

JOYCE SAYS:

Traits to treasure: Your lusty desires.

To transform: Avoid trying to manipulate and control your lovers.

Venus in the Ninth House

Values Adventure

You enjoy travel and have a fondness for people from cultures other than your own.

There is a love of education, knowledge, travel, and foreign cultures. In love and in friendship, you are attracted to people with whom you can share intellectual ideals and from whom you can learn. This is especially true of people from foreign cultures or backgrounds different from your own. It is possible to meet a mate at college, an educational seminar, or during foreign travels.

The love of travel may lead to visiting many foreign countries and possibly to living abroad. You have a free spirit that does not want to be contained. High ideals exist when it comes to love, and freedom and spontaneity must be part of any romantic relationship.

JOYCE SAYS:

Traits to treasure: Your love of travel and foreign horizons.
To transform: Avoid getting lost in wanderlust.

Venus in the Tenth House

Values Career

First-rate social skills and positive relationships with authority figures assist you on the road to success.

Your personal and professional lives are intertwined. Charm, beauty, and social grace help you get ahead in your career. You are adept at dealing with the public and get along well with authority figures (unless Venus receives difficult aspects). It is possible to meet a spouse at work or through work relationships.

You are attractive to the opposite sex, but when it comes to romance, your decisions are practical and conservative. You want a reliable mate you can count on, not one full of romantic promises. It is a priority for you to be with a mate who is successful and will enhance your status.

JOYCE SAYS:

Traits to treasure: The way you charm the boss or the public.
To transform: Avoid seeing marriage as solely a status symbol.

Venus in the Eleventh House

Values Friendship

Love and friendship go hand in hand.

You make friends easily, and friendship and love are of equal importance. For love to last, a lover must be your best friend, someone with whom to share ideas and ideals. At the same time, you enjoy the company of a wide variety of people, and a romantic partner must understand that falling in love for you does not exclude other friendships. Social acceptance is important, and yet love must include freedom and independence as well as closeness.

You enjoy socializing with groups of people in clubs and organizations, particularly those that unite around social causes. It is possible to meet a mate through these organizations or through friends.

JOYCE SAYS:

Traits to treasure: Your love of intellectual companionship.
To transform: Avoid being prejudiced against those who do not share your ideals.

Venus in the Twelfth House

Values Tranquility

You need peace and tranquility and enjoy the company of idealistic, spiritually-oriented people.

You love peace and tranquility, and your nature is sensitive. You need time alone every day in order to stay centered. This time may be spent meditating, reading, in some artistic pursuit, or just closing out the world.

You have an attraction to spiritually oriented people. You are kind and sympathetic and have a soft spot for those in need. When it comes to love, idealism makes it easy for romantic fantasies to prevail. You may over idealize your loved ones, or spend time in solitude, as no one measures up to your ideals. The desire to see the best in those you care about may lead to cloudy judgment, where you see the positive at the expense of the whole person. You are most easily taken advantage of when your sympathies are aroused. This is true in all relationships, but particularly with lovers. It is important to cultivate detachment.

JOYCE SAYS:

Traits to treasure: Your wish to associate with spiritually oriented people.
To transform: Avoid letting sympathies overwhelm rational judgments.

Chapter 9

MARS—HOW YOU ASSERT YOURSELF

***Keywords:** Drive, Energy, Assertiveness*
***Rules:** Aries, First House*
***Cycle:** Takes 22 months to revolve around the Sun*
***Somatic Influences:** Muscular System,*
Adrenal Glands, Male Sex Organs

Mars shows how we go after what we want. It is the planet of drive and initiative. The masculine warrior planet stands for assertion, separateness, and the ability to go it alone. Mars represents physical vitality, strength, courage, and ambition. It also represents anger, temper, conflict, and destruction. Mars rules fire, earthquakes, and violence.

Mars has to do with desire and sex, and reflects the manner in which we pursue whatever we desire. Sexually, Venus is the planet associated with attraction; Mars, with pursuit. Mars and the Sun are masculine indicators in the chart, and as such represent men in general.

Mars rules the fire sign of Aries. Mars was considered the ruler of Scorpio before Pluto was discovered. Some astrologers still maintain this ancient rulership, but the descriptions in this book give Mars' rulership to Aries and Pluto's rulership to Scorpio. Mars and Aries are an ideally matched planet and sign. Each represents unbridled direct action, the image of the first soldier going over the hill in battle. Each is quick, decisive, and courageous, loves freedom and dislikes interference.

Older astrology texts refer to Mars as the "lesser malefic," Saturn being the "greater malefic." In more ancient times, it is likely that individual initiative and pulling oneself up by one's bootstraps were seen as signs of hubris and inappropriate behavior.

Mars positively expressed gives self-confidence and the ability to stand up for ourselves appropriately. It conveys enthusiasm and courage. Negative expression of Mars may take one of two extremely different forms. An over-active Mars is overly aggressive, self-opinionated, and quarrelsome. It may be stepping on other people as a show of strength, or much more brutal behavior, such as soldiers in war killing civilians. At the other extreme, an under-functioning Mars is not assertive enough and conveys problems in standing up for ourselves. This may take the form of simply avoiding con-flict or the extreme of allowing ourselves to be victimized.

In the physical body, Mars rules the muscles, adrenal glands, red blood corpuscles, and the male sex organs.

The sign in which Mars falls shows how we assert ourselves. The house in which Mars falls depicts where we place our energy.

MARS IN THE SIGNS

Mars in Aries   ♂ ♈

Direct Action, Pursues Action
You are direct and straightforward in going after what you want. A competitive nature pushes you to be the best you can be.

Since Mars rules Aries, this is a very strong placement. You have great vital-ity, physical energy, and courage. Assertive, decisive, and impulsive, you excel at initiating situations. You straightforwardly pursue your aims, thrive on competition, and rebel against any sort of restraint. The desire to be the best you can be stimulates competition with yourself as well as others. A sense of honor is well ingrained, and you stand up for your principles. The courage of the first soldier over the hill in battle embodies this position.

Assertive qualities make patience difficult, so it is important to learn when to push, when to wait, and when to reevaluate. A hot temper and the tendency to perceive anger as self-expression also cause problems. It does not necessarily occur to you to temper your outbursts. You get over anger quickly and do not hold a grudge, so it is hard for you to understand when others do not get over these outbursts quite so easily. Learning to think before you act, particularly as you aspire to positions of authority, is important. Remember, the first soldier over the hill is usually the first soldier to get shot; so making sure your actions are well thought-out rather than impulsive goes a long way toward helping you achieve desired results.

JOYCE SAYS:

Traits to treasure: The fearless way you pursue what you want.
To transform: Exercise control over your temper and impulsiveness.

Mars in Taurus ♂ ♉

Steady Action, Pursues Finances
You are slow to take action, but once you do, you persevere. Effort is geared toward achieving practical, concrete results.

Taurus' fixed energy slows Mars down. Your actions are practical and geared toward concrete results. In new situations, you proceed cautiously. You are patient and begin only after planning appropriately. Once you set a course of action, you display great determination and finish what you start.

This placement gives a strong desire for money and possessions, which you work hard to acquire. It also gives a highly sensual, lusty nature. All physical pleasures, sex, food, or drink, are heartily enjoyed, and care must be taken to avoid becoming overly indulgent.

You dislike conflict, and go out of your way to avoid it. Yet you stand up for principles and do not allow others to push you around. You are slow to anger, but once you do become angry, you fight to the finish.

A stubborn streak comes with this placement. Finishing what you start is a plus when you are heading in the right direction, but it can become a minus if you have made a poor choice and refuse to reevaluate. It is important to be open to alternative ways of doing things and new ideas.

JOYCE SAYS:

Traits to treasure: Your patience and perseverance in pursuing your aims.
To transform: Be willing to change course when appropriate.

Mars in Gemini ♂ ♊

Active Intellect, Pursues Information
Action combines with intellect giving you versatility. You easily express yourself assertively, but avoid real conflict.

Mars in Gemini combines the intellect with action. You assert yourself intellectually. Your mind is active and restless, and there is constant need for mental stimulation. Before you take action, you want to be mentally prepared. The ability to come up with numerous ideas easily, combined with the need for variety and a dislike of routine, makes you excellent at multitasking. However, these traits bring two significant problems. If not mentally challenged, you become restless and bored, and varied interests may cause you to go off in too many directions at once. This makes it difficult for you to stick to any one project long enough to complete it. You work best in situations where you are the idea person and other people do the follow through (unless the rest of your chart has a preponderance of planets in fixed signs).

You excel in speaking and writing. You thoroughly enjoy debates and intellectual contests, but dislike real conflict. Not being particularly attached to any one idea, you can argue a point for the sake of intellectual stimulation. This makes it possible to be more combative than you realize. What you see as a conversation, others may see as conflict. Watch the tendency to be overbearing in speech.

JOYCE SAYS:

Traits to treasure: Versatility that allows you to see alternative ways of going after what you want.

To transform: Avoid going off in so many directions at once that you do not finish what you start.

Mars in Cancer ♂ ♋

Sensitive Actions, Pursues Security

Sensitivities and emotions have direct impact on your ability to take action. Feeling secure is important in order to move forward.

Mars in Cancer combines emotions with action. The need for security is directly tied to your actions, and the way you feel about a situation directly impacts your ability to act. In situations where you feel comfortable, you initiate effectively, particularly when your actions benefit the security of your family.

Difficulties occur when venturing forth into unknown territory. In unfamiliar areas, there is a tendency to procrastinate, waiting for some magical moment when you will feel secure, or for some indication that your actions will bear fruit. This procrastination may lead to undue delays, or even worse, complete avoidance of the unfamiliar.

Mars here is not outwardly aggressive. You dislike conflict and have the tendency to sidestep it whenever possible. But your emotions are easily triggered, and unexpressed emotions lead to moodiness and frustration. It is difficult for you to talk rationally when upset. Eventually, Mars' fiery energy can lead to steamy outbursts that release pent-up frustrations. This is particularly true on the home front, where you are more likely to feel safe and want to be the boss. Learning to stand up for yourself in an appropriate manner is important.

JOYCE SAYS:
Traits to treasure: The way you stand up for your family.
To transform: Avoid procrastination and holding onto anger.

Mars in Leo ♂ ♌

Dramatic Action, Pursues Self-expression
Self-expression comes naturally. You display courage and strength of purpose in pursuing your aims.

Mars in Leo puts Mars in the Sun's domain. This joining conveys abundant physical energy, enthusiasm, personal magnetism, and a fun-loving nature. The combination of the initiating ability of fire with the perseverance of fixed signs produces willpower, strength of purpose, and courage. You are competitive, desire to be at the forefront of your chosen arena, and are willing to do what it takes to get there.

Your actions are spontaneous, dramatic, and self-expressive. The self-confidence you exude, no matter how you feel inside, inspires others to have confidence in you. Your heart tells you what is right and which path to follow, giving you fixed convictions. These convictions, passionate self-will, and intense pride may lead to becoming overly opinionated or dogmatic. You can believe that your way is the only right way. Remembering to be tolerant of individual differences is a must.

On the more fun side, you enjoy life's pleasures, particularly love, romance, and sex. Being a passionate lover makes you particularly attractive to the opposite sex. As long as you are appreciated, relationships go well, but when you feel unappreciated, the tendency to become dominating, jealous, or possessive rears its head. Discussing differences rather than protecting your pride by trying to push others into to giving you what you want would actually go a lot further in helping you accomplish your aims.

JOYCE SAYS:

Traits to treasure: The courage and strength of purpose you display in going after going after what you want.

To transform: Avoid letting pride get in the way of achieving your goals.

Mars in Virgo   ♂ ♍

Detail Oriented Action, Pursues Perfection

You take action in a diligent and organized manner. An eye for detail assists you in methodical planning.

Mars in Virgo falls under Mercury's earthy intellect. You are hardworking, well-organized, and detail-oriented. You collect all needed information, then strategize and plan tasks methodically before taking action.

A perfectionist at heart, you believe the only way to do anything is the right way. Because of this, you do the best job possible no matter what the compensation. You work in an orderly fashion, proceeding logically one step at a time until completion. This makes you a master craftsperson. Your precision enhances performance; you do not miss fine points that others are likely to overlook. However, this perfectionism may lead to over fussiness and nitpicking, which in turn leads to spending too much time on minutiae at the expense of efficiency. It may also lead to being overly critical of other people's work, expecting the same perfection that you aspire to. Discerning what is important and what is not is a necessity.

Mars in Virgo is a highly discriminating sexual placement. Being very concerned with hygiene, you will not sleep with just anyone. And unless there are planetary placements to the contrary, more energy is likely to be channeled into work than into sex.

JOYCE SAYS:

Traits to treasure: The workmanship you display in any tasks you undertake.

To transform: Avoid letting perfectionism interfere with performance.

Mars in Libra ♂ ♎

Cooperative Action, Pursues Relationships

You act in a refined manner and sidestep conflict whenever possible. Working with others is a priority.

Mars in Libra falls under Venus' sociable, airy side. You have a graceful, intelligent, refined manner. Value is placed upon harmony and cooperation, and you prefer to act in partnership. Yet Mars here may cause you to behave in one of two very different ways, or to alternate back and forth between them. You can be diplomatic, persuasively bringing people over to your point of view. This first way stems from a dislike of conflict and a concern for what other people think. This may cause you to sidestep conflict whenever possible and to seek a middle ground. Of course this makes you charming, gracious, and easy to be around. Carried to an extreme, the desire for approval leads to letting the other people's opinions unduly influence your actions.

If persuasion does not work, you may become intellectually combative. This second way is particularly true in matters that involve fairness or justice. And in relationships or social settings, you want to be the leader, which can cause you to behave aggressively. It may feel safe to lose your temper in one-to-one relationships. Libra is associated with war and generals as well as peace. It is important to keep a balance between the two.

JOYCE SAYS:

Traits to treasure: Your persuasive use of diplomacy in pursuing your aims.
To transform: Avoid the alternatives of letting others exert too much influence over you, or being overly combative in getting others to do what you want.

Mars in Scorpio ♂ ♏

Powerful Desires, Pursues Desires

You exude power, strength, and sex appeal, and have great determination in going after what you want.

This is an extremely powerful placement. Before Pluto was discovered, Mars ruled Scorpio (and some astrologers still use it as the co-ruler). Intense emotions, feelings, and desires motivate actions. You exude power, strength, and sex appeal.

Once you make up your mind about something—a job, a relationship, or anything else—you doggedly pursue your aims. Naturally self-disciplined, you will put tremendous energy into accomplishing your desires. Secretive by nature, you excel in covert action. When it comes to a fight, you uncompromisingly stand up for principles but choose your battles rather than being thrown about by circumstances. Courage, stamina, and self-reliance give you the capacity to accomplish a great deal.

Carried to the extreme, determination, combined with the belief that you are always right, can result in obsessive-compulsive behavior. Lack of adaptability makes it difficult to reconsider positions or change courses of action. When headed in the right direction, it is possible for you to accomplish great feats. When headed in the wrong direction, uncompromising behavior can lead to self-destructive consequences.

Your nature is highly sexual, with a tendency toward being jealous and possessive. When it comes to anger, you have a long fuse but resentment gets built up over time. If anger festers too long, ruthless retaliation becomes possible.

You may sometimes find it hard to believe that no one can be right all the time and that those who disagree with you are not necessarily the enemy.

JOYCE SAYS:

Traits to treasure: Your incredible determination to make what you want happen.

To transform: Be willing to reconsider your actions and deal with anger before it turns into smoldering resentment.

Mars in Sagittarius   ♂ ♐

Straightforward Action, Pursues Adventure
Actions are direct and outgoing. You place a premium on freedom and independence.

You are independent and greatly value freedom. Action is taken in a direct, straightforward manner. There is a craving for travel and adventure and possibly risk-taking. Curiosity pushes you to discover what is around the next corner. The adventure you seek may be in gambling or dangerous sports or in more intellectual pursuits, such as education or philosophy, or combinations of these areas. You are attracted to the outdoors and to athletics.

Like a knight in shining armor, you are capable of gallant actions based on idealistic motives. However, the actions must be of your own choosing. You may expect to come and go as you please and do what you want, regardless of circumstances. You do not look for conflict but also do not sidestep it. The refusal to take orders from anyone or to be fenced in, carried to an extreme, can cause you to rebel against even the most legitimate requests.

You choose goals idealistically and are an effective crusader for beliefs you espouse. However, you should be careful of becoming overly dogmatic in your views. Also, you should take care not to scatter your energy. You tend to be overly optimistic about what you can accomplish, spread yourself too thin, and overlook important details that you find uninteresting.

JOYCE SAYS:

Traits to treasure: Your propensity for gallant actions in pursuit of idealistic aims.

To transform: Avoid scattering your energies and spreading yourself too thin.

Mars in Capricorn ♂ ♑

Pragmatic Action, Pursues Status
You are efficient and well-organized. Actions are geared toward concrete, practical accomplishments.

The action planet is contained under the influence of Saturn. Actions are based upon practical considerations. You have the capacity for hard work and decisive action and are well-organized, efficient, and conservative. Business instincts are innate, and discipline and self-control come naturally.

You aspire to professional status, recognition, and respect, and desire the material rewards that come from them. There is a respect for authority as you seek to become an authority figure. Not expecting anything to be just given to you, you work hard and smart in order to accomplish your goals. Aims are pursued patiently and persistently with actions that are competitive and well planned.

Problems may arise in dealing with others. When in positions of authority, you expect respect and obedience from those working for you. This may cause you to become an exacting boss. Even as a coworker, you may expect everyone, regardless of positions, to put in the effort that you do, and you can become heavy-handed and judgmental if they do not. If you are in a situation where your hard work goes unappreciated, you can build up frustration and resentment. A bit of tolerance goes a long way with this position.

JOYCE SAYS:

Traits to treasure: Your capacity for hard work and practical, decisive action in pursuing your aims.
To transform: Practice tolerance.

Mars in Aquarius   ♂ ♒

Individualistic Action, Pursues Intellectual Ideals
You act independently, wanting to be original and to have the freedom to do things your own way.

You possess high intelligence with good organizational ability. Your actions are based upon logic, although your logic may be quirky and unorthodox. Natural inventiveness helps you break new ground, and you enjoy the role of a detached reformer. Originality, intellectual competitiveness, and perseverance help you to accomplish goals.

You do not work well under authoritarian conditions. You enjoy teamwork but prefer to lead the team, as it difficult for you to cooperate when you disagree with a course of action. You distrust authority and only respect authority figures if you deem them worthy of respect. Likewise, you dislike tradition and prefer finding new, original ways of getting things done. This may lead to a tendency to throw out old methods despite their efficiency. Once you commit to a course of action, you doggedly pursue it, and may stubbornly disregard information that is contrary to what you already believe. Retaining an open mind is essential.

JOYCE SAYS:

Traits to treasure: Your ability to break new ground in pursuing your goals.
To transform: Make sure that you are open to new information after you have started on a course of action.

Mars in Pisces   ♂ ♓

Compassionate Action, Pursues Creativity
Not naturally competitive, you prefer to avoid conflict and disagreements.

Mars here does not display typical Martian characteristics of direct, assertive action or forceful aggressiveness. Instead, you lack competitiveness. You are sensitive and compassionate in how you proceed and may prefer to act in secret or behind the scenes and to avoid the limelight.

Expressing anger and taking direct action are difficult for you, and you should be careful not to scatter your energy. Your emotions are unpredictable, and strong feelings influence your capacity to act. When you are sad or upset, it is hard for you to act at all. You dislike disagreements and tend to avoid conflicts, even when that avoidance is to your detriment. This may lead to frustration, repressed anger, or brooding about the past. Learning how to stand up for yourself is of the utmost importance. Interestingly enough, you succeed far more easily in standing up for ideals or for those in need than for your own rights.

Your greatest accomplishments come when what you are doing is in line with a life vision. You have a strong imagination, creative and artistic abilities, and perhaps psychic abilities as well. You excel in pursuits where imagination and creativity are more important than competitiveness.

JOYCE SAYS:

Traits to treasure: The way you use imagination to help you attain goals.
To transform: Avoid letting emotions inhibit you from taking action.

MARS IN THE HOUSES

Mars in the First House

Action Geared Toward Immediate Environment
You have abundant energy, are action oriented, and have an intense need for activity.

Mars in the first house is a powerful placement, as Mars is associated with this house. You have a fiery temperament and tremendous energy, exuberance, and physical stamina. You are action oriented, competitive, and have an intense need for activity. Patience is not one of your strong points, and in new situations you jump in and take over. Because of this, people may perceive you as aggressive, whether or not that is how you see yourself. The sign Mars falls in shows the manner in which you actually assert yourself. If Mars is in a fire sign, it is particularly important for you to think before you act.

JOYCE SAYS:

Traits to treasure: Your action orientation.
To transform: Avoid being overly combative.

Mars in the Second House

Action Geared Toward Finances
You have a competitive drive geared toward making money.

You have drive and initiative in pursuing money and material possessions. You have no trouble working hard for what you earn and are competitive in financial arenas. Yet because you so dislike feeling in any way deprived, you may spend money impulsively rather than valuing it. Taken too far, you can tend to create financial ups and downs and crises based not on earning capacity but on spending habits. Typical Martian vocations include military or government work, engineering, mechanics, construction, and medicine.

JOYCE SAYS:
Traits to treasure: Your assertiveness in financial areas.
To transform: Temper overspending.

Mars in the Third House

Action Geared Toward Ideas
You have the capacity to forcefully express your ideas.

You are intellectually curious, restless, and competitive. You speak your mind, excel at repartee and debate, and have the ability to argue intensely about an idea without taking the argument personally. This makes it possible for you to come on too strong and offend people without realizing it. Learning a bit of tact in communicating ideas goes a long way toward avoiding unintended conflict. The third house also represents short-distance travel, so you may enjoy short, scenic trips, even though you are likely to drive much faster than the speed limit.

JOYCE SAYS:
Traits to treasure: Your debating skills.
To transform: Avoid being pushy verbally.

Mars in the Fourth House

Action Geared Toward Home and Family
You easily assert yourself in family matters.

With Mars in the fourth house, your early home life was Martian. You were taught assertiveness in the family, with one parent very likely playing a particularly dominating role. Since what is taught in early childhood affects the rest of our lives, aspects to Mars take on increased significance. If Mars has favorable aspects, you learned about courage by watching your parents display bravery and fortitude. If Mars has unfavorable aspects, aggressiveness and conflict were the family norm. In raising your own family later in life, you want to be in charge. If conflict ruled when you were young, be wary of repeating these family patterns as an adult.

JOYCE SAYS:
Traits to treasure: Your protectiveness of family.
To transform: Avoid bossy behavior on the home front.

Mars in the Fifth House

Action Geared Toward Self-expression
You readily assert yourself when it comes to creative expression, love affairs, and the interests of your children.

You have creative drive for self-expression. You want life to be play, and yet you possess leadership drive and hate losing at anything. You enjoy life's pleasures, including art, music, and theater, and you may possess artistic talent. In love and romance, you are sexual and romantic and directly pursue those you are interested in. The people you are attracted to are self-sufficient and independent, and a little bit of conflict keeps a romance exciting for you. Your actions directly influence your offspring, and your oldest is likely to be assertive.

JOYCE SAYS:
Traits to treasure: Your creative drive.
To transform: Avoid being bossy in romance and parenting.

Mars in the Sixth House

Action Geared Toward Work
You put forth significant drive and effort on the job.

You put a great deal of drive and energy into your job and are a bit of a perfectionist, albeit an impatient one. You are competitive in the workplace and relish on-the-job training. You finish tasks quickly and efficiently as long as you are allowed autonomy. If Mars receives unfavorable aspects, you dislike being told what to do or how to do it, which can lead to difficulties with authority figures. Your vitality is a plus when it comes to health, but you should be wary of overwork. Possible health problems come through accidents, fevers, inflammatory diseases, headaches, or burns.

JOYCE SAYS:

Traits to treasure: Your drive in the workplace.
To transform: Avoid conflict with coworkers and bosses.

Mars in the Seventh House

Action Geared Toward Relationships
You may be assertive relationally or attract an assertive partner, or both.

The seventh house represents both you and the type of people you attract. Typically, qualities of planets placed here get projected onto a spouse or business partner. With Mars here, you are attracted to assertive, take-charge, and possibly aggressive partners. Conversely, you may be the one who displays these characteristics. Developing a balance of power relationally is of prime importance. If you give up too much power, you grow to resent your spouse. If you are the one in charge, it is important for you to recognize your spouse's needs and not just your own. It is also possible that you see others as combative or trying to thwart you whenever you have a disagreement or do not get your way. Recognizing when compromise is appropriate is essential with this placement.

JOYCE SAYS:

Traits to treasure: Your drive toward relationships.
To transform: Look inside instead of blaming others for conflict.

Mars in the Eighth House

Action Geared Toward Desires
Intense desires propel you toward going after whatever you want.

You have a powerful sex drive and tend toward emotional intensity. A satisfying sex life is of prime importance. A strong nature gives you stamina in going after what you want, whether it is sex, money, or anything else. You are willing to sacrifice a great deal in order to accomplish goals. Being intense and possibly compulsive makes it difficult to detach and reevaluate situations once you set upon a course of action. If you have made a positive choice, you achieve goals well beyond reasonable expectations. If you have made a poor choice, results can be destructive. Learning to step back and reevaluate is essential.

Mars in this house also gives the potential for conflict over finances. It is possible that you and your spouse do not agree on spending or that your spouse controls the money. It is also possible to have difficulties over inheritances.

JOYCE SAYS:

Traits to treasure: Your powerful drive for accomplishment.
To transform: Avoid acting out of compulsions.

Mars in the Ninth House

Actions Geared Toward Adventure

You assert yourself when it comes to higher education, travel, and adventure.

You are enthusiastic and independent. There is a desire for travel, excitement, and adventure. You want to see the world. You are competitive in athletics and higher education, although you are just as likely to be self-educated as to attend institutions of higher learning. You have a willingness to stand up for social, moral, ethical, or religious beliefs, and you can be quite a proselytizer. Because of this, it is important for you to recognize that beliefs are personal and that no one person or belief system holds the key to the ultimate truth.

JOYCE SAYS:

Traits to treasure: Your desire for adventure.
To transform: Avoid believing you've cornered the market on truth.

Mars in the Tenth House

Actions Geared Toward Career

You display competitive drive in professional arenas.

Drive and energy are focused on achieving career goals. You are assertive and competitive. You like to be in positions of authority and to be looked up to and respected, and will work very hard to realize these aims.

It is possible that you were brought up in a home where there was conflict or the threat of force. As an adult, it is important for you to recognize your potential to create conflict, whether on the job or with family members. Professionally, you are likely to attract an authoritarian boss, and how you get along with this person determines your success.

How you handle your energy is of prime importance since planets in the tenth house have to do with public image. With Mars here, your actions are noticed. You may gain positive attention for courageously taking a stand, or you may gain negative attention and be dubbed a troublemaker.

JOYCE SAYS:

Traits to treasure: Your drive in achieving professional success.
To transform: Avoid direct conflict with authority figures.

Mars in the Eleventh House

Actions Geared Toward Friendship
You assert yourself with friends and in group or organizational activities.

You take the lead in friendships and group activities. The people you most enjoy socializing with are honest, direct, and assertive. If altruistic, your energy is directed toward social or humanitarian goals. Whatever your goals, you put drive and energy into their achievement and socialize with people who help you to attain them. Problems with associates can arise if you become overly aggressive or automatically see people who disagree with you as a threat.

JOYCE SAYS:

Traits to treasure: Your ability to take the lead in group activities.
To transform: Avoid being aggressive with friends or in group associations.

Mars in the Twelfth House

Actions Geared Behind the Scenes
You have difficulty directly standing up for yourself.

You dislike conflict. This makes it difficult for you to be assertive or to express anger. In conflict situations, you see yourself as the nice person and tend to blame others for aggressive behavior. Yet you tend to alternate between burying anger and unconsciously acting out with hostility. Your emotions strongly affect your actions, and acting out may be completely unconscious. This makes careful examination of all conflict situations important. Interestingly enough, you are better at asserting yourself when fighting for the underdog or acting compassionately on behalf of others than in standing up for yourself.

JOYCE SAYS:
Traits to treasure: Your capacity for compassionate action.
To transform: Avoid burying your anger.

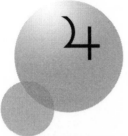

Chapter 10

JUPITER — WHAT YOU VALUE

Keywords: Expansion, Opportunity, Growth, Abundance, Faith
Rules: *Sagittarius, Ninth House*
Cycle: *12-year cycle-one year in each sign*
Somatic Influences: *Muscular System,*
Adrenal Glands, Male Sex Organs

Jupiter is the planet with the best reputation of the Zodiac. It rules opportunity, luck, ease, and prosperity—in essence, good fortune. Jupiter is associated with joy, levity, and having a good time. The ancients referred to Jupiter as the "greater benefic" and associated it with an abundant life.

Jupiter, the largest planet of the Zodiac, aptly embodies the principle of expansion. Jupiter provides the ability reach out, grow, and learn from experience. Called the planet of the "higher mind," Jupiter has to do with values. These values include moral or ethical standards, philosophical or religious beliefs, and attitudes toward life. Jupiter is contrasted with Mercury, the planet of the "lower mind," which is associated with day-to-day thoughts.

Jupiter rules the fire sign of Sagittarius and was considered to rule the water sign of Pisces before Neptune's discovery. Some astrologers continue to associate Jupiter with Pisces, but the descriptions in this book give Jupiter's rulership solely to Sagittarius and Neptune's rulership to Pisces. Jupiter and Sagittarius fit well together symbolically. Both planet and sign are associated with generosity, faith, optimism, joviality, and reaching out for what life has to offer.

Jupiter's positive expression endows an uplifting attitude toward life. Faith and self-confidence allow us to set and achieve goals. We believe we deserve to have the best, so we take advantage of opportunities that come our way. And seeing the world as plentiful allows us to share what we have with others.

A strong but negatively expressed Jupiter turns into self-indulgence. This takes the form of too much of a good thing, such as in overeating, overdrinking, and overspending. Too much may be expected for too little, for example, believing the world owes us a living.

If Jupiter is weak in a chart, optimism is difficult. If Jupiter is weak and Saturn is strong, there is a tendency to work too hard for too little.

The negative side of Jupiter is associated with wars over religious beliefs, such as the Crusades or Islamic jihads—wars that arise from the bigoted idea that a particular belief system embodies the truth at the expense of all others.

Jupiter is in a sign for one year. The sign it posits in our individual charts describes philosophical values. Whether these are actually values we live by or only those we espouse depends upon Jupiter's aspects with other planets. The house Jupiter falls in reflects the area of life we value and shows where we are likely to be lucky or indulgent.

JUPITER IN THE SIGNS

Jupiter in Aries ♃ ♈

Values Individuality
You hold individuality and self-sufficiency in high esteem.

You value individuality, independence, and self-sufficiency. You aspire to positions of leadership and respect those who gain leadership through individual ingenuity. You also value standing up for beliefs and fighting for good causes. You admire those who go their own way based on their principles rather than the need for approval or social conformity. This is a positive placement for self-acceptance.

JOYCE SAYS:
Traits to treasure: Your value of self-sufficiency.
To transform: Avoid underestimating the value of getting along with people.

Jupiter in Taurus ♃ ♉

Values Luxury
You highly value money and the good life.

You place a high value on money, security, stability, and possessions. There is a love of home and luxury. You appreciate the good life, from sensual pleasures to physical comforts to food and drink, and only the best feels good enough. Luckily, this is a favorable placement for attracting wealth. You admire those who are affluent and can afford to be extravagant, and you enjoy being generous to family members and close friends.

JOYCE SAYS:
Traits to treasure: Your value of material resources.
To transform: Avoid judging people's worth by their finances.

Jupiter in Gemini ♃ ♊

Values Intellect
You esteem education and intellectual pursuits.

Jupiter in Gemini combines the planet of the higher mind with the sign of the lower mind. You highly value knowledge, information, education, objective reasoning, and communication. You are intellectually curious and enjoy any type of learning that opens the mind to new ideas. Admiration for others is based upon their intelligence and possibly upon their advanced degrees. You enjoy local travel, whether visiting the next town or state, or taking a drive in the country. This is a favorable placement for intellectual endeavors.

JOYCE SAYS:
Traits to treasure: Your value of information.
To transform: Avoid intellectual arrogance.

Jupiter in Cancer ♃ ♋

Values Family
You value home, family, and family traditions.

You highly value stability and security. Your beliefs are traditional and conservative, and home and family traditions are held in high esteem. You are generous toward the family, and no matter what your background, you deeply believe family members should take care of one another. You admire those who are nurturing and caring and provide well for loved ones. This is a lucky placement for family matters and perhaps for ownership of real estate.

JOYCE SAYS:

Traits to treasure: The value you place on family.
To transform: Avoid expecting loved ones to conform to your values.

Jupiter in Leo   ♃ ♌

Values Self-Expression

You esteem self-expression, resourcefulness, and creativity.

You value creativity, resourcefulness, and courage. You look up to those with the ability to be true to their dreams and ideals. You appreciate the finer things in life, but you are more attuned to throwing lavish parties or having social gatherings than you are to attaining money for its own sake. When it comes to religion, you are more attracted to pageantry and grandeur than religious doctrine. This is a favorable placement for self-expression.

JOYCE SAYS:

Traits to treasure: The value you place on self-expression.
To transform: Avoid getting carried away with lavishness.

Jupiter in Virgo   ♃ ♍

Values Order

You value work, productivity, and order.

Virgo's detail-oriented nature is not a natural fit for expansive Jupiter. Your ideals are practical and conservative. You hold neatness and order in high regard and believe that any job worth doing is worth doing well. In a sense, you value hard work and perfectionism. There is an expectation that people's values to be tied to what they actually do, rather than to unreachable ivory-tower ideals. You enjoy accomplishment. This is a lucky placement for work.

JOYCE SAYS:

Traits to treasure: Your practical value of hard work.
To transform: Avoid being overly critical.

Jupiter in Libra ♃ ♎

Values Relationships
You value harmony, cooperation, and one-to-one relationships.

You value one-to-one relationships, diplomacy, and beauty. You believe that people should treat one another well and get along and that situations should be fair and equitable. Harmony and cooperation are important ideals. You appreciate beauty, whether the beauty of a person or a work of art. Your natural good taste makes it possible to choose works of art that appreciate in value. This is a lucky placement for marriage, partnership, and all one-to-one relationships.

JOYCE SAYS:
Traits to treasure: Your value of relationships.
To transform: Maintain balance between your values and those of others.

Jupiter in Scorpio ♃ ♏

Values Depth
You hold truth and justice in high esteem.

You value justice and admire truth. You are intense about your standards and love to see people get what they deserve, whether they deserve a reward or a punishment. There is an attraction to the mysteries of life, getting to the underlying meaning of situations, and uncovering the true motivations of people. There may be an interest in metaphysics or psychology. There is potential luck in investments or joint finances.

JOYCE SAYS:
Traits to treasure: Your value of truth.
To transform: Avoid getting caught up in wishing people their comeuppance.

Jupiter in Sagittarius ♃ ♐

Values Knowledge
You value knowledge, education, and the exploration of other cultures and belief systems.

Jupiter is the ruler of Sagittarius, so this is a strong, favorable, and lucky placement. Both Jupiter and Sagittarius are associated with the "higher mind" as well as with luck, faith, hope, and expansiveness. With Jupiter here, you value truth, ethics, and education. The search for truth may lead to the studies of philosophy, religion, metaphysical systems of thought, or foreign cultures. Learning is lifelong. There is an attraction to risk taking, whether in financial endeavors or mountain climbing. Having an innate sense of optimism, you look for the best in situations and usually find it. There is a love of travel, particularly to foreign places.

JOYCE SAYS:

Traits to treasure: The value you place on education.
To transform: Avoid getting caught up in looking for the "next truth."

Jupiter in Capricorn   ♃ ♑

Values Tradition
You have a high regard for tradition, common sense, and accomplishment.

Your social and political ideals are traditional and conservative. You hold hard work, practicality, and common sense in high esteem, and you value accomplishment. You aspire to positions of power and authority and the wealth associated with them. While you may be quite generous to those close to you, you believe that people should work for what they get, and have little sympathy for those unwilling to do so. This placement may be lucky for business opportunities and money.

JOYCE SAYS:

Traits to treasure: The value you place on accomplishment.
To transform: Maintain compassion for those less fortunate than you are.

Jupiter in Aquarius   ♃ ♒

Values Inventiveness
You value inventiveness, intellectual ideals, and friendships.

Your ideals are intellectual and humanitarian. You have disdain for traditional thinking and are attracted to inventive ideas that defy the norm. You like to associate with intelligent people. Beliefs about equality and social justice may lead to joining groups associated with social and humanitarian causes. You meet people as individuals and do not make judgments based upon socioeconomic class, ethnic identity, race, or religion. You tend to be lucky in associations.

JOYCE SAYS:

Traits to treasure: Your value of people as individuals.
To transform: Avoid intellectual arrogance.

Jupiter in Pisces ♃ ♓

Values Compassion
You hold compassion, empathy, and idealism in high regard.

Your values are idealistic and compassionate, and you have a generosity of spirit. You believe in sharing, particularly in helping people in need and those less fortunate. You are more in tune with mystical or spiritual pursuits than with organized religion. You are attracted to meditation, yoga, prayer, or other pursuits that provide a direct link to universal intelligence or God. There is also an appreciation of imagination and beauty. This appreciation may be of art, music, literature, or poetry.

JOYCE SAYS:

Traits to treasure: Your value of spiritual pursuits.
To transform: Avoid giving away more than you can afford.

JUPITER IN THE HOUSES

Jupiter in the First House

Overall Luck
A jovial, outgoing nature contributes to your openness to new experiences.

You are friendly, outgoing, and self-confident. Open to new experiences, you are forever seeking to expand your horizons through travel, education, or socializing. An optimistic nature provides faith and a positive outlook on life. You look for the good in situations and usually find it. Unless Jupiter receives difficult aspects, you are luckier than most people are. Being pleasure-loving and enthusiastic makes you fun to be around, and your self-confidence helps you gain the trust of others.

The danger of this position has to do with over-expansion. Too much of a good thing is not always positive. It is important that in your optimism that you do not promise more than is possible to deliver. This is more likely if Jupiter receives difficult aspects. Also, since the first house represents the physical body and Jupiter rules expansion, you may put on weight easily. Overindulgence over a period of time can negatively impact your health.

JOYCE SAYS:

Traits to treasure: Your generous spirit.
To transform: Avoid overindulgence.

Jupiter in the Second House

Lucky with Money

You earn money easily and can spend it just as easily.

You are optimistic about finances, and rightfully so, as you are lucky with money and material resources. Jupiter here represents the most propitious placement in the Zodiac for attracting wealth. You earn money easily—or it comes to you readily—and you take great joy in being both generous and extravagant. This creates a propensity to spend money as easily it is earned. In fact, your ideal around money is to make so much that you do not have to think about it. While generosity is a positive quality, unless it is tempered by practicality, it is possible to end up with little security regardless of income. If Jupiter receives difficult aspects here, carelessness with money is likely.

JOYCE SAYS:

Traits to treasure: Your luck with money.
To transform: Avoid an easy-come-easy-go attitude toward money.

Jupiter in the Third House

Lucky with Words

Your thinking is expansive, and you communicate facilely.

Your thinking is optimistic and your outlook broad. This placement conveys intelligence and expands your interest in intellectual horizons. Interests may lie in writing, publishing, and communicating. At the very least, you are a good talker.

You enjoy of short-distance jaunts such as driving to neighboring states and communities. You may also enjoy the outdoors.

If Jupiter receives favorable aspects, relationships with siblings and neighbors are favorable. If Jupiter receives unfavorable aspects, you may expect more of siblings than they deliver, or you may be the one who promises more than is possible.

JOYCE SAYS:

Traits to treasure: Your optimistic outlook.

To transform: Avoid talking for the sake of hearing your own voice.

Jupiter in the Fourth House

Lucky with Family

You grew up in a generous family environment and are generous with your own family.

If Jupiter receives favorable aspects, it is likely that you were the favored child in your family and that your childhood was happy. The family was supportive not just in material ways but by being loving and accepting, which helped you develop self-confidence and self-esteem. As an adult, kindness and generosity toward those you love help you create a happy family environment. Your ideal place to live is a large home in a country setting with lots of land and trees. Since the fourth house also represents real estate, you could be lucky with real estate investments.

If Jupiter receives unfavorable aspects here, very likely you encountered many unfulfilled promises in your early family life, and care must be taken not to repeat the same pattern with your own family.

JOYCE SAYS:

Traits to treasure: You value of home and family.

To transform: Avoid spoiling your children or promising your family more than you can deliver.

Jupiter in the Fifth House

Lucky with Love

Romantic prospects are numerous, and you are generous to loved ones.

You love a good time and enjoy grandeur. If Jupiter receives favorable aspects, there is luck in financial speculation, love affairs, creative endeavors, and with children. You socialize easily and readily attract suitors and generous lovers. Relationships with your children are a source of joy. You are generous to all those you love, and that generosity is returned.

If Jupiter receives difficult aspects here, you may expect to be luckier than you turn out to be with regard to financial speculation, love affairs, creative endeavors, and your children. The tendency to be overly generous or to expect too much from others may be the cause of disappointments.

JOYCE SAYS:

Traits to treasure: Your love of grandeur and appreciation of a good time.
To transform: Avoid expecting too much from lovers and children.

Jupiter in the Sixth House

Lucky with Work
Your opportunities in the workplace exceed the norm.

You have the potential to prosper at work. If Jupiter receives favorable aspects, you are lucky both in the work environment and with your health. Generally, you enjoy being productive and have a cheerful attitude toward work. Generosity and the willingness to lend a helping hand make you popular with coworkers and employers and help you to get ahead.

If Jupiter receives unfavorable aspects, there is a tendency to promise more than you can deliver, which can come from an overly optimistic assessment of circumstances or a lackadaisical attitude toward work.

JOYCE SAYS:

Traits to treasure: The value you place on day-to-day work.
To transform: Avoid optimistically taking on more daily tasks than it is possible to complete.

Jupiter in the Seventh House

Lucky with Partnership
You may be generous in marriage or business partnerships, or you may attract generous partners, or both.

You value relationships, enjoy meeting people and socializing, and are generous to others. If Jupiter receives favorable aspects, you are lucky in one-to-one relationships. This includes close friends and peers at work as well as marriage and partnerships. In marriage, you attract a spouse who treats you lovingly and provides well. In business, you attract virtuous and generous partners. At work, you readily set up alliances with peers. If Jupiter receives difficult aspects, you either give too much in relationships or expect too much or both. There is a danger of being attracted to charming, unreliable people who promise more than they ultimately deliver, or of your becoming the one who breaks promises despite what may be the best of intentions.

JOYCE SAYS:

Traits to treasure: Your value of one-to-one relationships.
To transform: Avoid being taken in by charm or taking in others by it.

Jupiter in the Eighth House

Lucky with Partnership Resources or Investments
You can benefit financially from joint resources.

You have the potential to benefit through joint finances, inheritance, and insurance. If Jupiter receives favorable aspects, you are lucky when it comes to other people's money. Financial benefit may come through marriage and from investments. If Jupiter receives unfavorable aspects, the likelihood is that you are not as lucky as you believe. You should be careful of get-rich-quick schemes, partners that squander your money, or you yourself promising others overly grandiose financial returns.

No matter what Jupiter's aspects, a strong sex drive and abundant opportunities for sexual partners exists. Your attitude toward life and death is positive, and you may be interested in the occult or reincarnation.

JOYCE SAYS:

Traits to treasure: The value you place on joint resources.
To transform: Avoid getting involved in get rich schemes.

Jupiter in the Ninth House

Lucky with Knowledge
Opportunities come to you through education, long-distance travel, publishing, or writing.

As Jupiter rules the ninth house, this represents a strong placement. You value knowledge and higher education. There is a life-long interest in learning. Areas of study that have appeal are philosophy, religion, ethics, and belief systems. Success through writing, publishing, lecturing, and teaching is possible.

This placement increases wanderlust. Travel and adventure are appealing, and living in foreign countries is a possibility.

If Jupiter receives difficult aspects, you may be lazy about education and overly opinionated about your own beliefs. Wanderlust is increased, and settling down may prove difficult.

JOYCE SAYS:

Traits to treasure: The value you place on higher education.
To transform: Be careful of getting caught up in wanderlust.

Jupiter in the Tenth House

Lucky with Profession
Connecting with people in authority helps you achieve career success.

You value success. You are likely to be lucky in achieving prominence in your career, and tend to be in the right place, at the right time, with the right contacts. If Jupiter receives favorable aspects, you have leadership potential and get along well with people in positions of authority who may become mentors and help you to achieve status and recognition. You, in turn, are generous in helping others when you are in a position of authority. Ethics play a large role in business decisions.

If Jupiter receives unfavorable aspects, you can be lucky for a while. However, if you promise more than you deliver, whether through over optimism or blatant exaggeration, reversals of fortune occur. You must be careful to have integrity.

JOYCE SAYS:

Traits to treasure: The value you place on success.
To transform: Make sure business dealings are conducted with integrity.

Jupiter in the Eleventh House

Lucky with Friends
You easily attract friends and socialize with diverse groups of people.

You value friendship and organizational activity and are lucky when it comes to associates. You have many friends, are popular with peers, and enjoy socializing with diverse groups of people. You are generous to friends, and they in return are generous to you. Acquaintances are helpful in assisting you achieve goals. If life affords you the time to give back to society, you are interested in organizations with charitable or humanistic goals.

If Jupiter receives difficult aspects, friends may be less reliable, or you may be less reliable in friendship. You need to be discerning about who you trust and make sure that you are trustworthy.

JOYCE SAYS:

Traits to treasure: The value you place on friendship.
To transform: Avoid unreliable associations and make sure that you are not an unreliable friend.

Jupiter in the Twelfth House

Lucky with Spirit
You have a "guardian angel" looking out for you.

This is the guardian angel placement for Jupiter. Luck somehow comes through, even in the worst of times and even if it appears at the eleventh hour. There is deep sympathy for and generosity to those in need. Your beliefs are metaphysically and spiritually oriented. There is a strong inner voice, which meditation helps you gain access to.

If Jupiter receives unfavorable aspects, idealism can be impractical and sympathy may lead to being taken advantage of by those in need.

JOYCE SAYS:

Traits to treasure: The value you place on matters of spirit.
To transform: Avoid getting caught up in impractical idealism.

Chapter 11

SATURN — YOUR WORK ETHIC

Keywords: Work, Discipline, Responsibility
Rules: Capricorn, Tenth House
Cycle: 29.5 Years, 2 ½ Years in Each Sign
Somatic Influences: Skeletal System, Bones, Teeth

Saturn is associated with the serious areas of life. It is the planet of work, discipline, duty, and responsibility. It rules reliability and stability. Saturn is associated with structure, boundaries, and rules, and as such is considered the planet of limitation. Saturn, also known as Father Time, rules time, delays, and old age. Saturn's concerns are concrete and practical. Its injunction is "Do what you are supposed to do. Work hard, be responsible, pay the mortgage, put bread on the table." Through Saturn we get what we earn—one way or the other.

Older astrology texts referred to Saturn as the "great malefic" and associate it with misfortune. We tend to think of Jupiter, expansion, as good, and Saturn, limitation, as bad. Because boundaries and limitations stop us, they are perceived as negative. Yet boundaries also provide safety and protection. The walls and ceilings of our homes represent boundaries. Outdoors gazing at the sky on a clear summer night, we may not feel the need for these boundaries; but we feel differently on a stormy, snow-driven winter night. Ideally, Jupiter and Saturn balance one another. Jupiter implores us to reach for more; Saturn lets us know when to stop.

Saturn rules the sign of Capricorn and was considered the ruler of Aquarius before Uranus was discovered. Some astrologers continue to use this dual rulership. In this book, Saturn is considered the ruler of Capricorn, and Uranus the sole ruler of Aquarius. Saturn and Capricorn represent a perfect fit between sign and planet. Both represent hard work and responsibility. Both convey caution and conservatism. Capricorn is an ambitious sign that wants to be in an executive position and expects to gain that position through hard work and responsibility. Both planet and sign look to the past and learn from established traditions.

Positively expressed, Saturn helps us realistically assess the world around us and ourselves. We approach situations with common sense and discipline, learn from experience, and live up to appropriate responsibilities. Appropriate is the key word because knowing when to live up to expectations and when to set limits is a must for Saturn's positive expression.

If Saturn is negatively expressed, we are more likely to see what is wrong with the world than what is right with it. This gives us a pessimistic attitude toward life and possibly inhibits self-expression. After all, what is the point of doing anything if nothing good can happen. This attitude can also make us cold and calculating in order to protect ourselves from a cruel world.

Both an overemphasized and an underemphasized Saturn can lead to problems. An overemphasized Saturn causes an overdeveloped sense of responsibility. This leads to assuming responsibilities where none should exist, such as overwork due to taking on tasks that are not our own. It may also take the form of blaming ourselves for other people's behavior or for outcomes over which we have no control—in essence, seeing situations as our fault and believing we have a duty to fix them, whether or not this is the reality of the situation. This may lead to low self-worth, fearfulness, and pessimism. Alternatively, we can be critical of others who we do not see as responsible enough.

Additional difficulties associated with Saturn's negative expression have to do with boundary issues. There are likely to be problems with authority figures that manifest in one of two ways. Either we give in to the authority figures out of fear, or we rebel against them, regardless of what is appropriate in a given situation. Also, we may feel easily rejected and see barriers where none exist. This separates us from other people or inhibits our ability to achieve. This is handled in one of two extremely different ways. Seeing the barriers, we either push through to ultimate achievement, or we give up in fear. In either case, the tendency is to see life as hard, perhaps harder than is accurate. The glass looks half empty, not half full.

A weak Saturn conveys completely opposite behavior—an underdeveloped sense of responsibility. This is particularly likely to be the case if Jupiter and/or Neptune are strong and Saturn is weak. In this case, we blame other people for our lack of achievement instead of realistically assessing situations and learning from experience.

Saturn has a 29.5-year cycle. It stays in each sign two and a half years. The sign it falls in shows the lessons of responsibility that must be learned by our peer age group, how our age group seeks status, and what are its fears or inadequacies. The house it falls in shows where we take life seriously, assume responsibilities, and perhaps where we are fearful.

SATURN IN THE SIGNS

Saturn in Aries   ♄ ♈

Personal Responsibility
Lessons in your life come through the necessity of combining responsibility with personal autonomy.

In general, the lessons of your age group are in combining responsibility with independence and self-sufficiency. Aries' natural expression is to jump into action and think about it later. Saturn here does not hamper initiative but requires that the action be taken responsibly. Fears about being restricted may lead to problems dealing with people in authority. There may also be fears about lacking initiative or ability. This is a positive placement for working independently, initiating new systems, or being in your own business.

JOYCE SAYS:
Traits to treasure: Your responsible self-sufficiency.
To transform: Avoid seeing authority figures as the enemy.

Saturn in Taurus   ♄ ♉

Financial Responsibility
Lessons in your life come through money and the accumulation of material resources.

Saturn and Taurus are a positive combination, as they both relate to work and money. Your life lessons have to do with financial resources. Career stability and security are of primary importance, and your attitude toward money is conservative. You may have fears of not having enough money or success, but these fears can be motivating forces for achievement. This is a positive position for careers in banking, finance, investments, or business management.

JOYCE SAYS:

Traits to treasure: Your responsible handling of money.
To transform: Let go of fears surrounding finances.

Saturn in Gemini   ♄ ♊

Intellectual Responsibility
Lessons in your life come through education and learning.

The lessons of your age group have to do with mental attitudes and education. Learning may be seen as work, and it is possible that you fear not being "smart enough," regardless of your actual intellectual capacity. This may spur you to achieve advanced degrees or cause you to avoid educational environments altogether. Despite any fears, this position is positive for careers that have to do with organized mental abilities. These include education, mathematics, science, writing, research, and engineering.

JOYCE SAYS:

Traits to treasure: Your serious thinking.
To transform: Let go of fears surrounding intelligence.

Saturn in Cancer   ♄ ♋

Family Responsibility
Lessons in your life come through home and family.

The lessons of your age group have to do with family responsibilities and security. It is possible that too much was expected of you from an early age in your family, or else that you just felt duty-bound to be responsible for family members. As an adult, providing for your family is a top priority. There can be fears of not having enough emotional or financial security. This may lead to being an overprotective parent. Careers associated with Saturn in Cancer are real estate, home improvement industries, restaurants, and food industries.

JOYCE SAYS:

Traits to treasure: Your serious concern for family.
To transform: Let go of being overbearing with family members.

Saturn in Leo ♄ ♌

Responsible Self-expression

Lessons in your life come through the use of will and power.

The lessons of your age group have to do with creativity, will, love, and authority. Leo's natural expression is dynamic, outgoing, and lavish. It is the sign of self-expression. Saturn adds a strong sense of personal responsibility. Your desire to be important may be coupled with the fear of not being important enough, and creative urges may be coupled with a fear of not being creative enough. You may see self-expression as work.

You may also have issues in personal relationships and a fear of being unloved. These fears tend to be handled in one of two ways. You push through fears and accomplish your heart's desire, or back away from whatever you perceive as too challenging. Careers associated with Saturn in Leo are positions of authority in education, entertainment, management, business, and finance.

JOYCE SAYS:

Traits to treasure: Your serious concern for creative abilities.
To transform: Let go of fears about self-worth.

Saturn in Virgo ♄ ♍

Work Responsibility

Lessons in your life come through day-to-day work and responsibilities.

The lessons of your age group have to do with discrimination. Virgo is a perfectionist sign and is most associated with work in the sense of making sure a job is well done. It is also associated with health. Lessons here involve discriminating between what is important and what is not. You may have a fear of not accomplishing enough or of your work being less than perfect. This can lead to being overly critical. There is an obvious association between overwork and health problems. Careers associated with Saturn in Virgo have to do with traditional and alternative medicine, health care, science, accounting, and any other field involving attention to detail.

JOYCE SAYS:

Traits to treasure: Your serious concern for work standards.
To transform: Let go of perfectionism.

Saturn in Libra ♄ ♎

Relational Responsibility
Lessons in your life come through one-to-one relationships.

The lessons of your age group have to do with fairness, cooperation, and relationships. Libra is the sign that represents relationships and the ability to get along in them. Relationships are taken seriously, and you may have fears of relational loss or social disapproval. This can make setting appropriate boundaries with people difficult. The tendency is to either to inappropriately go along with other people's demands, or to set rigid standards of relational behavior. It is important to distinguish when acceptance and compromise represent the best course of action and when standing up for principles is more appropriate. Careers associated with Saturn in Libra are law, mediation, organizational planning, and systems analysis.

JOYCE SAYS:

Traits to treasure: Your serious concern for cooperation.
To transform: Let go of rigid relational standards.

Saturn in Scorpio ♄ ♏

Responsible Sharing
Lessons in your life come through the sharing of resources.

The lessons of your age group have to do with joint resources. Scorpio rules power, sex, deep-rooted desires, passion, intensity, and other people's money. Sharing, whether it is sexual or financial, is taken seriously. You may have fears of not having enough power, control, intimacy, or money. Because of this, you can become overly authoritarian, or avoid situations where you feel threatened. Neither of these alternatives works.

You take sex seriously, which is not a problem if it means that you are selective about your sexual partners, but may become one if you let unconscious fears stifle intimate relationships. Tests involving power and control may come through the handling of other people's money or with inheritances. These issues may propel you to look for the deeper meaning in life.

It is important to find a balance between your personal power and the power of others. and to become aware of what you really want rather than letting unconscious motivations guide your actions. Careers associated with Saturn in Scorpio are banking, finance, insurance, medicine, psychology, psychiatry, research, and chemistry.

JOYCE SAYS:

Traits to treasure: Your concern for sharing resources equitably.
To transform: Let go of fear surrounding joint resources.

Saturn in Sagittarius ♄ ♐

Ethical Responsibility

Lessons in your life come through higher education, philosophy, and personal values.

The lessons of your age group have to do with values. Sagittarius rules higher education, philosophy, religion, and belief systems. You value higher education, which may propel achievement of advanced degrees. Regardless of your chosen profession, you have a tendency to underrate your self-worth if you are not as educated as you think you should be.

Developing personal ethical, religious, or philosophical values to live by is a must. Once developed, it is important to realize that your values are not necessarily "the truth" and that other have the right to choose their own. Careers associated with Saturn in Sagittarius are writing, teaching, philosophy, religion, politics, travel, law, and science.

JOYCE SAYS:

Traits to treasure: Your serious concern for values.
To transform: Let go of believing that you have the only key to values.

Saturn in Capricorn ♄ ♑

Career Responsibility

Lessons in your life come through responsibility and use of authority.

Saturn rules the sign of Capricorn, so this is a very strong placement. Both Saturn and Capricorn stand for rules, order, discipline, work, success, authority, and achievement. Both are traditional and conservative. The lessons of your age group have to do with the right use of authority. You respect those in authority and believe in working hard in order to achieve positions of power, prestige, and authority. Yet an underlying fear of not being successful enough may cause you to judge yourself harshly. No matter what your success quotient, you are likely to believe that you should be at the next level. You also expect others to achieve by their own efforts, and it is possible for you to be callous toward those you deem as not doing enough to help themselves. It is important to learn the difference between constructive and destructive forms of criticism of both yourself and others. Success is regarded in traditional terms, and you are more likely to be comfortable in a Fortune-500 company than in a start-up venture. Careers associated with Saturn in Capricorn include traditional business in general, corporate executives, chief financial officers, chief executive officers, economists, chiropractors, religious leaders, engineers, government officials, political leaders, real estate, and medicine.

JOYCE SAYS:

Traits to treasure: Serious concern for success.
To transform: Let go of rigid professional standards.

Saturn in Aquarius   ♄ ♒

Social Responsibility
Lessons in your life come through friends, associates, and belief systems.

The lessons of your age group have to do with humanitarianism, friendship, and group associations. At its most ideal, Saturn here gives you a sense of duty toward humanity. Aquarian ideals embrace individual freedom and altruism. This gives a strong sense of duty to friends and to the ideals of associations that you join.

You have a reverence for intellectual freedom. Yet intellectual pride and the conviction that you have the truth may cause you to become rigid in your opinions. This can take the form of not listening to those who disagree with you or avoiding them completely. Lessons here involve the ability to live up to your own intellectual ideals. Careers associated with Saturn in Aquarius involve humanitarian causes, science, education, engineering, occultism, organizational work, psychology, and research.

JOYCE SAYS:

Traits to treasure: Your serious concern for humanitarian ideals.
To transform: Let go of believing you have the corner on truth.

Saturn in Pisces   ♄ ♓

Spiritual Responsibility
Lessons in your life come through balancing the ideal with the mundane.

Saturn is the planet that most represents being down-to-earth and responsible. Pisces is the sign that most represents spiritual ideals as well as compassion and sensitivity. Surprising as it may seem, both are motivated to "do what's right," albeit from different perspectives. Saturn's perspective is one of duty and doing what is correct. Pisces' perspective is one of compassion and being a good and kind person. Yet, both may lead to taking on responsibilities that are not one's own.

The lessons of your age group have to do with discrimination and detachment. There may be strong sympathy for the underdog. It is important to recognize when it is appropriate to help others and when it is appropriate to hold them accountable for their behavior. Careers associated with Saturn in Pisces are fishing, seafaring, veterinarians, medicine, drug and alcohol treatment, hospital work, prison work, relief work, oil industry, hypnotism, spiritualism, and occultism.

JOYCE SAYS:
Traits to treasure: Your serious concern for compassionate responsibility.
To transform: Let go of responsibilities that are not your own.

SATURN IN THE HOUSES

Saturn in the First House

Responsibility Plus
Mature and dependable, you started at an early age to take responsibilities seriously.

You approach situations cautiously and with reserve, behavior learned in youth. Very likely, you were mature and responsible at an early age and growing up was not easy. Whether it was an inner compulsion that motivated you to act like an adult early on or the circumstances warranted it, you were accountable for responsibilities far beyond your years.

As an adult, you face life pragmatically. You are hard working, serious, and have a strong sense of duty. You behave in a correct manner because it is the right thing to do. Being responsible is a positive trait that can help you succeed in life, but it can also be carried too far. Being overly dependable and trustworthy can lead you to take care of situations and other people far better than you take care of yourself. A sense of inadequacy may lead you to believe that you are only as good as what you accomplish. Because of this, you may take on undue burdens and actually refuse help because you see it as weakness or proof of inadequacy. Yet you end up feeling taken advantage of and become critical of others for not behaving responsibly enough. Because of this, you may become self-protective and build a wall around yourself that keeps others out more than it protects. It is important to recognize that giving and receiving require balance, and having more fun and developing a sense of humor is a good idea.

JOYCE SAYS:

Traits to treasure: Your sense of responsibility.

To transform: Take care of yourself as well as you take care of other people or situations.

Saturn in the Second House

Practical Finances

Having to work for what you earn, you are practical when it comes to money.

With Saturn in the second house, you get what you earn financially. Money and security come through hard work. The positive side of Saturn is productivity; the negative side, fear. You may be fearful about finances, afraid of poverty, or worried that there will never be enough money. This fear increases ambition and engenders the practical handling of resources. Since you do not expect something for nothing, you work hard and responsibly in order to achieve financial aims.

You know the cost of goods, spend wisely, and perhaps enjoy bargain-hunting. You tend to save money for the future and old age. Because of this, you may hesitate spending on even necessary items—irrespective of your actual financial worth. By looking at the realities of financial situations rather than at your fears, you may find that you do not necessarily lack money or opportunity for financial gain, but that you must work for what you earn.

JOYCE SAYS:

Traits to treasure: Your financial responsibilities.

To transform: Recognize that you have the ability to earn money through work.

Saturn in the Third House

Pragmatic Thinking
Your thinking is practical, and you put effort into learning.

You are mentally disciplined and have the capacity for deep concentration. Effort goes into learning. Thinking is serious, methodical, and pragmatic, and ideas are judged according to their workability. Speech is measured and deliberate.

Yet despite intellectual prowess, you are likely to be afraid that you are not smart enough. This fear may manifest in one of two ways. Either it pushes you to study hard to become knowledgeable and thereby prove your intelligence, or it causes you to drop out educationally so as to avoid failure or the fear of it. As a child, difficulty in adjusting to school may have added to inherent intellectual fears. It is important to remember that fears are not realities unless you act in ways that make them so.

This placement promotes worry and causes you to look for what can go wrong in a situation. This provides the ability to anticipate problems and resolve them before they manifest. Negative, gloomy thinking may cause you to miss opportunities, or at the very least, spend a lot of time worrying about things that never become problems. It is important to distinguish between pragmatism and pessimism.

This placement can also cause difficulties with, or responsibilities for, siblings.

JOYCE SAYS:
Traits to treasure: Your critical thinking.
To transform: Avoid letting fears about intelligence get in the way of learning.

Saturn in the Fourth House

Family Responsibilities
You grew up in a family that stressed duty, and as an adult feel a sense of obligation toward family members.

Very likely you had family responsibilities at an early age. You were brought up with strict rules and were expected to behave like an adult during childhood. These experiences taught you maturity and responsibility. As an adult, you have a strong sense of duty toward family, and you take care of and protect those you love.

Saturn can create structure or limitation. It is possible that during childhood you were deemed worthy only as long as you conformed to family expectations. Particularly if Saturn receives difficult aspects, it may be hard to feel worthy for being yourself. Self-worth may be defined in terms of what you do for others, or what you accomplish, rather than in who you are. As an adult, guilt may push you into helping out family members whether or not it is appropriate to do so.

Childhood lessons run so deep that, as an adult, you may define right and wrong in the way you were taught during childhood rather than developing your own views. As a parent, you should be wary of creating a rigid environment for your children. It is important to differentiate between structure and limitation. Building sound structures creates a sense of safety and security. Yet when structures become overly demanding, they damage self-worth and repress growth.

JOYCE SAYS:
Traits to treasure: Your serious concern for family members.
To transform: Avoid setting up rigid, authoritarian familial standards.

Saturn in the Fifth House

Romantic Responsibilities
Romance is more serious than fun for you.

You are serious when it comes to creative endeavors, responsibilities toward children, and love affairs. If you pursue creative endeavors, it is in a hardworking manner. Creativity is expressed through organization and discipline. You find it hard to believe in your talents until you see tangible results.

If you have children, high standards are set for them. Because of this, it is important to recognize the difference between structure and restriction, as there is a tendency to be overly strict in trying to propel offspring toward their potential.

You take romance seriously, and may actually view it as work. Particularly if Saturn receives difficult aspects, you may fear that no one will ever love you or love you enough, and fear of rejection may make you self-conscious about expressing love. In relationships, you have a tendency to either make your partner the authority figure or to become the authority figure yourself. This may lead to choosing an older, mature lover who you look up to, or a person your own age who "feels" older, and one who will take care of you. Or you may be the one who does the taking care of. Either way, you have a strong sense of responsibility for preserving the relationship, and a great deal of effort is put into living up to perceived expectations.

Healthy relationships require more effort than most people care to admit, and with Saturn here, this is especially true. If fear stops you from confronting differences, romances end up being restrictive and oppressive rather than open and loving. In this case, if the lover is the authority figure, you feel smothered. If you have become the authority figure, you tire of playing a parental role. Either way, it is easier to blame the lover than to recognize your own choices in the situations. If this happens, you may tend to withdraw and become cold, as changing the relationship may not feel possible. It is important to recognize that good relationships require openness and risktaking. This insight gives you the tenacity and wherewithal to resolve differences.

JOYCE SAYS:

Traits to treasure: Your sense of responsibility toward lovers and children.
To transform: Avoid letting duty or fear stop you from expressing love.

Saturn in the Sixth House

Hard Work

Being naturally disciplined and organized, you are an efficient, reliable worker.

There is a natural tie-in between Saturn and the sixth house since Saturn rules work and responsibility (as well as fears and inhibitions) and the sixth house depicts work (as well as health). With Saturn here, you are an efficient, reliable worker who takes responsibilities seriously. Being naturally disciplined and organized, you aspire to do a good job because that is what one is supposed to do. Yet there may be fears about whether your performance is good enough and whether you are living up to your employer's expectations. In part, these fears push you to become more detail-oriented and to execute tasks even more conscientiously.

You demand a great deal of yourself, possibly too much, and expect the same of others. In positions of authority you may either be a great mentor or an overbearing taskmaster. Becoming too critical of coworkers or subordinates may cause problems on the job. You also take on more work than is appropriate for your position and expect to be rewarded because you are "doing it right." It is possible for you to miss out on getting ahead because you are paying too much attention to work and not enough to office politics. If this happens, you can become bitter and angry. You are quite capable of career strategy once you put your mind to it.

It is possible for overwork to create health problems, particularly if you are overly worried about performance. Health problems related to Saturn include colds, chronic fatigue, skin blemishes, skeletal problems, and blockages and obstructions.

JOYCE SAYS:

Traits to treasure: Your serious concern for day-to-day responsibilities.
To transform: Pay attention to getting ahead not just to tasks on the job.

Saturn in the Seventh House

Responsible Relationships

You may have a sense of duty when it comes to marriage or partnership, or you may attract partners with a sense of duty, or both.

You have a strong sense of responsibility in all one-to-one associations. You take relationships seriously and believe it is important to fulfill duties to others, whether they are good friends, colleagues at work, business partners, or spouses. Not wanting to make commitments that you cannot keep makes you cautious about entering into significant relationships.

Marriage, in particular, may be seen as synonymous with responsibility. On one hand, Saturn's placement here may make you fear that you will never marry. On the other hand, you want to make sure that you marry a trustworthy person. There is a tendency to look to a partner to become a parental figure—someone who will take care of you. You may marry late in life or choose a hard-working spouse who is older than you or one your age that seems mature. Or, although it is less likely, you may become the mature authority figure. Either way, you see it as your duty to preserve the relationship and live up to the perceived expectations of your spouse.

If Saturn receives favorable aspects, your mate provides stability in your life. Particularly if Saturn receives difficult aspects, it is possible to end up with a mate who is cold and unloving, or for you to end up that way. If you give up too much authority to a spouse early in marriage, you later feel inhibited or restricted, and it is easy to forget that you relinquished the authority in order to feel protected. If you are the one who has become the authority figure, you may tire of taking care of your spouse. Either way, it is important to maintain relational balance. Saturn in the seventh house makes it important for both parties to have equal relational responsibilities if the marriage is to be a happy one.

These same issues of responsibility and authority may also arise in business partnerships, with close friends, or with colleagues at work. Saturn here makes it imperative that your wishes and those of significant others are treated equally. Problems arise when the scale tips too far to one side or another.

JOYCE SAYS:

Traits to treasure: Your serious concern for one-to-one relationships.
To transform: Make sure that authority is shared equally in marriage or partnership.

Saturn in the Eighth House

Serious Sex

You are cautious and responsible when it comes to sex, investments, and shared finances.

You are serious about the fruits of relationships, from sex to joint finances. You are careful about who you have sex with. You may be sexually inhibited, but this arises from a sense of caution. In addition to not wanting to be a sex object, you want to make sure sexual partners have no communicable diseases. There is a need to get to know and trust someone before you feel amorous. If Saturn receives favorable aspects, these issues work out over time. If Saturn is afflicted, deep-rooted, irrational fears about sex as well as death and mortality may exist.

Since this house also represents joint finances, you are very responsible in handling other people's money. (The second house determines how you handle your own finances.) You are likely to marry someone who is conservative financially and possibly restricts your spending. In the case of divorce, significant conflict over money is likely, and it is important to take measures to ensure that you are treated fairly in financial settlements. If Saturn is afflicted, problems may arise over inheritance or insurance matters.

On the more positive side, you are practical with investments and cautiously tuck away money for old age.

JOYCE SAYS:

Traits to treasure: Your serious concerns about joint finances and long-term investments.

To transform: Discern people's attitudes toward money before entering into partnerships.

Saturn in the Ninth House

Conservative Beliefs

Your beliefs are conservative and higher education is a means to success.

You take religion, philosophy, belief systems, and higher education seriously. Self-worth is tied to educational achievement, and a lack of advanced degrees may be perceived as personal failure. Yet you can be fearful about scholastic ability, which may be handled in one of two ways. You may work very hard to attain entrance to, and academic achievement in, institutions of higher learning. Or, you may avoid higher education altogether. If you take the higher education route, you are practical in choosing schools, preferring ivy-league settings (if you can get in) and using these settings to make contacts that advance future career goals.

Philosophical and religious views are traditional and conservative. There may be healthy skepticism, or complete distrust of new ideas, leading to a closed mind. You can become dogmatic and believe that everyone else should conform to your personal religious or moral standards. Carried to the extreme, this leads to intolerance and fanaticism. It is important to remember each person has a right to his or her own views.

Travel is much more likely to be related to work than pleasure.

JOYCE SAYS:

Traits to treasure: Your serious concern for higher education.
To transform: Be open-minded about other people's beliefs.

Saturn in the Tenth House

Practical Career

You aspire to positions of authority and take professional responsibilities seriously.

This is a powerful placement, as Saturn rules the tenth house. You take your career and family responsibilities seriously. It is likely that as a child you were brought up with strict rules, were expected to behave like an adult early, and were pressured to live up to family expectations. These early experiences taught you responsibility and a strong sense of duty, but they also make it difficult for you to feel worthy within yourself. Self-worth is likely to be defined through achievements: no achievement, no self-worth.

Your background makes you ambitious on one hand and insecure on the other. The reinforcement of success is needed in order to feel good enough. Yet, despite your fears, or possibly because of them, you have strong career ambitions and direct your innate organizational and managerial abilities to achieve status, positions of leadership, and wealth.

If Saturn receives difficult aspects, it is possible to have difficulties with authority figures and be particularly sensitive to criticism by them. The tendency to take remarks personally may get in the way of career achievement.

It is important to watch the tendency to become successful at all costs. Family relationships suffer if too much time is spent at work. Also, it is possible for you to become dictatorial once you are in a position of leadership. With Saturn in this house, you ultimately get what you earn, whether that is reward or punishment. Lasting success must be achieved with integrity.

JOYCE SAYS:

Traits to treasure: Your serious concern for professional achievement.
To transform: Avoid becoming dictatorial once you attain positions of power.

Saturn in the Eleventh House

Serious Friendships

You choose your friends cautiously and are conscientious with regard to them.

You take friendship and organizational participation seriously. Friends are chosen with care. You are attracted to older or conservative people or those who can help to advance your career. You are loyal and feel a sense of responsibility toward those with whom you associate. Friends know they can count on you, and you expect the same consideration in return. Because of this, you prefer having a few close, reliable friends to being involved with lots of people. You have a desire for status and respect from peers. It is possible, particularly if Saturn receives difficult aspects, for you to damage relationships by being overly authoritarian or keeping too strong a balance sheet in terms of who did what for whom.

If you get involved in associations or group activities, you work hard for those groups, taking on positions of leadership or responsibility. Because of this, you may expect everyone else to work as hard as you do, and you can become overly critical of friends or associates if they do not live up to your standards.

JOYCE SAYS:

Traits to treasure: Your serious concern for friendship.
To transform: Avoid being authoritarian with friends or in group associations.

Saturn in the Twelfth House

Serious Solitude

You may fear responsibilities, yet feel compelled to take them on.

You enjoy solitude and need time alone to recharge your batteries. You have a subconscious wish to retreat. This may lead to a preference for working behind the scenes rather being center stage. You can tend to fear the unknown, whether or not you are consciously aware of this. Subtle fears may cause doubts, lack of self-confidence, and feeling easily threatened. This may cause you to stick with what you are familiar with rather than to reach out to new experiences, despite what may be your better logical judgment. Your tendency to isolate can cause loneliness and depression.

You may fear responsibilities, yet feel compelled to take them on. Sympathy for the underdog or holding yourself to the standard of what a good person would do draws you in. Because of this, you have to be careful of ending up in situations where you feel stuck and put-upon. This can lead you to believe that the world is hard and that self-protection is necessary. It is important to realistically assess responsibilities before making commitments.

JOYCE SAYS:

Traits to treasure: Your serious concern for those in need.
To transform: Avoid taking on too much responsibility out of sympathy or guilt.

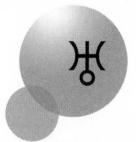

Chapter 12

URANUS—YOUR FREEDOM NEEDS

Keywords: Freedom, Originality, Rebellion
Rules: Aquarius, Eleventh House
Cycle: 84-Year Cycle, 7 Years in Each Sign
Somatic Influences: Nervous System, Pituitary Gland

Uranus is the planet of freedom, independence, and individuality. It is associated with originality, breakthroughs, and disrupting the status quo. It is also associated with mind-oriented studies such as science, computer technology, psychology, astrology, and occultism, which ideally lead to breakthroughs in human consciousness. Uranus' energy is disruptive and unexpected, and thereby associated with accidents, injuries, rebellions, revolutions, and natural disasters.

Uranus is sometimes linked with Mercury. Mercury is seen as the everyday mind, and Uranus as the higher-level intellectual mind, which includes intuition. Interestingly enough, Uranus was in the sign of Gemini, which Mercury rules, when it was discovered in 1781.

Uranus is the ruler of Aquarius, which is perhaps the worst planet-sign combination in the Zodiac. Both planet and sign relate to mind-oriented studies. However, Uranus' action is quick and sudden. Aquarius is attracted to extraordinary ideas, but is a fixed sign that does not readily change its mind.

The discovery of new planets brings about changes in consciousness. Before the discovery of Uranus, Saturn was the outermost planet. Saturn represents, among other things, limitation. It can be hard for us, after the turn of the millennium, to recognize that individual freedom and human rights have short histories in humankind. Uranus' discovery broke the bounds of Saturn, challenging the concept of limits. It changed the long-held image of the solar system and coincided with the American Revolution and French Revolution, which proclaimed individual rights.

Positively expressed, Uranus is the planet that urges us to be honest with, and true to, ourselves. It is associated with resourcefulness and pioneering spirit. It drives us to break through fears or other barriers to self-expression. In a societal context, it challenges social structures that are inequitable or devoid of freedom and helps to create more egalitarian systems. Uranus rules inventors and entrepreneurs, people who, inspired by their own vision, step outside of traditional structures.

Negatively expressed, Uranus' urgings cause unwarranted disruption, lack of personal responsibility, and flaunting of inappropriate behavior. Any social propriety or convention can be seen as restrictive and be rebelled against, regardless of its appropriateness. It can resemble a child screaming, "I'm doing what I want and you can't make me do anything else." On a societal level, it represents the negative side of revolutions, where cold, radical forces take over, and human beings are butchered under the guise of progress.

Uranus has an eighty-four-year cycle and spends seven years in each sign. The sign it falls in, along with those of Neptune and Pluto, represents the Zeitgeist at the time of one's birth. In our individual charts, its house placement and aspects give greater indications of its influence than its sign.

URANUS IN THE SIGNS

Uranus in Aries ♅ ♈

Individual Freedom

You were born into a generation of people for whom freedom, originality, and independence take precedence.

You were born into a generation of trailblazers. Uniqueness of the individual is emphasized. Freedom, independence, initiative, and originality are paramount virtues. Your generation has the courage to be different and to challenge the status quo. These challenges may take the form of individual expression, scientific thought, or social reform. Uranus was in Aries from 1927 to 1935.

JOYCE SAYS:

Traits to treasure: Your trailblazing generation.
To transform: Avoid rebelliousness for the sake of rebelling.

Uranus in Taurus ♅ ♉

Financial Freedom

You were born into a generation of people who bring forth innovative ways of managing money.

Uranus and Taurus have opposite energies. Uranus is quick and revolutionary. Taurus is slow, deliberate, and security conscious. Your generation combines these qualities with inventive ideas about practical concerns such as money, resources, and comfort. Good financial instincts and possibility for innovation in making money and managing resources exists. Uranus was in Taurus from 1935 until 1942.

JOYCE SAYS:

Traits to treasure: Your generation's inventiveness in making money.
To transform: Avoid disrupting security by impulsive spending.

Uranus in Gemini ♅ ♊

Intellectual Freedom

You were born into a generation of people who bring forth new ways of thinking.

Uranus has a natural affinity for Gemini. Both planet and sign enjoy freedom and are mind oriented. You were born into a generation of free thinkers. Bringing forth innovative ways of thinking, particularly in science, technology, and education are a part of this generation's destiny. Uranus was in Gemini from 1942 to 1949.

JOYCE SAYS:

Traits to treasure: Your generation's innovative intellectual pursuits.
To transform: Avoid becoming intellectually scattered.

Uranus in Cancer ♅ ♋

Family Freedom

You were born into a generation of people who seek freedom from traditional family structures.

There is no natural affinity between Uranus and Cancer. Cancer is the sign of the home and family. Cancer seeks emotional and financial stability and security; Uranus seeks change. You were born into a generation seeking freedom from traditional family structures. Equality within the family is sought. This equality may take the form of a mother working, a father staying home with the children, or the definition of family extending beyond biological roots. Uranus was in Cancer from 1949 to 1956.

JOYCE SAYS:

Traits to treasure: Your generation's unique way of defining family.
To transform: Don't overlook the positive sides of tradition.

Uranus in Leo ♅ ♌

Creative Freedom

You were born into a generation of people destined to be free and independent when it comes to love, creativity, and childrearing.

Your generation seeks freedom and independence in love, romance, creativity, and child rearing. This placement corresponds with a deep desire for self-expression and a strong value on being true to oneself. There is a desire for love and romance to include individual freedom as part of personal commitment. Uranus was in Leo from 1955 to 1962.

JOYCE SAYS:

Traits to treasure: Your generation's unique approach to self-expression.
To transform: Balance freedom needs with commitments when it comes to love.

Uranus in Virgo ♅ ♍

Work Freedom

You were born into a generation of people who revolutionize the work place.

Your generation is one that revolutionizes the work place and health care. Innovative, practical, and efficient ideas are the norm. New approaches include advanced uses of computers and technology and the introduction of alternative types of healing. Restlessness at the work place can lead to frequent job changes. Uranus was in Virgo from 1962 to 1968.

JOYCE SAYS:

Traits to treasure: Your generation's innovative approach to work.
To transform: Avoid being rebellious on the job.

Uranus in Libra ♅ ♎

Relational Freedom

You were born into a generation of people who revolutionize human relationships.

Your generation is one that revolutionizes relationships and social conduct. Relationships include marriage, partnership, close friendships, and treaties among nations. Personal relationships must support individual freedom, independence, and autonomy. International relationships must respect the rights and autonomy of individual countries, regardless of the size. Uranus was in Libra from 1968 to 1975.

JOYCE SAYS:

Traits to treasure: Your generation's innovative approach to relationships.
To transform: Avoid flaunting your autonomy with significant others.

Uranus in Scorpio ♅ ♏

Sexual Freedom

You were born into a generation of people destined to bring forth liberated attitudes toward sex, birth, and death.

Your generation is one that revolutionizes attitudes toward sex, birth, and death, and joint resources. Organ transplants and other medical miracles that keep people alive longer may lead to questions involving quality of life and not just longevity. The possibilities of reincarnation, life on other planets and other mysteries of the universe may be examined as your generation ages. Your generation is also likely to have a hand in the fading of gender roles. Uranus was in Scorpio from 1974 to 1981.

JOYCE SAYS:

Traits to treasure: Your generation's innovative approach to shared resources.

To transform: Avoid recklessness when it comes sexual activity.

Uranus in Sagittarius   ♅ ♐

Philosophical Freedom

You were born into a generation of people who seek independent thought in philosophy, religion, and higher education.

Your generation revolutionizes philosophy, religion, higher education, travel, and international relations. Not being bound by the orthodoxy of conventional beliefs, your generation explores new and innovative ways of looking at the world. It breaks down international barriers, and travel may literally become out of this world by exploring outer space. Uranus was in Sagittarius from 1981 to 1988.

JOYCE SAYS:

Traits to treasure: Your generation's innovative ways of looking at the world.

To transform: Avoid being attracted to beliefs for their shock value.

Uranus in Capricorn   ♅ ♑

Professional Freedom

You were born into a generation of people who challenge conventional wisdom in government and big business.

Your generation revolutionizes government and business structures. During the generation of your birth, the Berlin Wall fell and Eastern Block countries took their first steps toward democracy. As adults, you help to overthrow governments that do not support freedom. You also make practical changes that revolutionize the work place. Uranus was in Capricorn from 1988 to 1995.

JOYCE SAYS:

Traits to treasure: Your generation's innovative attitudes toward government and business.

To transform: Avoid disrupting the status quo just for the thrill of doing it.

Uranus in Aquarius ♅ ♒

Humanitarian Freedom
You were born into a generation of people destined to challenge society's prevailing ideas and social structures.

Uranus rules Aquarius, so this is a strong placement. Your generation revolutionizes society's structures and prevailing attitudes. Humanitarian ideals and the demand for liberty and equality are triumphed. This generation is inventive. The search for truth can lead to unprecedented scientific discoveries and further investigation of outer space. Uranus was in Aquarius from 1995 to 2002.

JOYCE SAYS:
Traits to treasure: Your generation's innovative attitudes toward humanitarian ideals.
To transform: Avoid seeing your ideals as the only ones.

Uranus in Pisces ♅ ♓

Spiritual Freedom
You were born into a generation of people destined to revolutionize the compassion of humanity.

Your generation revolutionizes spirituality and compassion. You seek freedom from the entrapment of materialistic conventions. There is an orientation toward the aesthetic. Mystical leanings include meditation, yoga, and Eastern philosophies. There is compassion in helping those less fortunate, but with an eye toward helping them attain self-sufficiency. Uranus is in Pisces from 2003 to 2010.

JOYCE SAYS:
Traits to treasure: Your generation's innovative attitudes toward spirituality and helping those less fortunate.
To transform: Avoid getting caught up in eerie spiritual communities.

URANUS IN THE HOUSES

Uranus in the First House

The Individual

You are a nonconformist par excellence.

You are freedom oriented and independent. Your strong belief in individuality, that each person should find and follow his own way, makes you a nonconformist par excellence. You abhor conventional behavior, and fitting in is nowhere near as important to you as being true to yourself. Because of this, others may see you as eccentric or unusual, and very likely, you take pride in being seen this way.

Uranus here gives rise to restlessness. You crave excitement and adventure and dislike routine. The last thing you want is for each day to be like the day before. Inventive, and frequently ahead of your time, these characteristics may lead you to make new discoveries or to promote new ideas.

Your motto is like Shakespeare's injunction in *Hamlet* of "to thine own self be true." Positively, this message conveys honesty, candor, and honor. You are willing to courageously stand up for your principles, even in the face of seemingly overwhelming odds. However, particularly if Uranus receives difficult aspects, your dislike of authority may cause you to rebel against even the most reasonable expectations of others. This can lead to erratic behavior, unreliability, and rebelliousness for the sake of rebellion rather than for a higher purpose. With this position, individuality is a given, but it is equally important that you recognize the rights of others and responsibilities you have toward them.

JOYCE SAYS:

Traits to treasure: Your individuality.
To transform: Avoid flaunting eccentricities.

Uranus in the Second House

Erratic Finances

You have a propensity for risk in financial arenas.

There is a desire financial freedom. You are more likely to be attracted to entrepreneurial ventures or commission sales jobs than to more traditional, secure ways of making a living. Unusual talents or insights in financial arenas help you to earn money through inventions or original ideas. Yet, the challenge of making money, or playing the game, may be more interesting than the money itself. A propensity for risk-taking can lead to being on top one day and on the bottom the next, particularly if Uranus receives difficult aspects. Yet money is desired for the independence that it brings.

The tendency to spend money impulsively may cause financial ups and downs. Learning money management is a must with this placement, as is recognizing the difference between a calculated risk and gambling.

JOYCE SAYS:

Traits to treasure: Your entrepreneurial skills.
To transform: Avoid impulsive spending and taking financial risks solely for excitement.

Uranus in the Third House

Unconventional Thinking
Your thinking is original and independent, and you find new ideas enticing.

You are open to new ideas. Your mind is keen and alert and your thinking original and independent. A combination of intuition and logic produces inventive ideas.

You have an interest in unusual studies and a quest to chart unknown intellectual territory that can lead to interests in science, technology, or the occult. Being ahead of your time, your farsighted ideas may be seen as either genius or weird. Whatever the case, you are open, honest, and you readily speak your mind. You are not easily influenced by the ideas of others, and it is possible for you to become intellectually opinionated, believing that your ideas represent ultimate truth.

This placement is somewhat accident prone, so it is important to concentrate on the road while driving a car and to curb your propensity for speeding. When feeling trapped, even a short journey may provide the necessary relief of getting away from it all.

In your family you may feel like a stranger and have very different beliefs than siblings.

JOYCE SAYS:

Traits to treasure: Your innovative mind.
To transform: Avoid being so blunt that you offend others when it is not your intention.

Uranus in the Fourth House

Unconventional Family

You learned freedom early in a home life that was out of the ordinary.

Your early home life was unconventional or in some way unusual. Possibly you moved a lot, with changes in residence coming suddenly, or your family greatly differed from those of your neighbors.

Lessons of freedom of expression and individuality came from the family at an early age. If Uranus receives favorable aspects, you learned to believe in yourself, that your individuality counted, and that being true to yourself should be a life-long priority.

If Uranus receives difficult aspects, individuality was more likely to have been foisted upon you at the expense of stability and security, as Uranus can bring an inconsistent, perhaps erratic, home life. As a child, it was hard to know what to expect, or who to count on. One or both parents were either inconsistent or absent. Behavior could be rewarded one day and punished the next, making it difficult to feel secure. You learned self-sufficiency and how not to depend upon others.

Either way, as an adult, there is an inner restlessness and the possibility of rebelling against convention or the idea of being tied down by family obligations. Examining the personal meaning of freedom is a must.

JOYCE SAYS:

Traits to treasure: The individuality at the roots of your being.
To transform: Avoid flaunting your refusal to conform in family situations.

Uranus in the Fifth House

Eccentric Romances

You are attracted to the unusual when it comes to entertainment, romance, and child-rearing.

Your inclinations in art, romance, and child-rearing are out of the ordinary. You may be creative in unusual ways; in art, music, or entertainment, you are attracted to the avant-garde.

With this placement, either you inspire individuality in your children, or they have a natural propensity for it. If you inspire individuality, you strongly advocate freedom of expression for youngsters. Because of this, you tend toward unconventional relationships with your offspring, and your oldest in particular is treated like a friend from an early age. Your children may be unusual or gifted in some way. Particularly if Uranus receives difficult aspects, you may give a child more freedom than he can handle, or a child may be extremely individualistic, rebel against authority, and behave disruptively.

You need freedom and independence in romance, and love should never stand in the way of being true to yourself. You may recognize your own need for freedom, or you may project it onto a lover. You are attracted to an independent and, if Uranus receives difficult aspects, perhaps unpredictable lover. The lover's independence and unpredictability then give you precisely the freedom you require. You may be quite unconscious about this motivation and see your paramour as commitment-phobic rather recognizing this issue as emanating from your own psyche.

Whatever the case, there is a tendency for you to jump into relationships quickly. To be interesting, a relationship must be exciting, but it is possible for you to get more excitement than you bargain for, which can leave you feeling alone and abandoned. Learning to look before you leap is essential, as is recognizing your own needs so that they are not unconsciously projected onto another.

JOYCE SAYS:

Traits to treasure: The freedom you need to be yourself when in love.
To transform: Avoid satisfying freedom needs in romance by behaving erratically or choosing a romantic partner who does so.

Uranus in the Sixth House

Freedom on the Job
You work best in an environment that allows you to be inventive.

With Uranus in the sixth house, freedom and independence are of prime importance on the job. Autonomy is essential. You work in a highly individualistic way and perform best when you are given an assignment and left alone to do it.

You excel at finding new and inventive ways of handling tasks and frequently have ideas that are ahead of their time. The more innovative and entrepreneurial the company you work for, the more you thrive in the environment. Since you dislike routine and bristle at being told what to do, a conservative workplace is a bad fit. Particularly if Uranus receives difficult aspects, problems with authority are likely. You may overreact to what you perceive as being told what to do and perhaps rebel against even reasonable requests of superiors. As a boss, you expect self-sufficiency from subordinates and should be careful of giving subordinates too much freedom before you know their capabilities.

Uranus in the sixth house can also result in job-related accidents. Physically, you may be nervous or high strung, and illnesses may have on-again, off-again symptoms that make diagnosis difficult.

JOYCE SAYS:

Traits to treasure: Your innovative abilities in the workplace.
To transform: Avoid flaunting autonomy on the job.

Uranus in the Seventh House

Eccentric Relationships
You may be independent relationally or attract a highly independent mate or both.

With Uranus in the seventh house, individual freedom cannot be sacrificed in marriage or partnership. However, planets in this house can easily be projected onto other people. In relationships, you may be the free-spirited, independent partner, or you may attract a mate who fits this description, or you may both possess these characteristics. You have a tendency to jump into relationships quickly, and, if things do not go well, to jump out just as suddenly.

Your mate may be unusually intelligent, entrepreneurial, or in some way eccentric. Excitement is a necessary relational component, and with excitement comes ups and downs. Particularly if Uranus receives difficult aspects, you may choose a mate who is unreliable, refuses to be demanded of, or just plain believes that he should be able to do as he pleases. These qualities actually provide you with the personal autonomy you desire, whether that desire is conscious or unconscious.

Uranus in this house makes cooperation in partnerships difficult. The same type of issues may arise in business partnerships as in marriage or significant romantic relationships. Workable relationships require that individual autonomy be balanced with respecting the rights of others.

JOYCE SAYS:

Traits to treasure: Your need for personal freedom in marriage or partnership.
To transform: Avoid maintaining freedom by choosing erratic, unreliable partners or by being one yourself.

Uranus in the Eighth House

Sudden Changes in Fortune
Your shared resources are subject to unexpected ups and downs.

Sudden changes of fortune can occur with regard to joint finances or other people's money. This includes marital finances, business partnership finances, inheritances, insurance, taxes, or corporate finances. If Uranus receives positive aspects, you have a knack for choosing unusual investments and sudden windfalls are likely. If aspects are negative, unexpected losses can occur. You and a mate or business partner may disagree about how to spend money or invest long-term finances.

Uranus here gives an interest in metaphysics, the desire to discover why all things are the way they are, and to question what is life's purpose. This may lead to an interest in reincarnation.

This placement also conveys an unconventional attitude toward sex. This may mean that you seek freedom by having many partners or may just mean that you are liberated and desire varied experiences.

JOYCE SAYS:
Traits to treasure: Your unique approach to joint finances.
To transform: Avoid making joint financial decisions impulsively or going along with a mate who does.

Uranus in the Ninth House

Liberated Beliefs
You disdain orthodoxy and are attracted to innovative ways of looking at the world.

You have avant-garde beliefs with regard to philosophy, religion, or higher education, and perhaps have an interest in New Age topics. You have disdain for orthodoxy and intellectualism. You may be a political reformer, a fanatic, or merely an armchair philosopher. Whatever the case, it is important to be tolerant of other people's views.

You greatly enjoy learning, but dislike following a prescribed curriculum, and are unlikely to perceive professors as authority figures. The more liberal the educational environment, the more it is to your liking. Not wanting to be hemmed in may lead to disruptions in education, possibly attaining degrees in fits and spurts. Internet or long-distance learning environments may fit your needs better than traditional campus settings.

Traveling to foreign lands, particularly undiscovered, out-of-the-way places, fulfills needs for excitement and adventure.

JOYCE SAYS:

Traits to treasure: Your independent approach to higher learning.
To transform: Avoid letting freedom needs interfere with educational pursuits.

Uranus in the Tenth House

Unconventional Career

You are at your best when you are self-employed or when you work in an environment that values inventiveness.

Since both the fourth and tenth house have to do with family upbringing, the information under Uranus in the fourth house also applies to the tenth.

With Uranus here, you are individualistic, politically liberal, or even radical or revolutionary. You excel in fighting for social causes or for whatever you believe in. Your respect for authority goes only to those you deem worthy of respect.

At work, you are naturally original and inventive, and you dislike being told what to do or how to do it. Ease in coming up with new ideas or innovative ways of performing tasks makes leadership in science, humanitarian fields, New Age areas, or business possible. Yet innovation is a double-edged sword. As you are frequently ahead of your time, others may see your ideas as ingenious or as "too far out" to be useful.

Ideally, you are self-employed or work in an atmosphere where innovation is prized. If not, your dislike of authority may to lead to difficulties with superiors, who you may consider intellectual inferiors and whose authority you are likely to openly disregard. Because of this, your career is subject to sudden changes. You may be on top one day and quit your job the next or be fired with seemingly no warning. If you work in a hierarchical environment, learning to enroll people in your originality rather than flaunting your independence and intellectual superiority is a necessity. In a social or humanitarian context, these same qualities make you a great leader.

Traits to treasure: Your innovation in professional arenas.
To transform: Avoid flaunting your disregard for authority.

Uranus in the Eleventh House

Eclectic Friendships
You enjoy friendships with intelligent, forward-thinking people.

Uranus rules the eleventh house, so this is a "good" placement. You are an intellectual nonconformist. Open-minded and concerned with truth, you are not interested in traditional views. Your political views are likely to be unconventional, but whether or not you live by these views depends upon the entire chart. Leadership in humanitarian groups is possible.

You are attracted to mentally stimulating people. You seek friends who are intelligent, forward-thinking, and out of the ordinary, or possibly those who are exciting and likely to step over the edge. Conventional people are "boring" to you. You have friends of both sexes and make no distinctions based upon gender. Goals can be both individualistic and humanitarian. Your friends influence your goals, and you influence theirs in return.

If Uranus receives difficult aspects, you may attract exciting but unreliable associates, or due to independence needs, you may be the unreliable person. Your Achilles heel is feeling pushed around, and while autonomy and self-sufficiency are important, it's important for you to remember that no one can do precisely as he pleases all the time and maintain relationships.

JOYCE SAYS:
Traits to treasure: Your attraction to avant-garde people.
To transform: Avoid unreliable associates or becoming an unreliable friend.

Uranus in the Twelfth House

Unconscious Freedom Needs
You have a deep-seated need for self-sufficiency, whether or not you are consciously aware of it.

You have strong needs for freedom and independence, but since the twelfth house rules the unconscious, it may take time in life to consciously recognize these needs. You may have fears of entrapment or being compelled to conform. These fears may manifest consciously as thoughts, such as "You can't push me around," or as compelling urges to break out of situations, or less consciously, as feeling trapped and wanting to get out when in uncomfortable situations. If Uranus receives difficult aspects, these urges are even more compelling and disruptive and are likely to leave you wondering why you behave the way you do. The more you recognize your own uniqueness and are true to yourself and your own individuality, the easier this placement is to handle.

You may also be interested in mystical studies such as astrology, yoga, meditation, or psychic phenomena, and have a wish to discover the mysteries of the universe.

JOYCE SAYS:

Traits to treasure: Your need for independence.

To transform: Avoid behaving disruptively based on unconscious urges.

Chapter 13

NEPTUNE—YOUR IDEALISM

Keywords: *Spirituality, Imagination, Universal Love, Escapism*
Rules: *Pisces, Twelfth House*
Cycle: *168 Year Cycle, 14 Years in Each Sign*
Somatic Influences: *Pineal Gland*

Neptune is the planet of imagination, idealism, creativity, and spirituality. It represents the capacity to experience beauty, feel universal love, and express compassion. Neptune rules the psychic world. It has domain over the subconscious mind, hypnosis, dreams and visions, and intuitive insights.

Being overly idealistic can lead to the not-so-positive side of Neptune, which is illusion and deception. Deception may emanate from seeing situations the way we want them to be rather than as they are, or we may actually be victimized by our own gullibility. Escapist behaviors such as drug and alcohol addiction also fall under Neptune's domain.

Neptune rules all arenas that combine imagination, creativity, and beauty. This includes music, art, literature, movies, theater, decorating, and design. Under Neptune's rule, visions created in the mind's eye take form in what is ultimately created.

Neptune's spirituality takes the form of direct union with God. Jupiter rules religion and belief systems that ideally connect us with the divine. Under Neptune, that connection is made directly through meditation, prayer, or purely divine inspiration. It occurs on a feeling, intuitive level that defies logical explanation. Somehow we are just in tune.

Neptune's spirituality also takes the form of the ideals of universal love and acceptance. This differs from Venus' love, which in essence says, "You love me, and I'll love you." Neptune and the sign it rules, Pisces, say "I love you because you exist."

A highly emphasized Neptune in the horoscope conveys psychic or strongly intuitive abilities. We know things before they happen. We make decisions based upon feelings. We perceive the undercurrents in situations, and those undercurrents in turn affect our well-being. In a positive environment, we feel uplifted; in a negative environment, energetically drained.

In line with being spiritual, when Neptune is highly emphasized, we believe we must live up to the way a good, kind person would behave. We believe that we must help others if we can, and we look for the best in people and situations. In a therapeutic relationship, the ability to see the best in others allows the therapist to help the patient reach for what he is capable of and seeming miracles can occur.

In personal relationships these traits can be more problematic. The belief that we must help others in order to be a good person can lead to being indiscriminate about who we help. Focusing on another's potential makes it possible for us to miss what the actual person is like. At a minimum, this leads to future upsets when we discover that all is not as we believed it to be. We can easily be deceived or victimized by trusting the wrong people based upon overly idealistic assumptions. It is also possible to feel victimized even if there has been no attempt to do so. This leads to disappointment.

Paradoxical as it may seem, with highly emphasized Neptunian, we can either be too accepting or not accepting enough. We may naively overlook faults and flaws that we should pay attention to. Yet it can be difficult to accept people's all-too-human faults and flaws that make them less than ideal. The difference between the way life is supposed to be and the way it is can be hard to live with.

Neptune's last rulership is that of escapism. Escapism may take the form of denial—ignoring problems or pretending they do not exist—or it may take the form of drug or alcohol addiction. Neptune links creativity and escapism, so it is not an accident astrologically that people who are psychic, artistic, or creative are more typically extra sensitive to their environment and therefore more in need of escaping from it.

Neptune is in a sign for fourteen years and is more important in personal charts by house and aspect than it is by sign. The sign it posits, along with that of Pluto, has to do with social, political, and historical trends.

Neptune's sign represents the cultural ideals of the time, while Pluto's effect is one of muckraking.

The house that Neptune falls in tends to be where things are not seen clearly. Situations are seen as better than they are or worse than they are; it is difficult to see them as they are.

NEPTUNE IN THE SIGNS

Neptune in Aries ♆ ♈

Idealized Individuality
Your generation idealizes individuality, independence, and self-sufficiency.

Neptune was in Aries from 1861 to 1875. As a generation, people born during this time frame idealized freedom, individuality, independence, self-reliance, personal initiative, and new beginnings.

Aries traits were idealized during this timeframe. The Civil War in United States, which took place between 1861 and 1865, extended individual liberty to slaves, and the Fourteenth Amendment to the United States Constitution that prohibited voting discrimination was passed in 1866. Russian serfs were also emancipated during 1861.

JOYCE SAYS:
Traits to treasure: Your ideal of self-reliance.
To transform: Avoid idealizing freedom at the expense of relationships.

Neptune in Taurus ♆ ♉

Idealized Material Resources
Your generation idealizes business, material resources, and security.

Neptune was in Taurus from 1874 until 1889. As a generation, people born during this time frame idealized business, material resources, and security. This included land, property, money, food, and nature.

Pluto was also in Taurus until 1884, which to some degree has the effect of thwarting Neptune's idealism. Economic growth and prosperity exemplified this period, yet workers were exploited and labor unions seen as anarchist.

JOYCE SAYS:
Traits to treasure: Your ideal of financial resources.
To transform: Avoid wasting valuable resources.

Neptune in Gemini ♆ ♊

Idealized Intellect
Your generation idealizes ideas, intellectual creativity, and communication.

Neptune was in Gemini from 1887 until 1902. This generation idealized ideas, intellectual creativity, and communication.

The media began to influence public opinion during this time frame. Pluto was also in Gemini, which to some degree thwarts Neptune's idealism. Communication, education, books, writing, intellectualism, neighbors, and short-distance travel all fall under Gemini's rule. The idealization and destruction of literary figures that took place combines the influences of both Neptune and Pluto. Oscar Wilde went to prison on charges of homosexuality, and Emile Zola was jailed for an article protesting the frame-up of Captain Alfred Dreyfus. Spiritual writing disseminated the teachings of Christian Scientists and theosophists.

JOYCE SAYS:
Traits to treasure: Your ideal of ideas.
To transform: Watch the tendency to believe everything you read.

Neptune in Cancer ♆ ♋

Idealized Family
Your generation idealizes home, family, and security.

Neptune was in Cancer from 1901 until 1916. This generation idealized home, family, and security. These ideals can be generalized to include country as part of family.

Pluto entered Cancer in 1914. Religious and spiritual pursuits were part of familial ties and provided a sense of community. Waves of immigrants came from Europe to the United States (a Cancer country) in search of a better life. World War I occurred, incited by patriotic ties.

JOYCE SAYS:
Traits to treasure: Your ideals of family life.
To transform: Avoid overlooking faults and flaws of family members.

Neptune in Leo   ♆ ♌

Idealized Entertainment
Your generation idealizes youth, romantic love, and glamour.

Neptune was in Leo from 1915 to 1929. This generation idealized youth, romantic love, glamour, and artistic expression.

The Roaring Twenties were wild times. Prohibition brought speakeasies, and women dancing and drinking became the rage. Interest rates rose to all-time highs, and speculation brought the stock market to new heights.

JOYCE SAYS:
Traits to treasure: Your ideal of creative expression.
To transform: Avoid choosing glamour at the expense of substance.

Neptune in Virgo   ♆ ♍

Idealizes Work
Your generation idealizes the work ethic.

Neptune was in Virgo from 1929 to 1943. This generation idealizes work, work-related education, and health. Born during or just after the Great Depression, this generation romanticizes work ethic.

Fortunes were lost during the Stock Market Crash in 1929, and many of the rich needed jobs like everyone else. Labor unions were born, and the common man was idealized in film.

JOYCE SAYS:
Traits to treasure: Your ideal of work.
To transform: Avoid losing yourself in your daily tasks.

Neptune in Libra   ♆ ♎

Idealizes Relationships
Your generation idealizes relationships.

Neptune was in Libra from 1943 to 1957. This generation idealizes marriage and one-to-one relationships, as well as law and justice.

Libra also rules treaties and alliances. After World War II, international relationships changed as the Cold War began with the United

States and Western Europe on one side and Russia, Eastern Europe, and China on the other.

JOYCE SAYS:

Traits to treasure: Your relational ideals.

To transform: Avoid setting relational ideals so high that no can live up to them.

Neptune in Scorpio   ♆ ♏

Idealizes Sex

Your generation idealizes sexual pleasures and the search for personal understanding.

Neptune was in Scorpio from 1957 to 1970. This generation idealizes sexual pleasures on one hand and the search for self-understanding and transformation on the other.

The sixties were the time of flower children and the sexual revolution. "Make love, not war" was the slogan protesting the Vietnam War. Promiscuity and experimental drug use were commonplace and idealized as a way toward transcendence.

JOYCE SAYS:

Traits to treasure: Your ideal of transformation.

To transform: Avoid sex or drugs as means of escape.

Neptune in Sagittarius   ♆ ♐

Idealizes Belief Systems

Your generation idealizes philosophical, religious, or spiritual meaning in life.

Neptune was in Sagittarius from 1971 to 1985. This generation idealizes philosophy, religion, and belief systems. They seek a spiritual meaning for life. Freedom, independence, and travel are also idealized.

This time frame was one of spiritual searching. Groups promising transformation, like EST and evangelist television shows, prospered. People sought more leisure time and a freer lifestyle.

JOYCE SAYS:

Traits to treasure: Your spiritual ideals.

To transform: Avoid getting taken in by cult-like groups.

Neptune in Capricorn ♆ ♑

Idealizes Business
Your generation idealizes success and conservative values.

Neptune was in Capricorn from 1984 to 1998. This age group idealizes success as defined by tradition, conservative ideas, big business, money, and the work ethic. The task of incorporating spirituality into business falls to this generation.

During this time frame, work and business became idealized. Working sixty to seventy hours a week became commonplace, and those failing to do so were seen as lazy. Initial public offerings of businesses surged, and the rush to make money was on.

JOYCE SAYS:

Traits to treasure: Your ideal of success.
To transform: Avoid over-idealizing money and big business.

Neptune in Aquarius ♆ ♒

Idealizes Common Man and Free Thinking
Your generation idealizes free thinking and inventiveness.

Neptune is in Aquarius from 1998 until 2012. This generation idealizes the intellect, free thinking, and inventiveness. As they become adults, they will want to throw out the old to make way for the new.

September 11, 2001, changed the world as we knew it in the United States. Firemen, policemen, and everyday workers became the idealized heroes. Neptune in Aquarius brings into the norm the idealizing of the average person.

JOYCE SAYS:

Traits to treasure: Your humanistic ideals.
To transform: Avoid over-idealizing any one system of belief.

Neptune in Pisces   ♆ ♓

Idealized Spirituality
Your generation idealizes spirituality and compassion.

Neptune was in Pisces from 1847 to 1861 and will be in Pisces again from 2012 to 2026. Neptune rules Pisces, so this represents a strong placement. This generation will idealize spirituality, sensitivity, compassion, universal love, and creativity and imagination.

JOYCE SAYS:
Traits to treasure: Your spiritual ideals.
To transform: Avoid seeing any one system of belief as coming from the only true God.

NEPTUNE IN THE HOUSES

Neptune in the First House

Psychic Sensitivity
You are kind and compassionate and look for the good in people and situations.

You are a romantic idealist with an eye for, and an appreciation of, beauty. Sensitive to the needs of others, you look for the good in people and situations. You may be a dreamer or a visionary, depending upon what you do with your dreams. Whether you realize it or not, you exude glamour and charisma. Very likely you do not see yourself clearly or the way that others see you.

Neptune here makes you somewhat psychic and extremely sensitive to your environment, and gives spiritual longings. You may sense things before they happen, or pick up subliminal cues about people and situations. Your environment also subliminally influences you. If you are not consciously aware of this influence, it may appear as if your mood-swings occur for no apparent reason. Some time alone every day is needed to retreat and rejuvenate. Meditation helps keep you centered, and metaphysical studies help to fulfill spiritual aspirations.

You are kind and compassionate. Helping others may be seen as a spiritual obligation, or what a good person would do. This attitude is caring and compassionate, but must be practically tempered. In therapeutic settings, seeing the best in people helps to bring it out, but in personal settings, it may lead to unrealistic expectations that can bring about disappointments or being taken advantage of. Developing discrimination is a must.

Neptune here also gives escapist tendencies. While you readily help others, you may ignore problems in your own life, hoping that somehow situations will magically improve. This can lead to greater difficulties down the road when reality sets in. Given the tendency for escapism and since your body is physically sensitive, care should be taken with regard to drugs and alcohol.

JOYCE SAYS:

Traits to treasure: Your compassionate spirit.
To transform: Be careful who you trust.

Neptune in the Second House

Confusion with Finances

Your intuition can help you make money, and you spend easily.

Your intuition may help in financial arenas, and money may be earned through creative, spiritual, or psychic endeavors. Being idealistic about money and the use of material resources, you may donate generously to spiritual or humanitarian causes.

However, this is a difficult placement for Neptune. You do not think of yourself as money-oriented. Yet you spend money extremely easily and very likely without ever thinking about where it goes or whether you will have enough for later. You may feel as if you should have whatever you want whenever you want and that somehow the Lord will provide. This makes the use of credit cards potentially dangerous. It is important to avoid overextending financially. It is also important to avoid naïve investments. A good policy to remember is that if it sounds too good to be true, it probably is.

JOYCE SAYS:

Traits to treasure: You intuition in financial arenas.
To transform: Avoid letting money slide through your fingers.

Neptune in the Third House

Visionary Thinking
Your thinking is creative, imaginative, and possibly escapist.

Your conscious, subconscious, and superconscious minds all work together. You are much more likely to rely on intuitive, creative, and possibly psychic insights than to think practically. Learning by osmosis and absorbing what goes on around you, whether or not you are paying attention, is normal for you. When interested in a topic, you can totally immerse yourself in it and lose all track of time. However, when uninterested, you may tune out and escape into a dream world—regardless of the importance of the information.

A powerful imagination helps with creativity or vision. There is potential for talent in art or creativity in writing fantasy, science fiction, or romance novels. You are likely to be interested in the occult or mystical topics.

Intuition helps you to be a persuasive communicator. In sales, you know just when to close the deal. In public relations, you know how to best sell your point.

JOYCE SAYS:
Traits to treasure: Your intuition and creative ideas.
To transform: Avoid daydreaming to the point of tuning out pertinent information.

Neptune in the Fourth House

Illusionary Family
You have close emotional ties to family, coupled with a sense of obligation.

You have close emotional ties to family, coupled with an idealized picture of the way family life should be—one that real families rarely live up to. This is the way you see your own family—as better than they are or worse than they are, but not realistically. This position for Neptune may denote a creative or spiritually oriented family, or one with a skeleton in the family closet. One parent was likely to have been escapist in some way, possibly by avoiding unpleasant realities, or more seriously by using drugs or alcohol or through mental illness.

The early family message was not to look at or deal with disagreeable situations. This created confusion as to what you could count on. Yet despite this, you have close ties to relatives. As a child, you may have been placed in a caregiving role. As an adult, you have a compelling sense of obligation. While you may long to be rescued by loved ones, you may be the one doing the rescuing. You are loving and nurturing toward family. A part of you, possibly unconscious, feels the need to mother the world. Learning to discriminate as to when to take care of others and when not to is a must.

Living by, or being near, the ocean can provide much needed tranquility. Your home must be an aesthetically pleasing place where you can escape from the pressures of the world.

JOYCE SAYS:

Traits to treasure: Your loving tenderness toward family.
To transform: Learn to discriminate as to when to take care of others.

Neptune in the Fifth House

Idealistic Romances

You possess creativity and are idealistic when it comes to love affairs and relationships with your children.

You are highly creative and imaginative. There is a love of beauty, art, music, theater, movies, and all forms of entertainment. The possibility of excellence in artistic or creative endeavors exists.

When it comes to love, Neptune in this house conveys an idealistic wish for romance. At the most fanciful, you both want and expect to fall in love with Prince/Princess Charming and have all of life's difficulties dissolve when the slipper fits. This makes relating to mere mortals a problem that gets handled in one of two ways, or by fluctuating back and forth between both. One, upon meeting someone interesting, the joy of having found such a wonderful person takes over and you put that person on a pedestal and ignore his foibles. Feeling lucky to have found someone so wonderful, you do all you can for that person. You are happy as long the relationship stays idyllic.

Even though you are the one who wants to be rescued, a high degree of sympathy and compassion, and the feeling of being loved when needed, may attract needy lovers. Your lovers may be creative or talented or have difficulties handling life's ups and downs, or have drug or alcohol problems. You may choose a person who takes advantage of you and unrealistic expectations can lead to disappointments.

The first stage of falling in love for everyone includes over-idealization—seeing what might not really be a handsome or beautiful face, but finding it handsome or beautiful to you. But this stage typically gives way to the second stage, which is recognizing the person, as he is, warts and all. This acceptance stage proves difficult. Recognizing a lover's flaws, you are likely to try to change him into what he is capable of, anticipating how wonderful the relationship will be later, and ignoring how it is now. At some point the recognition that people do not change quite so easily sets in. Disappointment and disillusionment follow, and you may feel taken advantage of, or at the extreme, victimized. At this point a choice is made as to whether to stay in the relationship.

The second way relationships are approached is to stay out of them. If no one meets the Prince/Princess Charming criteria, you decide to go it alone. Or, you can go back and forth, alternating between putting a current lover on a pedestal and then having difficulty finding anyone else to love, only to later find someone else and repeat the pattern. The problem with these choices is that relationships exist more with your fantasies than a real person. It is important to recognize that no one, no matter how lovely, is perfect.

The fifth house also represents children, and Neptune here conveys the wish for idealistic relationships with your offspring. You may sacrifice for your children or spoil them by giving in to their whims so that they can be happy. Children, particularly the oldest, are likely to be creative, imaginative, or prone to escapism. It is important to watch the tendency for them to overuse drugs or alcohol.

JOYCE SAYS:
Traits to treasure: Your creative imagination.
To transform: Recognize what romantic partners and children are like, as distinguished from the way you might want them to be.

Neptune in the Sixth House

Idealistic Work
You are most absorbed in your work when it is creative or helps people.

You excel in creative or helping professions. Your performance is best when work creates beauty, pleasure, entertainment, or helps those in need. Intuitive ability helps in the workplace. You are inclined toward such diverse fields as traditional medicine, alternative medicine, humanitarian work, decorating or design, animal communication, or creative endeavors. If you care about your job, you are capable of becoming so totally absorbed in it that you lose all track of time. If you have a humdrum job unappealing to your soul, you are more likely to daydream about where you would rather be than to pay attention to tasks at hand. This makes it very important to be in tune with your work.

This placement also makes you very sensitive to the atmosphere of the workplace. You feel the vibes around you and your moods fluctuate depending upon the environment.

This house ties work and health together. With Neptune here, your body is especially sensitive, and being overly stressed at work can directly lead to health problems. Care should be taken in the use of drugs and alcohol, and even small doses of prescription drugs may prove too strong. You are prone to infection, and illnesses may have vague symptoms and be difficult to diagnose. Eating healthy, avoiding sugar, and minimizing stress works wonders.

JOYCE SAYS:

Traits to treasure: Your enrapture with work you love.
To transform: Eat healthy and avoid stress (as much as possible).

Neptune in the Seventh House

Romantic Marriage

You may be romantic and idealistic in significant relationships, or attract a highly idealistic mate, or both.

You want marriage to be forever romantic—candy, flowers, and all the rest. The ideals of marriage with Neptune in the seventh house are much like the ideals of romance of Neptune in the fifth house. You want to fall in love, get married to Prince/Princess Charming, and live happily ever after without ever having conflicts or disagreements. Early on, an idyllic marriage is possible. Very likely, you put your mate on a pedestal and overlook his all-too-human foibles. If you have not chosen wisely, idealism turns into disappointment down the road, and relational problems that are ignored become crises.

It is your nature to want to see what is good in all people, not just in your mate. This inclination is exceptionally charitable but not realistic. With Neptune here, it is possible to attract creative, imaginative people, needy ones, alcohol or drug users, or con men. This is particularly problematic since you feel what might be characterized as a spiritual calling to help those in need who are close to you. It is difficult to say no in any significant one-to-one relationship. This makes it imperative to take time to get to know others so that in marriage, business partnership, or friendship, you see people for who they really are and not just the facades they present or the reflections of your own ideals. Otherwise, it is all-too-easy to be taken advantage of by spouses, friends, or business partners.

JOYCE SAYS:

Traits to treasure: Your love of romance.
To transform: Get to know people before you put your trust in them.

Neptune in the Eighth House

Confused Joint Resources

Your intuition shines when it comes to metaphysical areas. More care is needed with joint finances.

Neptune fits well with the occult side of the eighth house. Interests in the mysteries of life, spiritual quests, and reincarnation are likely. It is possible to be psychic or a medium. Vivid dreams may supply you with otherworldly information, and may include talking to people on the other side.

In the more earthly domains of the eighth house, Neptune may create confusion and possibly deception. Romance must be part of sex, but be careful not to overly idealize sexual partners. Problems with joint finances are possible. Differences with a spouse or business partner over how to spend money may occur, and you may tend to attract a financially irresponsible, or even dishonest, spouse, business partner, or financial planner, particularly if Neptune receives difficult planetary aspects. You can be intuitive about investments, yet financial naivete can prove costly. With Neptune here, all matters of joint resources must be scrutinized carefully to make sure that what you anticipate is actually what you are likely to get. This includes investments, inheritance matters, insurance, taxes, as well as marital and partnership monies. It is important to be very careful about who you trust financially.

JOYCE SAYS:

Traits to treasure: Your interest in the occult or mysteries of life.
To transform: Be careful about who you trust when it comes to money.

Neptune in the Ninth House

Spiritual Beliefs
You are more attracted to spiritual studies than to organized religion or traditional beliefs.

Your beliefs are mystical or metaphysical rather than religious. Yoga, meditation, or oriental studies may be of interest, as there is a longing for a direct connection to God or a higher universal intelligence. If you seek a spiritual teacher, discrimination in distinguishing between real spiritual leaders and cult leaders or charlatans is a must.

Idealistic beliefs extend to how people should be treated, including the belief that people should lend a helping hand to those in need.

Spiritual or creative studies may be more interesting to you than practical ones. This placement makes achieving higher degrees in anything other than what you are truly interested in difficult. You learn by osmosis when you care about a topic. Otherwise, daydreaming is more likely.

The ocean provides a soothing atmosphere when you want to get away, and travel by ship can be relaxing.

JOYCE SAYS:
Traits to treasure: Your interest in spiritual or philosophical studies.
To transform: Be discerning about belief systems.

Neptune in the Tenth House

Creative Career
You work best when your career involves beauty or entertainment or helps people.

The tenth house, along with the fourth house, represents family life and upbringing, so the section on the fourth house also applies to Neptune in the tenth.

It may be difficult to decide upon a career. You are at your best when your work creates beauty, pleasure, entertainment, or helps people. A glamorous public image helps in careers such as acting, music, or politics. There is a sincere wish to give to others, and intuition helps you to perceive what they need.

If your work is not creative or people oriented, it may be difficult to go to work at all. You are more likely to daydream about where you would rather be. This may be problematic, as unreliable or dishonest behavior in the workplace does not go unnoticed. If you care about your work, you are so completely committed that you can lose all track of time and possibly ignore other areas of life. You may idolize a boss or authority figure. If you are in a subordinate role, it is important to make sure that you get appropriate credit for professional contributions.

JOYCE SAYS:

Traits to treasure: Your capacity for enrapture in a profession you love.
To transform: Do an honest day's work and be sure to get credit you deserve.

Neptune in the Eleventh House

Idealistic Associations

You enjoy friendships with creative, idealistic people.

You are idealistic about friendship. Friends are likely to be creative, visionary, romantic, and humanistic, or escapist, possibly with drug or alcohol problems. You look for the best in people with whom you associate and do whatever you can to help them. Because of this, particularly if Neptune receives difficult aspects, you should be wary of overlooking people's faults or motivations to such a degree that you get taken advantage of.

The desire to associate with like-minded people may prompt you to join associations concerned with metaphysical or spiritual teachings or those with humanitarian goals. You thrive with this type of camaraderie so long as your wish to belong is balanced with good judgment.

JOYCE SAYS:

Traits to treasure: Your attraction to creative, spiritually oriented people.
To transform: Avoid putting yourself in a position where friends and associates take advantage of you.

Neptune in the Twelfth House

Spiritual Longings

You possess heightened intuitive abilities and are likely to have vivid, insightful dreams.

Neptune rules the twelfth house, and both have to do with subconscious urges and superconscious connections. You possess heightened intuition and possibly psychic capabilities. Vivid dreams provide much insight into your own psyche, that of others, and possibly the future. You want to understand the mysteries of life and seek spiritual connection with what is beyond this world. Mystical studies, such as meditation, yoga, astrology, or metaphysics help you in this pursuit.

You are very sensitive to the moods and vibrations of your environment. This, combined with your call to the mystical, makes spending time alone every day in meditation or contemplation important in keeping you balanced. But it is just as important not to allow yourself to retreat too far. Too much time with others can cause overwhelm; too much time alone, depression.

JOYCE SAYS:

Traits to treasure: Your intuition.

To transform: Avoid retreating too far.

Chapter 14

PLUTO — YOUR INNER DRIVE

Keywords: *Transformation, Death and Rebirth, Inner Drive*
Rules: *Scorpio, Eighth House*
Cycle: *248 Year Cycle, 12 to 32 Years in Each Sign*
Somatic Influences: *Sex Organs, Elimination System, Pituitary Gland*

Mythologically, Pluto was the god of the underworld, and as such represents the underworld within ourselves. Pluto comprises our unconscious and inner drives or compulsions that we are hard-pressed to explain. It represents will, focused attention, and power. It is associated with death, rebirth, and transformation.

A highlighted Pluto in the horoscope conveys a tremendous capacity for "good or evil." It gives the innate ability to pierce through situations and instinctively get to the bottom of what is going on. It helps us recognize the underlying causes in events and the underlying motivations of people. Yet under Pluto's domain, we are motivated by unconscious urges, which can make our actions and beliefs extreme. There is difficulty finding middle ground when we combine the belief that we are right with the compelling feeling that nothing other than exactly what we want will do. This energy used in a positive manner can achieve what seems like miracles. Used in a negative manner, this same energy is destructive to oneself or others.

Pluto's energy is also magnetic. When it is strong in a horoscope, we exude power and can be intimating without trying to be. People are drawn to us or repulsed by us with little middle ground.

Pluto is associated with doctors, therapists, healers, religious leaders, and politicians—ideally those who want to transform the world. It is also associated with dictators, organized crime, gangs, mob violence, and terrorism—those willing to gain control by any means or those who are completely out of control.

Pluto rules the sign of Scorpio and the planet-sign combination is one of the best fits of the Zodiac. Both Pluto and Scorpio are deep and intense. Both are mysterious, hard to get to know, and know no moderation. Scorpio and Pluto are also associated with the desire principle. Desires relate to sex but are not limited to it.

The positive expression of Pluto is linked with the urge for wisdom and knowledge, to become the best that we can be. It conveys the desire to transform ourselves and possibly the world we live in.

Pluto's negative expression is linked with the urge to dominate and control. We attempt to control our circumstances or other people because we are unable or unwilling to control ourselves.

Pluto is seen as the higher octave of Mars. Mars rules the individual warrior. It has to do with guns and knives, personal combat, and direct confrontation. Pluto rules bombs and atomic energy. Atomic energy has the capacity to supply heat and warmth and alternatively to destroy the planet.

Pluto is the slowest moving planet in our solar system, taking approximately 248 years to make one complete revolution through the Zodiac. It is the only planet with an eccentric orbit, spending from 12 to 32 years in one sign. During its fastest moving time frame, it is within the orbit of Neptune, which spends 14 years in each sign.

Pluto's sign, along with Neptune's, marks generational differences. The sign it posits has more to do with historical, social, and political trends than with personal attributes. Like a volcano erupting, the dark side of the sign comes to light in ways that affect people and cultures. Conflict ensues that is typically characterized as good versus evil, with vast differences of opinion as to which is which. This precipitates healing crises that transform these issues. By the end of Pluto's time in the sign, permanent and irrevocable changes have taken place in the areas it rules. Current conflicts fade and new ones arise as Pluto moves into the next sign.

In our individual charts, Pluto's placement affects us more through its house position and aspects than through its sign. Pluto intensifies the energy of any planet in it comes in contact with. The area of life represented by that planet takes on a driven quality.

PLUTO IN THE SIGNS

Pluto in Aries   ♇ ♈

Transform Personal Power
Your generation shares an unconscious urge for transformation in the area of self-determination.

Pluto was in Aries from 1823 to 1852. Aries is a sign of self-reliance, initiative, independence, and new beginnings. As a generation, people born during these years share an unconscious urge for, and seek to gain power from, self-determination.

In the United States, this was the era of the Wild West. As settlers moved westward, personal initiative was pitted against the hardships of the elements, danger from bandits, and wars with Indian tribes. Violence was rampant, and individuals had to fend for themselves. Yet, despite it all, pioneering settlers carved out a new nation.

JOYCE SAYS:
Traits to treasure: Your inner drive for self-determination.
To transform: Avoid one-upmanship in putting your needs before those of others.

Pluto in Taurus   ♇ ♉

Transform Material Resources
Your generation shares an unconscious urge for transformation in the areas of personal resources and material wealth.

Pluto was in Taurus from 1852 to 1884. Taurus is a sign that represents the earth, money, and material production. As a generation, people born during these years share an unconscious urge to gain material wealth and to control their resources.

In the United States, this was a period of economic expansion. Factories and cotton mills were established, railroads built. It was also the time of the Civil War (1861 and 1865), which pitted brother against brother and destroyed much property. The Civil War was fought over whether human beings could be considered property.

JOYCE SAYS:
Traits to treasure: Your deep drive for material resources.
To transform: Avoid avarice.

Pluto in Gemini ♇ ♊

Transform Ideas
Your generation shares an unconscious urge for transformation in the ability to gain power from ideas and education.

Pluto was in Gemini from 1884 to 1914. Gemini is a sign that represents communication, education, intellectualism, neighbors, and short-distance travel. In the physical body, Gemini rules the lungs and respiratory system. Individuals in this generation had an unconscious urge for education and to gain power from ideas.

New inventions both changed and threatened the way people lived. Ford produced the Model T. Alexander Graham Bell and Thomas Edison discovered uses for electricity. The Wright Brothers flew the first airplane.

Two new ideas particularly challenged prevailing beliefs: Albert Einstein's Special Theory of Relativity and Sigmund Freud's theories about unconscious sex drives. Health problems of the time included global influenza epidemics.

JOYCE SAYS:
Traits to treasure: Your inner drive to develop intellectual concepts.
To transform: Avoid trying to dominate other people's thinking.

Pluto in Cancer ♇ ♋

Transform Family Life
Your generation shares an unconscious urge for transformation in the areas of family and security.

Pluto was in Cancer from 1914 to 1939. Cancer is a sign that represents the home and family, feelings in general, security, domestic concerns, and food. Individuals born in this generation have an unconscious urge to for security and to protect and control what is seen as their own, whether family or country.

This timeframe included World War I, the roots of World War II, the Suffragette Movement culminating in women's right to vote, and the Roaring Twenties followed by the 1930s Depression. War and depression are readily seen as threats to security, but women's right to vote was seen as a threat to the family, and like the Civil War, it pitted family members against one another.

Traits to treasure: Your deep drive to protect your family.
To transform: Avoid trying to dominate family members.

Pluto in Leo ♇ ♌

Transform the Ego

Your generation shares an unconscious urge for transformation in the areas of personal power and creative self-expression.

Pluto was in the sign of Leo from 1939 to 1957. Leo is a sign of leadership, individual power, and creative expression. Those born in this generation share an unconscious urge for personal power. The urge for power created worldwide destruction. This was the time of dictators and global power struggles. World War II pitted Germany, Japan, and Italy against France, Britain, Russia, and the United States. Millions were killed in concentration camps, and the first atomic bomb was exploded. World War II was followed by the Cold War between the capitalist democracies of United States and Western Europe and the communist totalitarian countries of Russia, China, and Eastern Europe.

JOYCE SAYS:
Traits to treasure: Your deep drive for creative self-expression.
To transform: Avoid egotistical power plays.

Pluto in Virgo ♇ ♍

Transform the Work Environment

Your generation shares an unconscious urge for transformation in the areas of work and education.

Pluto was in Virgo from 1957 to 1972. Virgo is the sign of health and hygiene. It is also the sign of work, education relating to work, and work tools. Those tools can range from simple hammer and nails to advanced scientific, medical, or industrial technology. This generation has an unconscious urge for control of their work life.

Russia's launching of Sputnik, the first earth satellite, spurred the technological innovation in the United States that led to the launching of the first moon rocket and men being sent into outer space. Struggles between labor unions and employers led to increased workers' rights. Medical science made vast strides. Technology was revolutionized, and it was feared that newly invented computers would replace workers (which occurred when people born during this time frame reached adulthood).

JOYCE SAYS:

Traits to treasure: Your inner drive to transform the workplace.
To transform: Avoid power struggles in the work arena.

Pluto in Libra ♇ ♎

Transform Relationships
Your generation shares an unconscious urge for transformation in the areas of marriage, partnership, and law.

Pluto was in Libra from 1972 to 1984. Libra is the sign of marriage and partnerships, social relations, law, justice, and treaties and alliances. This generation has an unconscious urge for control over associations and for justice.

The women's movement started in the 1960s and took further hold in 1970s. Pluto's trek through Libra coincided with a skyrocketing divorce rate. What some would characterize as a deathblow for marriage, others would see as the emancipation of women.

The Watergate scandal occurred during this timeframe, and President Nixon resigned in disgrace. Watergate showed that not even a president was above the law.

JOYCE SAYS:

Traits to treasure: Your inner drive for justice.
To transform: Avoid power plays in one-to-one relationships.

Pluto in Scorpio ♇ ♏

Transform Sexual Mores
Your generation shares an unconscious urge for transformation in the areas of sex and joint resources.

Pluto was in Scorpio from 1984 until 1996. Pluto is the ruler of Scorpio, making its time frame in this sign particularly potent. Both Pluto and Scorpio are associated with sex, death, other people's money, the underworld (whether that of the psyche or organized crime), therapy, and transmutation. This generation has an unconscious urge for power and control as well as for transformation, particularly in arenas having to do with sex and finances.

Sex and abuse were key newspaper headline topics for these years. Domestic violence was no longer ignored or sanctioned by law. This led to the creation of women's shelters and the issuance of restraining orders against violent husbands or boyfriends. The image of rape victims changed from that of women who enticed men to women who were victimized.

The AIDS epidemic represented the association of sex with death, both of which are associated with Scorpio. This worldwide epidemic killed millions and brought to the forefront civil rights issues based upon sexual orientation.

The "other people's money" side of Pluto in Scorpio was typified by bank failures that accompanied the real estate crash at the end of the 1980s and early 1990s.

JOYCE SAYS:

Traits to treasure: Your inner drive for transformation.
To transform: Avoid power struggles over sex or joint resources.

Pluto in Sagittarius   ♇ ♐

Transform Religion

Your generation shares an unconscious urge for transformation in the areas of religion and belief systems.

Pluto is in Sagittarius from 1996 until November, 2008. Sagittarius is the independent fire sign associated with philosophy, religion, higher education, long-distance travel, and law. This generation has the unconscious urge for personal freedom and to gain power from belief systems.

This time frame has been fraught with religious extremism. Terrorist attacks by extreme Islamic fundamentalists brought down the United States World Trade Center on September 11, 2001. Christian fundamentalists found a champion in President George W. Bush. Religious extremists in Israel attempted to block Prime Minister Ariel Sharon's efforts at attaining peace with Palestinians by removing Israeli settlers from Gaza.

The Catholic Church has been rocked by scandals of not only rampant sexual abuse by Catholic priests worldwide, but cover-ups by the Church hierarchy. Lawsuits against the Church have netted millions of dollars in settlements for abuse victims.

JOYCE SAYS:

Traits to treasure: Your inner drive for personal freedom.
To transform: Avoid religious and national prejudices.

Pluto in Capricorn ♇ ♑

Transform Big Business and Government
Your generation shares an unconscious urge for transformation in the areas of authority, business, and government.

Pluto was last in Capricorn from 1762 until 1777. It will enter Capricorn again in 2009 and remain there until 2024. Capricorn is the sign associated with authority, professional leadership, ambition, status, business (particularly big business such as multinational corporations), government, and economic policies. This generation has an unconscious urge for power, control, and authority.

The American Revolution began during Pluto's last trek through Capricorn. The Declaration of Independence, written by Thomas Jefferson, proclaimed, "We hold these truths to be self-evident, that all men are created equal, and that they are endowed by their Creator with certain unalienable rights, that among these are life, liberty, and the pursuit of happiness." In 1776, these were radical ideas. The United States was a British colony, and ordinary men were not seen to have unalienable rights. What was considered freedom in the then-forming United States was considered treason by Britain. In essence, this was the beginning of the overthrow of authority.

Pluto's next trek through Capricorn is likely to see this same type of revolution with uprisings against repressive governments throughout the world. Multinational corporations are also likely targets as oppressed people overthrow corrupt governments and ordinary people demand just wages. A time of worldwide economic difficulties is the likely result.

JOYCE SAYS:

Traits to treasure: Your inner drive for authority.
To transform: Avoid abusing positions of authority.

Pluto in Aquarius   ♇ ♒

Transform the Rights of Masses
Your generation shares an unconscious urge for transformation in the areas of humanitarianism and intellectual ideals.

Pluto was last in Aquarius from 1777 until 1799. It will transit Aquarius again from 2024 to 2043. Aquarius is the sign associated with freedom and independence as well as friendship, group activity, equality, brotherhood of humans, humanitarianism, intellectual development, and scientific achievement. This generation has an unconscious urge for power and control over their destiny, as well as overthrowing prevailing intellectual ideals.

The United States Revolutionary War and the French Revolution occurred during Pluto's last trek through Aquarius. The United States was formed and the Constitution and the Bill of Rights formulated. Individual rights, justice, and equality are all Aquarian principles.

Pluto's next trek through Aquarius is likely to see a continuation of revolutions that begin with Pluto in Capricorn. New governments will form once again based on the ideas of freedom and democracy. However, the formation of these governments will not be without internal strife, as was seen in the French Revolution.

This time frame is also likely to include significant scientific breakthroughs, including greater emphasis on outer space. Major changes in educational systems are also likely.

JOYCE SAYS:
Traits to treasure: Your inner drive for equality.
To transform: Avoid power struggles over ideals.

Pluto in Pisces   ♇ ♓

Transform Spirituality
Your generation shares an unconscious urge for transformation in the areas of creativity, spirituality, and compassion.

Pluto was last in Pisces from 1799 until 1823. It will transit Pisces again from 2043 until 2067. Pisces is the sign of sympathy, compassion, universal love, spirituality, mystical experiences, the unconscious mind, imagination, and artistic creativity.

During this era, many works of musical and literary genius were produced that are still enjoyed today. Mozart, Beethoven, and Haydn composed symphonies. Jane Austin, Thomas Moore, Washington Irving, and Aleksandr Pushkin wrote novels.

The Church Missionary Society was founded in London in 1799 with the vision of spreading spirituality by making Christ known throughout the world. Peace in 1801 marked the end of the Holy Roman Empire, and in 1807, England prohibited slave trade.

Pisces is the sign that ties creativity and spirituality together. The next transit of Pluto through Pisces is likely to once again bring forth great artistic pieces in music and literature. Space travel may become the next spiritual frontier. And the spread of spirituality will likely threaten religious organizations.

JOYCE SAYS:

Traits to treasure: Your inner drive for spiritual ideals.
To transform: Avoid power struggles surrounding spiritual ideals.

PLUTO IN THE HOUSES

Pluto in the First House

Intense Persona

You exert a powerful presence, without even saying a word.

Pluto in the first house is a strong placement. You possess depth, intensity, ego strength, and may be a bit of a loner. In new situations, you prefer to stay in the background until you get your footing by observing what is going on. Yet you exude a powerful presence and either magnetically attract or repel people. Early in life, most likely unaware of your persona and seeing yourself more as a quiet kind of person, you were probably surprised, possibly shocked, at people's reaction to you.

Moderation is not a strong point for you. An intense all-or-nothing personality makes you either completely committed to a person, a job, or an ideal or not interested at all. Choices are not made consciously but stem from desires deep within your psyche. On the positive side, your drive, determination, and perseverance make things happen. If you are headed in the right direction, you accomplish unbelievable feats.

On the not so positive side, being so sure you are right about what you want, and how you want to go about attaining it, makes it difficult to cooperate with others. Differences of opinion feel like attacks, and you are more likely to go your own way than give in. If working with others is essential to achieving goals, power struggles are likely to ensue and making enemies is possible.

A second problem also exists. Your desires are so strong that they can become addictions—you have to have what you want; nothing else will do. This makes it difficult to examine if what you want is actually good for you. If you are headed in an unhealthy direction, your actions take you on a self-destructive course. It is essential to step back, examine your motivations, and avoid letting the objects of your desires become more important than you are.

JOYCE SAYS:

Traits to treasure: Your intense commitment to whatever you do.
To transform: Avoid letting unconscious urges override better judgment.

Pluto in the Second House

Good Financial Instincts
Delving and researching abilities help you to acquire material resources.

You are ambitious in acquiring wealth and material resources. Your income may involve other people's money, such as banking, corporate finance, accounting, insurance, taxes, or possibly being self-employed. Good instincts help you to be enterprising in financial situations and to perceive financial opportunities that others would overlook. Money is important, as it allows you to have what you want, and you enjoy owning the best of possessions.

Particularly if Pluto receives difficult aspects, it is possible to become obsessed with accumulating money and possessions. If this happens, greed may overtake you in your quest for riches, and at the extreme, you can become unscrupulous. With this position, it is important not to let possessions become more important than your own well-being.

JOYCE SAYS:

Traits to treasure: Your uncanny perceptions in moneymaking arenas.
To transform: Avoid becoming obsessed with possessions.

Pluto in the Third House

Deep Thinking

You have a delving, researching mind that instinctively perceives the core of ideas.

A delving, researching mind makes you capable of deep thinking and profound insights. You are opinionated about your beliefs and speak or write persuasively when showcasing those beliefs.

You have an intense desire to know all about whatever you choose to study. Wanting to know the meaning of life and why we are here may lead to the study psychology, metaphysics, history, science, or the humanities.

Your capacity to be somewhat obsessive helps in studies and research but has the potential to become problematic in other arenas. When something upsets you, it is all you can think about. Yet you are secretive and more likely to dwell on the situation than to communicate in such a way as to resolve it. Particularly if Pluto receives difficult aspects, you are instead likely to make sarcastic remarks as a way of letting off steam. In all communications you tend to say exactly what you mean or nothing at all. Recognizing how your communications impact others is essential.

JOYCE SAYS:

Traits to treasure: Your capacity for profound insights.
To transform: Get your point across without going for the jugular.

Pluto in the Fourth House

Powerful Parent

One parent dominated your early life, and you tend toward dominating your own family.

An early family loss is possible. One parent exerted great power and influence in the household during your childhood. This power may have been acted out dictatorially or merely implied, but whatever the case, the message was clear, and fear of disregarding this parent's wishes existed. Perhaps the control was seen as for your own good, such as a parent being overprotective in order to save you from perceived harm.

As an adult, you should be careful not to recreate this same dynamic with your own family. While your motivation for control is the belief that you know what is best for everyone, it is still possible to become overbearing. This is particularly true if Pluto receives difficult aspects in this house.

Traits to treasure: Being a dynamic influence in your family circle.
To transform: Avoid being dictatorial in family matters.

Pluto in the Fifth House

Intense Love Affairs
You are passionate in romance and in dedication to your children.

You are intense and passionate when it comes to affairs of the heart. Sex and love go hand in hand for you, and attraction is based almost exclusively upon chemistry. When the chemistry is right, there is no such thing as too much sex. And without chemistry, a goodnight kiss can be excruciating.

You put all you have into romance. But too much intensity can lead to problems, particularly if Pluto receives difficult aspects. You can become obsessive and love can become an addiction. The chemistry between you and a lover may be so powerful that that you actually have a relationship with the chemistry rather than really getting to know the person. Within the relationship, either you or your lover may play a dominant role, or you may switch back and forth between who has the upper hand. Your feelings are easily hurt, but you do your best to hide them. Fear of losing loved ones makes it easier for you to have covert power struggles than to directly address relational problems. Ultimately, extreme blowups are likely. With this position, it is important to spend time getting to know someone and building a relationship before having sexual relations.

The fifth house represents children as well as love affairs. Relationships with children are also likely to be particularly intense. You may be a dominating parent who tries to push your children into being the best of they can be, or you may have strong-willed children (particularly the oldest) determined to do what they want. If Pluto receives difficult aspects, care must be taken to avoid power struggles.

Traits to treasure: Your intense loyalty and devotion to loved ones.
To transform: Avoid covert power struggles or being dictatorial with lovers or children.

Pluto in the Sixth House

Intense Work

You are deeply desirous of being an expert at your job.

The ability to instinctively perceive better and more efficient ways to get things done gives you the capacity to transform the work place. If you are working in a profession of your choosing, you care deeply about your work and are desirous of being an expert at it. You work hard and long to accomplish goals. The one thing you require is autonomy in what you do. You hate being told what to do or how to do it. Particularly if Pluto receives difficult aspects, it is difficult for you to cooperate with superiors or coworkers when you disagree with them. This may create actual power struggles, or hostility may brew beneath the surface. It is essential to learn how to work effectively with others.

Seething, or unresolved anger, can lead to health problems.

JOYCE SAYS:

Traits to treasure: Your ability to transform the workplace.
To transform: Avoid overt or covert power struggles with superiors or coworkers.

Pluto in the Seventh House

Intense Marriage

You may be dominant and strong-willed in marriage, or you may attract a mate who displays these characteristics, or both.

You have intense devotion and loyalty in one-to-one relationships. Yet issues of power and control are likely to arise in marriage or partnership. You may choose a dominant, strong-willed mate or business partner, or you may play the dominant role. Since this house is frequently projected, it is more likely that you choose dominating mates or partners rather than being one yourself.

Whatever the case, your life dramatically changes when you marry. You are attracted to your mate's strength. Yet if you give away too much power and let your mate control the relationship, eventually you feel trapped, resent him or her because of it, and fight to reclaim your power. Whether or not the marriage survives depends upon the strength of the relationship. If you are the one who dominates the relationship, you should be wary of being overly controlling—even when you feel it is in your mate's best interests—or your mate may end up feeling trapped by you. It is necessary to pay attention to the balance of power in all one-to-one relationships.

JOYCE SAYS:

Traits to treasure: Your loyalty and devotion to your mate.
To transform: Make sure there is a balance of power in marriage or partnership.

Pluto in the Eighth House

Passionate Sex

You have a powerful sex drive and need a passionate mate.

Since Pluto rules the eighth house, this is a powerful placement. An interest in metaphysics and reincarnation is likely. It is possible that you have abilities as a medium. If Pluto receives favorable aspects, wealth can be derived from marriage or partnership. If Pluto receives unfavorable aspects, a spouse or business partner can be the cause of financial losses, and conflict over money is likely.

This placement gives you a powerful sex drive and an intense sexual connection with your mate. If Pluto receives difficult aspects, be careful of developing sexual addictions.

JOYCE SAYS:

Traits to treasure: Your desire to get to the bottom of situations.
To transform: Avoid letting sex dominate relationships.

Pluto in the Ninth House

Strongly Held Beliefs

Higher education, foreign travel, or philosophical studies can transform your beliefs.

Pluto in the ninth house gives intense desire and the ability to understand the world around you. Transformation may come through adherence to religious or philosophical beliefs, through higher education, or by travel and adventure in foreign lands. At your best, you have little tolerance for hypocrisy and have the ability to pierce through belief systems and see their fundamental ideas.

Once you adopt a belief system, you have a total commitment to it. Because of this, you can become extreme. You should be wary of believing that you have found the way and that everyone else should believe what you do. Particularly if Pluto receives difficult aspects, there is danger of refusing to listen to another's point of view, and at your most fanatical, trying to coerce others into agreeing with you.

JOYCE SAYS:

Traits to treasure: Your intense desire to understand the world around you.
To transform: Avoid developing fanatical beliefs.

Pluto in the Tenth House

Passionate Work

You exert a commanding influence in your chosen career.

The descriptions of Pluto in the fourth house apply here, as both the fourth and tenth houses depict family influence.

Pluto in this house gives intense commitment and relentless drive in pursuing professional aims. Control in your professional life is of prime importance. Your determination to achieve may border on or be obsessive and compulsive, but it also provides courage and tenacity. You stand up for what you believe in, and crave authority so that you can to transform your chosen professional world. Whether you are in government, politics, business, or an ordinary job, you are capable of farsighted leadership. Handling this energy positively, you are an innovator; handling it negatively, a dictator. In either case, you exert a powerful influence on what goes on around you.

If you are not in a position of authority, issues of power and control are likely to arise with superiors, particularly if Pluto receives difficult aspects. It is possible to make powerful enemies as well as powerful friends. If you gain power dishonestly, a fall from grace is likely to follow. The right use of power is essential with this position.

JOYCE SAYS:

Traits to treasure: Your intense desire to transform your profession or the world around you.
To transform: Avoid misusing power when you are in positions of authority.

Pluto in the Eleventh House

Intense Friendships
You enjoy friendships with strong-willed, deep people.

You have intense friendships with carefully chosen, select people. You are attracted to those who are to strong-willed, dynamic, and powerful. Friendships have a transformational quality. Your friends may exert a great influence over you or you over them, or the influence may be mutual. Wherever Pluto is found, the possibility of becoming dictatorial exists. It is important to respect the rights of others and to choose friends who respect your rights. Particularly if Pluto receives difficult aspects, abrupt endings to friendships are possible.

You may get involved in associations, especially those with scientific, spiritual, or humanistic goals. If you do, you may become a dynamic change agent and end up in a position of leadership. Particularly if Pluto receives difficult aspects, power struggles can ensue. In all associations, it is important to listen to other people's points of view.

JOYCE SAYS:
Traits to treasure: Your inner drive to engage in friendships that have transforming power.
To transform: Avoid getting into power struggles in friendships and group associations.

Pluto in the Twelfth House

Powerful Subconscious
You have a profound capacity to understand human nature.

Both Pluto and the twelfth house have an otherworldly quality. With Pluto in this house, no matter what you do for a living, you are drawn to psychology and metaphysics. Your intuition is strong, and you are capable of deep meditation. Sensitivity to other people's thoughts, feelings, and motivations makes it possible for you to have profound insight into human nature. Your dreams may be profound. Abilities as a medium may exist and healing capabilities are possible.

Both Pluto and the twelfth house function below the level of normal awareness, so it is possible to have a greater need for power and control than you are consciously aware of. If this need is thwarted, deep-seated feel-ings of anger and resentment can fester below conscious awareness and eventually lead to health problems. Being honest with yourself about your own motivations is of prime importance.

JOYCE SAYS:

Traits to treasure: Your inner drive to understand human nature.
To transform: Consciously examine feelings of anger and resentment.

Chapter 15

ASPECTS—HOW THE PLANETS RELATE TO ONE ANOTHER

The 360 degrees of the Zodiac are divided into twelve signs containing 30 degrees each. Aspects are angular relationships between planets at specific degree intervals. The energies of the planets that form aspects with one another become intermingled. Aspects may be harmonious or inharmonious, and the ease or difficulty of the planetary intermingling depends upon the nature of the planets combined and the type of aspect between them.

Harmonious or favorable aspects are typically perceived as good and inharmonious or unfavorable aspects as bad. Yet harsh aspects stimulate activity. They push us to learn, grow, and change, albeit it may be because we have no choice. Favorable aspects connote ease, so change is not necessarily perceived as needed in these areas. A more apt way of looking at aspects is that when aspects are harmonious, we behave willingly, naturally. When aspects are inharmonious, we are forced to do something. Whether what we actually do is good or bad depends as much upon our own consciousness as on the nature of the planets involved and the aspects between them.

All of us have a combination of harmonious and inharmonious aspects in our horoscopes. It is true that the more difficult aspects we have in our charts, the more difficult life is. Yet, a preponderance of easy aspects does not mean we necessarily experience life as easy. It may mean the expectation of ease actually makes it more difficult to cope as problems occur. Conversely, if our horoscope contains a preponderance of difficult aspects, we may be better able to handle problems—unless we get to the point where we are so overwhelmed we give up.

Success in life comes from balancing contradictory needs as shown in the chart by signs and planetary aspects that pull us in conflicting directions. A high level of personal awareness is necessary to achieve this balance as it is difficult to recognize the internal conflicts and how they can be reconciled. It is far easier to blame unhappiness on other people or the world around us than to look inside and see how our choices affect our happiness quotient.

Conjunction ♂

A conjunction takes place when two or more planets fall from 0 to 8 degrees from one another. Planets in conjunction are close to one another. Conjunctions typically occur in the same sign but may occur in two signs when one planet is at the end of a sign and the second is at the beginning of the next sign. In a conjunction, planetary energies combine to form a unit and work together. This powerful combination can be harmonious or inharmonious depending upon the nature of the planets. For instance, a conjunction of Mercury and Venus is harmonious as it combines communication with sociability, making us more likable. On the other hand, a conjunction of the Moon and Saturn is inharmonious as Saturn inhibits the feeling nature of the Moon, making emotional expression difficult.

HARSH OR DIFFICULT ASPECTS: MULTIPLES OF TWO

Difficult aspects occur in multiples of two. They represent arenas of the personality that pull against one another and must be worked on for situations to come out harmoniously. These aspects push us to change.

Opposition ☍

An opposition forms when two planets are 180 degrees (plus or minus 8 degrees) away from one another. It divides the 360-degree Zodiac in half. Oppositions by sign are Aries-Libra, Taurus-Scorpio, Gemini-Sagittarius,

Cancer-Capricorn, Leo-Aquarius, and Virgo-Pisces. The opposition is an aspect that connotes confrontation and conflict. The energies of the planets pull against one another creating a polarity, a pulling apart, or a separating. Conflict may seem to come from the outer world or another person rather than from within. The degree of difficulty of the opposition depends upon the planets and signs involved. Reconciliation of oppositions requires balancing the opposing forces expressed by the planets and signs. An opposition that is not balanced may have a seesaw effect where each planet takes its turn being up or down, or one planet may completely dominate the other.

Square   ☐

A square forms when two planets are 90 degrees (plus or minus 8 degrees) from one another. Since there are 360 degrees in the Zodiac, the square divides the circle in four. Squares usually occur between signs in the same quadruplicity. This serves as the basis for the erroneous notion of sun-sign incompatibility, the idea that, for example, Aries, Cancer, Libra, and Capricorn cannot get along.

The square connotes stress and conflict between the planets involved. Squares form what is best described as an internal battle. The planets involved seem to be fighting one another and pulling in cross directions. This creates a sense of being boxed in, which forces us to take action to get out of the box. The action taken may resolve the conflict or create more.

EASY OR FAVORABLE ASPECTS:
MULTIPLES OF THREE

The easy or favorable aspects divide the circle by three. They represent a harmonious blending of planetary energies. There is no push to change, as the areas of life that are ruled by the planets and signs involved come together easily. Human nature being what it is, we enjoy ease, so harmonious aspects are perceived as favorable. Yet they can represent areas where we take the easy route rather than the best possible one. The planetary combinations are not as intense as with the conjunction, square, or opposition.

Trine   △

The trine is 120 degrees (plus or minus 8 degrees). This division of the circle by three is the most favorable aspect. Trines depict natural talents, are lucky, and represent things that fall in our lap. The flow of energy between the planets involved requires no effort.

An unintended consequence can be to become lazy in these areas of life. We may do what comes naturally rather than what is best. For instance, suppose we have trines in the work segments of our chart, so jobs are attained easily. While that sounds great, it may mean that since "good enough" jobs get offered, we take what is in there rather than look for what is truly fulfilling.

Sextile   ✱

The sextile is 60 degrees. It represents a division of the circle by six. Since six is a product of two times three, it combines the energy of the trine with that of the opposition. It is favorable but requires conscious effort to get the most out of the combination of planetary energies.

ASPECTS BY SIGN

The signs in which the planets fall strongly affect the ease or difficulty of aspects. While all oppositions and squares imply difficulty, not all signs forming these aspects pull against one another to the same degree. The following descriptions assume equal planetary weight of each sign. For instance, if the Sun and Moon fall in opposite signs, the pull between the ego and the emotions is equal. If the Sun and Saturn fall in opposite signs, Saturn's influence is stronger than that of the sign it falls in, so Saturn's energy will predominate.

Oppositions   ☍

Aries and Libra are opposite signs. Aries is the sign of the individual. "I'm doing what I want and no one can tell me different." Aries are direct and straightforward, stand up for themselves easily, and enjoy a bit of conflict.

Libra, on the other hand, is the sign of relationships. To be in a relationship, we have to get along with other people. We need to look at all sides of an issue, not just our own. Compromise is necessary for the sake of harmony. The opposition between Aries and Libra is one of the most difficult of the Zodiac to reconcile. It can make us feel as if we have to choose between following our principles or being involved with other people. In actuality, Aries has much to learn from Libra's ability to get along with others, and Libra has much to learn from Aries' honesty and self-direction. The solution comes from balancing being true to ourselves with social appropriateness.

Taurus and Scorpio are opposite signs. Both are fixed and stubborn and believe they have the right answers. Taurus has to do with personal resources, including money and possessions. The planet Venus rules Taurus, like Libra, so Taurus also seeks harmony. Taurus are just more likely to seek this harmony by quietly and graciously doing what Taurus wants rather than compromising. Taurus also likes to relax and enjoy life. Scorpio, on the other hand, is intense and driven. Scorpio has an all-or-nothing quality and stands up for beliefs. Scorpio also has to do with joint resources. This is also the sensual-sexual axis of the Zodiac, Taurus for pure physical pleasure, Scorpio for a deep emotional connection. This opposition is more difficult in relationships than internally for those who have it. Jealousy and possessiveness are likely. The solution comes from balancing our own wants and needs with those of others and not treating people like possessions.

Gemini and Sagittarius are opposite signs. Gemini, an air sign ruled by Mercury, is considered the "lower mind." Gemini is concerned with personal ideas, reason, and logic. Sagittarius, a fire sign ruled by Jupiter, is considered the "higher mind." Sagittarius is concerned with social concepts and belief systems such as philosophy and religion. Both signs crave freedom and independence and balk at being hemmed in. Both signs are flexible, adaptable, and curious, making this is one of the easier oppositions to balance. Intellectually, personal beliefs and social concepts are not necessarily in conflict.

Cancer and Capricorn are opposite signs. Cancer is an emotional water sign concerned with family and security. Capricorn is the practical earth sign representing business and concerned with structure and responsibility. Yet these signs have much in common. Both are conservative and traditional. Both have strong family values and protect their own. Cancer and Capricorn are typically seen as of the mother-father figures of the Zodiac. The major pull between these two signs centers on issues of sensitivity.

Cancer is sensitive, emotional, and Cancer's feelings are easily hurt. Capricorn provides financial security but has difficulty in expressing feelings. Cancer has much to learn from Capricorn's ability to keep it together, and Capricorn has much to learn from Cancer's emotional expressiveness.

Leo and Aquarius are opposite signs. Leo is the fire sign ruled by the Sun. It represents individual self-expression. The symbol for Leo is the lion, the king of the jungle. Likewise, the Sun is the center of our solar system, and all the planets revolve around it. In essence, Leo is the star. Aquarius is an air sign concerned with intellectual principles. Aquarius represents friendship, group activity, and the brotherhood of man. While Aquarius also represents the individual, it symbolizes Everyman. Leo's concerns are personal. Aquarius' concerns are for the group. Leo wants to be a big fish. Aquarius wants everyone to have an equal say. Both are fixed signs. This is one of the more difficult oppositions to balance, as Leo wants to be the star and Aquarius does not believe anyone should be seen as better than anyone else. This opposition requires balancing the recognition Leo wants for individual creative effort with Aquarian concerns for the whole.

Virgo and Pisces are opposite signs. Virgo is the discriminating worker of the Zodiac. Virgo thinks along the lines of, "this is step one, this is step two." Virgo sees the details and excels at breaking things down into their component parts. Pisces sees beauty and potential. Pisces' vision and ability to see things the way they should be may lead to avoiding looking at them the way they are. Pisces has compassion. These two opposing ways of viewing the world create one of the more difficult oppositions. But if balanced successfully, Virgo keeps Pisces' feet on the ground rather than in the clouds, and Pisces uplifts Virgo's mundane view to see a vision of what is possible.

Squares ◻

The cardinal signs form squares as well as oppositions to one another. Squares create internal conflict. Aries squares Cancer and Capricorn, and Cancer and Capricorn square Libra. The Aries-Cancer square creates an internal struggle between the "me" concerns of Aries and the family concerns of Cancer. There is also a pull between the fiery emotions of Aries with the more sensitive ones of Cancer. The Cancer-Libra square creates an internal struggle between the family, symbolized by Cancer, and primary relationships, symbolized by Libra. This presents the dilemma of who comes first, the children or the spouse. There is also a pull between Cancer's emotions and Libra's intellect. The Libra-Capricorn square creates an internal struggle between relational needs and ambition. Libra wants to get along with others and have equal relationships, and Capricorn wants to get ahead and be the authority figure. The Capricorn-Aries square creates an internal struggle between responsibility and authority and the desire to be an authority to oneself.

The fixed signs form squares as well as oppositions to one another. Taurus squares Leo and Aquarius, and Leo and Aquarius square Scorpio. Taurus' earthy desire for comfort, money, possessions, and security can be in conflict with Leo's priority of self-expression and the need to be true to oneself. Leo's needs for attention, to be center stage, and to be admired are at odds with Scorpio's preference for secrecy and for controlling situations from behind the scenes. Scorpio's intensity and strong desires interfere with Aquarius' detachment and objectivity. Aquarius' preference for people and ideas over possessions gets in the way of Taurus' enjoyment of pure physical pleasures.

The mutable signs form squares as well as oppositions to one another. Gemini squares Virgo and Pisces, and Virgo and Pisces square Sagittarius. Gemini's wish for information to satisfy intellectual curiosity is at odds with Virgo's focus on useful information, and Gemini's flitting from one task to the next gets in the way of Virgo completing its work. Virgo's detail orientation conflicts with Sagittarius' big picture view. Sagittarius' philosophical or religious beliefs can be at odds with Pisces more idealistic, spiritual inclinations, and Pisces' idealistic, spiritual inclinations can conflict with Gemini's attention to facts and information.

Trines   △

Signs of the same element trine one another. Since a trine is a harmonious aspect, the energies of the signs flow together easily.

The fire signs, Aries, Leo, and Sagittarius, form trines to one another. As fire is the most yang element, aspects among the fire signs promote direct action. Aries, the cardinal fire sign, plays the role of the initiator. Aries starts the action. Leo, the fixed fire sign, plays the role of sustainer. Leo completes what is started. Sagittarius, the mutable fire sign, spreads ideas. Fire sign trines represent ease of spontaneity, spirit, and individual initiative.

The earth signs, Taurus, Virgo, and Capricorn, form trines to one another. The fixed earth sign Taurus represents concerns for finances, possessions, and security. The mutable earth sign Virgo represents the worker who makes sure gets the job done correctly. The cardinal earth sign Capricorn represents the boss or authority figure. Trines in these signs represent ease in the work or financial arenas.

The air signs, Gemini, Libra, and Aquarius, form trines to one another. Air signs are associated with intellect, communication, and connections among people. The mutable sign Gemini has an interest in diverse ideas and disseminating those ideas. Gemini acquires information. The cardinal sign Libra's interest lies in people and communicating as a way of making connections. The fixed sign Aquarius represents the associates who share the information and affix it into principles. Trines in air signs represent ease in mental activities.

The water signs, Cancer, Scorpio, and Pisces, form trines to one another. Water signs are associated with feelings and emotions. Cancer symbolizes the mother who nurtures her offspring and takes care of family members. Scorpio's emotions are tied up in the passion and intensity of close, intimate relationships of their choosing. Pisces feels for the entire world, not just those Pisces personally relates to. Trines in water signs reflect ease in emotional expression.

Sextiles   ✶

Fire and air signs sextile one another. Aries initiates situations. Gemini spreads ideas that assist Leo's creative endeavors. Leo's loving nature helps pave the way for Libra's one-to-one relationships of marriage or partnership. Libra's sense of justice assists Sagittarius' principles. Sagittarius' principles reinforce Aquarius' humanistic ideals, which assist Aries' initiative ability.

Earth and water signs sextile one another. Taurus' practical financial orientation assists Cancer's security urges. Cancer's security urges and family concerns assist Virgo in accomplishing day-to-day tasks. Virgo's analytical abilities combine well with Scorpio's ability to see what is beneath the surface. Scorpio's insights help Capricorn get ahead. Capricorn's practicality helps Pisces keep both feet on the ground, and Pisces' vision of beauty and the future can assist Taurus in making money.

Chapter 16

ASPECTS OF THE SUN

The Sun represents the basic sense of self. The sign it falls in reflects how we express our identity, willpower, and creativity. The house the Sun falls in reflects the area of life where we want to shine. The Sun is our core, and aspects to it affect how we think and feel about ourselves. Because of this, all aspects to the Sun affect self-expression, work, money-making potential, and all relationships.

SUN AND MOON

The Sun and Moon reflect the building blocks of character. The Sun represents the ego, identity, and individuality. The Moon represents the subconscious, habit patterns, and emotions.

Sun Conjunct Moon ☉ ☌ ☽

This occurs when the Sun and Moon come together at the New Moon or just before it. A New Moon represents a beginning. The sky is dark and the Moon unseen. In a similar manner, being born at the New Moon reflects a new emerging identity. By contrast, being born just before the New Moon represents the ending of a cycle, so it reflects coming to completion rather than a beginning.

In either case, when the Sun and Moon are conjoined, identity and feelings are tied together, creating an intertwining of feelings, emotions, and ego desires. The intertwining provides focused interests, great commitment to whatever you care about, and not much interest in other areas. The sign and house positions of these celestial bodies are of the utmost importance as the qualities of the sign the Sun and Moon fall in get expressed to the nth degree. The house where this conjunction falls in is the most important arena of your life.

No matter what your sign, the blending of the ego and the emotions creates sensitivity and vulnerability. The ups and downs of your emotions affect how you feel about yourself. This creates an emphasis on the self and may make it difficult to see situations from another's point of view. Watch out for the tendency to overdo the qualities associated with the sign this conjunction falls in and the tendency to be self-absorbed.

Sun Sextile or Trine Moon   ☉ ✳ / △ ☽

Your emotional nature and your character complement one another. There is harmony between the masculine and feminine sides of your nature, and your moods, feelings, and subconscious habit patterns support your ego. Unless there are contrary indications in the chart, you pursue goals with no internal conflict pulling you in opposing directions, and you get along equally well with men and women.

Sun Square or Opposite Moon   ☉ □ / ☍ ☽

Your feelings and sense of identity pull in differing directions. This challenges the ego. It is difficult to feel good emotionally and achieve ego satisfaction simultaneously. What satisfies the emotions pulls at the ego, and vice versa. This may create inner restlessness and a sense of never being quite satisfied.

The key to working out this aspect depends upon the signs and houses that these celestial bodies fall in. A big enough vision of life must be created to include satisfaction of all the needs expressed by the signs and houses involved rather than alternatively choosing some needs and then others. For instance, suppose you have a square between the Sun in Aries and the Moon in Cancer, and you want to open your own business. Aries requires individual initiative and self-sufficiency. Cancer requires safety and security. Going out on your own after you have accumulated a sufficient financial reserve to provide a safety net satisfies the needs of both Aries and Cancer.

Traits to treasure: The importance of both the masculine and feminine sides of your nature.
To transform: Avoid letting the ego or the emotions overrule one another.

Sun Conjunct Mercury ☉ ♂ ☿

Since Mercury is never further than 28 degrees away from the Sun, Mercury is found in the same sign as the Sun or the sign before it or after it. The conjunction is the only aspect possible. Mercury represents the conscious mind. When these two celestial bodies conjunct, the ego and identity are tied to the thought processes. This gives good communication skills, the capacity for decisive decision-making, and the will to back up decisions. At the same time, the intertwining of ego and thinking makes it difficult to be objective about yourself or situations in which you have a vested interest. There is a need to be on guard against the tendency for the will to overpower better judgment. The sign and house this conjunction falls in reflect how you communicate, what you pay attention to, and where you are likely to be overly invested.

JOYCE SAYS:

Traits to treasure: Your persuasiveness.
To transform: Avoid letting ego drives overpower your better judgment.

Sun Conjunct Venus ☉ ♂ ♀

The proximity of Venus to the Sun makes the conjunction the only major aspect possible between them. Venus represents love, beauty, and sociability. These two celestial bodies' conjunct provides charm and social grace and very likely a pleasing appearance. You are easygoing and affectionate, and you get along well in social situations. You appreciate the finer things in life and enjoy beautiful surroundings. It is possible for the expectation of the good life to add an element of narcissism or self-centeredness.

The sociability of Venus makes being liked and well thought of important. Significant relationships affect your sense of identity and self-worth. Because of this, you seek harmony with those with whom you associate. The sign that this conjunction falls in describes more fully what you are like in terms of your identity and in relationships. Assuming this conjunction occurs between Venus and the Sun in the same sign, the people to whom you are attracted are more like you than unlike you.

JOYCE SAYS:
Traits to treasure: Your charm and good taste.
To transform: Avoid trying to get by on charm alone.

SUN AND MARS

The Sun and Mars represent the masculine indicators in the chart. Together they represent the ego drive and how we go after what we want. This assertive combination of planets conveys will and determination. All aspects between the Sun and Mars heighten the likelihood of acting upon principles. The type of aspect shows how this action takes place. The signs that these planets fall in describe the ego needs and the manner of assertion.

Sun Conjunct Mars ☉ ☌ ♂

This conjunction conveys a fighting spirit. You have a great deal of energy coupled with physical stamina and a strong sex drive. You are not just action oriented, but need activity in order to be happy. You are self-sufficient, have strong will and determination, and have the capacity for hard work. This makes you ambitious, direct, assertive in going after what you want, and a fierce competitor. Let no person stand in your way.

These qualities add up to being courageous or foolhardy or both. You stand up for what you believe in and let no one push you around. This gives you integrity. If this conjunction falls in a fire sign or Scorpio, you are particularly fearless. Yet you can jump into situations without stopping to think about the consequences. You may lose your temper easily and be feistier than you realize, believing that you are simply expressing yourself. You hate confinement of any kind, and you can overreact if you perceive that someone is telling you what to do.

The sign this conjunction falls in determines how you express this energy and what you stand up for. For instance, this conjunction in Aries brings out the extreme macho side, very much "I'm doing what I want and no one can tell me anything." If the conjunction falls in Pisces, you are much more assertive than would typically be true for Pisces, but the assertion would be more likely directed in artistic projects or in standing up for the underdog.

Sun Sextile or Trine Mars   ☉ ✻ / △ ♂

The favorable combination of these planets heightens physical vitality, endurance, and sex drive. The ability to go after what you want goes hand in hand with the drive for significance. You are ambitious, self-sufficient, and competitive. You naturally pursue goals of your own choosing and have the courage of your convictions.

You find challenges enjoyable and act in a quick and decisive manner. While the sextile and trine are positive aspects, it is still possible for you to be pushier than you recognize. Very likely, you expect to get your way in situations and will push to make sure this happens.

The type of challenges you enjoy and where you put your energy are very much determined by the signs and houses these planets fall in. For instance, trines between the second and tenth houses would put the emphasis in work and money arenas. Sextiles between the fifth and seventh houses would place emphasis on children and marriage.

Sun Square or Opposite Mars   ☉ □ / ☍ ♂]

Like the conjunction, sextile, and trine, a square or opposition between the Sun and Mars heightens will, determination, ambition, and competitiveness. You are self-sufficient, courageous, enjoy challenges, and easily stand up for your principles. However, a difficult aspect between the Sun and Mars makes greater discipline necessary to handle this energy positively.

Patience is not one of your strong points. You are action oriented, but the actions you take do not necessarily benefit you. Rash actions can actually make you accident-prone. It is possible to act at the wrong time or alienate others by being too forceful. You may perceive conflict where none exists, lose your temper quickly, or be overly aggressive in the pursuit of goals. You detest being told what to do or how to do it. This may build up inner resentment or bring about conflict with authority figures. Learning to think before you act and to express anger in an appropriate manner is essential to avoid conflict.

JOYCE SAYS:
Traits to treasure: Your ability to stand up for yourself and go after what you want.
To transform: Avoid creating unnecessary conflict.

SUN AND JUPITER

Aspects between the Sun and Jupiter combine the ego and sense of identity with possibilities for growth, expansion, and good luck. All aspects convey optimism and positive views of the world, but also the possibility for excess and extravagance.

Sun Conjunct Jupiter   ☉ ♂ ♃

This is a good-luck, expansionary aspect, which makes you a fortunate person. There is a desire to experience all that life has to offer. Travel and adventure beckon, whether it is travel of the body, mind, or spirit. You are optimistic and self-confident and inspire others to believe in you. Generally you are lucky and instinctively put yourself in the right place at the right time. Being outgoing, enthusiastic, and generally happy, you enjoy yourself easily. Qualities of looking for the best in people and situations, being generous, and a willingness to lend a helping hand endear you to others. There is a bit of a proselytizer in you, and you excel in enrolling people in your ideas.

Zest for life combined with faith in the future helps you through even the worst of times. You look at problems with an eye toward finding solutions, and assume that situations will work out well.

This expansive planetary combination tends toward excess and extravagance. Eating too much, drinking too much, or spending too much are all possible, as is the tendency to gain weight easily.

Sun Sextile or Trine Jupiter   ☉ ✳ / △ ♃

These are good luck aspects. With the trine, things just happen. With the sextile you need to put in a little more effort. Still, it is possible to end up at the right place and have situations go your way. You are outgoing, optimistic, and self-confident, and happy most of the time. There is a desire to reach out and experience life. Travel beckons, as does education and knowledge.

You are also idealistic and philanthropic and look for the best in people and situations. Generosity and a willingness to lend a helping hand make you well liked. You know how to enjoy life and generally do.

The major problem with favorable aspects, particularly the trine between the Sun and Jupiter, is that they can be too much of a good thing. When life is easy and situations typically go your way, it is possible to become lazy and accept what is in front of you rather than exerting effort to reach for what might be better and even more satisfying. The desire to enjoy life may also cause you to overindulge in eating, drinking, or spending.

Sun Square or Opposite Jupiter ☉ □ / ☍ ♃

These aspects, like the more favorable ones between the Sun and Jupiter, make you outgoing, optimistic, enthusiastic, and self-confident. You enjoy a good time, are generous to others, and look for the best in people and situations.

You also are a bit of a proselytizer. You fervently stand up for causes you believe in and therefore need to avoid unfairly judging those who disagree with you.

Problems between the Sun and Jupiter have to do with exaggerated expectations and excess. You are a risk taker and you enjoy a challenge. However, it is possible to overestimate your luck, and risks do not necessarily pan out as easily as you anticipate. Over-optimism can cause you to promise more than it is possible to deliver in a timely fashion or cause you not to deliver at all. It may also lead to an exaggerated sense of self-importance. Generosity and love of a good time can lead to spending more than you can afford. Eating too much and drinking too much may cause problems with weight management and health.

The square or opposition between the Sun and Jupiter is still lucky if you manage expectations and develop self-discipline and a practical gage of reality. This may sound like negative thinking, but overly positive thinking leads to unfulfilled expectations.

JOYCE SAYS:
Traits to treasure: The generous way you are willing to share.
To transform: Avoid promising more than it is possible to deliver.

SUN AND SATURN

Aspects between the Sun and Saturn have to do with how the ego and sense of identity combine with duty, responsibility, limitations, and restrictions. This is a work-oriented, conservative combination of planets, and success in life comes through effort.

Sun Conjunct Saturn   ☉ ♂ ♄

The conjunction is an aspect that can be beneficial or difficult depending upon the nature of the planets involved. The conjunction between the Sun and Saturn is one of the more difficult ones, as it makes positive ego formation difficult.

Positively, this conjunction conveys patience, practicality, self-discipline, and reliability. A strong sense of purpose, good organizational ability, and the capacity to handle responsibilities well help you work hard in order to achieve goals. Others know they can trust you, as you do what you believe is right.

Very likely you were mature, serious, and responsible at an early age. This made it easier during childhood to get along with adults than with peers with whom you did not readily fit in. Life becomes easier at the point where your age catches up with your maturity.

This conjunction may be better for the people around you than it is for you. Difficulties arise from how you feel about yourself as very high standards may affect your self-esteem. You may define being "good enough" as living up to perceived expectations of your parents, boss, friends, or spouse. It is hard to realize that these expectations are just as likely to emanate from within. Being responsible is a positive quality, but it can become negative if it leads to assuming responsibilities that are not yours and taking care of other people or situations at the expense of taking care of yourself. This ultimately leads to feeling overburdened and building up resentment at being the one who somehow always gets stuck. It is very important to distinguish between what is your responsibility and what is not.

Another difficulty of this conjunction comes from the inhibiting quality of Saturn. You expect life to be work and are prone to seeing barriers. This may lead to pessimism, isolation, and actually creating barriers that make life harder than it needs to be. A person with a positive sense of self-worth assumes that he is included and joins in activities while one who is less sure of his acceptance is quick to perceive rejection. It is possible to easily feel unappreciated and excluded and then to blame others for not recognizing your worth. You may handle these feelings in very different ways. You may retreat in fear when you come up against a barrier or feel rejected, or you may push through to overcome your fears. The results you achieve in life are a direct result of these choices. It is important to distinguish between realistic assessments and negative ones and to recognize what you are responsible for and what you are not.

The sign this conjunction falls in affects what you feel responsible for, and the house it falls in determines where you place your priorities.

Sun Sextile or Trine Saturn ☉ ✳ / △ ♄

Your ego needs and sense of identity easily combine with responsibility and the work ethic. This gives you patience, practicality, organizational ability, and the capacity for hard work. You have the ability to realistically assess yourself, the world around you, and to learn from life experiences. Common sense and discipline come naturally. You work hard, assume responsibilities easily, and respect authority. You can slip into being overly responsible, but you possess a realistic gauge of what you are responsible for and what you are not. This helps you set appropriate limits with people and in situations so that responsibilities do not turn into burdens.

Sun Square or Opposite Saturn ☉ □ / ☍ ♄

With difficult aspects between the Sun and Saturn, achievement takes hard work. Like those with the conjunction, trine, or sextile, you are patient, practical, methodical, and self-disciplined. You labor earnestly and handle responsibilities well. It is not all in your imagination that life is harder and more work for you than it may be for others, but it is also important that you do not make life harder than it needs to be.

Like the conjunction, the square or opposition can create problems with self-esteem. Very likely, you grew up in a difficult, critical household where a lot was expected of you from an early age. Being mature and responsible early and somewhat inhibited as a child, it was probably easier to get along with adults than with children your age. This could set up a sense of isolation early on and give the tendency to easily feel left out or rejected. It is possible to see barriers where none may exist and therefore to exclude yourself.

Early responsibilities may lead to becoming very demanding of yourself as an adult and to somehow end up in situations where people expect a lot from you. You may believe that your worth is a function of what you do rather than who you are as a human being. The demands you make of yourself lead to two extremely different choices. Feeling overwhelmed and unworthy, you may give up when life seems too difficult. Or you may take the completely opposite approach. Recognizing that life is not easy and that it requires work and effort, you push through barriers despite their difficulties. Pushing through barriers obviously leads toward greater success. Although either way, you are likely to believe that life is hard.

The perception that life is hard may also cause you to become self-protective and distrustful. Because of this, it is possible to appear self-centered and coldhearted. This appearance may end up being true, or it may be a purely self-protective mechanism. If you continually assume responsibilities for others at the expense of yourself, you end up resentful. Yet it is difficult to let others do things for you even when they offer. Deep down you can believe that if you need anything from anyone else, it proves your unworthiness. Facing this and learning how to let others in is essential to overcoming this internal obstacle to personal satisfaction. It is imperative to face responsibilities and deal with the world as it is, but it is also necessary to see the difference between reality and burdens of your own creation.

JOYCE SAYS:

Traits to treasure: Your reliability and responsibility allow others to count on you.

To transform: Avoid letting responsibility turn into over-responsibility by assuming burdens that are not yours.

SUN AND URANUS

Aspects between the Sun and Uranus combine the ego and sense of identity with the needs of freedom and autonomy. This planetary combination heightens inventiveness, originality, and the ability to think out of the box.

Sun Conjunct Uranus   ☉ ☌ ♅

With this conjunction, the will and identity fuse with freedom and originality. You were born with a sense of independence and individuality. From an early age you wanted to go your own way and do your own thing. Strong-willed and adventurous, you are attracted to the unusual, and there is nothing you like better than forging into the unknown. The status quo is more difficult to live with. This makes you a born rebel, much more attuned to your inner voice than the conventions of society. Your talents lie in originality and inventiveness no matter what your field.

These same traits make it difficult for you to fit in. On one hand, your magnetic personality attracts people; but dancing to a different drum, you are seen as unpredictable and possibly unreliable. Trouble with authority figures is likely, as you refuse to be told what to do or how to do it, and you stand up for what you believe regardless of the circumstances. These traits make you a rebel or an entrepreneur. You work better in your own business or in start-up companies than in more traditional settings. You have the capacity to fight for just causes. On the less positive side, it is possible to take actions for their shock value, and the craving for autonomy can interfere with the give-and-take needed for intimate relationships. Balancing the rights and needs of others with your own is essential with this conjunction.

On the purely physical level, it is possible to be nervous and jittery and also accident-prone. Physical exercise is a must to relieve tension.

The sign this conjunction falls in has a lot to do with how you feel about yourself. For instance, if this conjunction falls in one of the naturally independent signs like Aries or Sagittarius, you are completely at home with being an individual. If it falls in a security-oriented sign like Taurus or Cancer, individualistic needs must be balanced with those of security and stability. The house these planets fall in show where you want to shine independently.

Sun Sextile or Trine Uranus ☉ ✳ / △ ♅

With the trine or sextile, the will and sense of identity combine easily with the urges toward freedom and originality. You are naturally free and independent. This is a broadminded association of planets. You believe in "live and let live." You follow your own path, but do so in such a way so as not to create conflict with others. Naturally original and inventive, you enjoy forging into the unknown. There is an attraction to what is out of the ordinary, whether in the realm of ideas or science or friends and social groups. Intuition and ingenuity contribute to success.

Sun Square or Opposite Uranus ☉ □ / ☍ ♅

With the square or opposition, there is conflict between the will and the sense of identity and freedom and originality. This conflict may be experienced in relation to other people as well as within you. You are a born rebel or entrepreneur—strong willed, independent, individualistic, and very likely impulsive. Inventive and original in thought and action, you derive pleasure from challenges. Joy comes from forging into the unknown, and there is little tolerance for conventional thinking or the status quo.

Problems are likely to arise with authority figures, as you take orders from nobody and all too willingly fight for what you believe in. At your best, you fearlessly stand up for just causes. However, the feeling of being pushed around is your Achilles heel , and the belief that you have to prove that nobody can do so can lead to acting rashly without thinking about consequences. It is possible to overreact to reasonable requests and flaunt an unwillingness to go along with convention. The desire for freedom at all costs may interfere not only with relationships but also with the ability to achieve results you desire. It is essential to recognize the difference between compromise and giving in, and that no one, not even you, can be right all the time.

Like the conjunction, the square and opposition may create physical nervousness and jitteriness and may cause a tendency to be accident-prone. Physical exercise is a must to relieve tension.

The signs these planets fall in significantly affect how these issues are acted out. In cardinal signs, responses are quick and immediate. In fixed signs, the internal responses are quick and immediate but take much longer to manifest on an outer level. Seething inside before taking action is more likely. In mutable signs, responses are likely to be more erratic.

JOYCE SAYS:

Traits to treasure: Your originality, inventiveness, and willingness to challenge the status quo.

To transform: Avoid behaving rashly and flaunting disrespect for authority or convention.

SUN AND NEPTUNE

All aspects between the Sun and Neptune combine the ego and sense of identity with spirituality, creativity, idealism, and imagination. This planetary combination heightens sensitivity, compassion, and psychic ability. All aspects can be creative or escapist.

Sun Conjunct Neptune   ☉ ♂ ♆

This planetary combination is one of psychic attunement and romantic idealism. You are sensitive, compassionate, and artistically creative. On an intuitive level, you feel the undercurrents of the moods and vibrations of people and places. You may know things before they happen. While the idea of being psychic or intuitive seems mysteriously pleasant, it also means that the moods and vibrations of your environment affect you more than they would someone else, and that your moods fluctuate depending upon where you are and whom you are with. If you are consciously aware of these feelings and pay attention to your instincts, you know who to associate with and who to stay away from. If you are not consciously aware, you may experience mood swings and wonder why. Spending time alone each day and meditating helps you pay attention to your inner voice.

You have an almost rapture-like enjoyment of music, theater, or art, and you may have creative imagination and talents in the arts or decorating and design. You not only appreciate beauty, you want life to be beautiful. Very likely, there is a call to the mystical, a longing for union with some higher power. You are a sensitive, compassionate soul, who wants to be the most ideal person possible. Because of this, you may be a visionary, or you may live in a world of fantasy, or possibly a bit of both.

You want to see virtues rather than flaws in yourself and others. You long to live in a world where everyone is kind to one another and you feel compelled to lend a helping hand. If you work as a therapist, you help people create a vision of what is possible. If you are an artist, you create beauty that leaves others in awe.

In your personal life, these same traits can be problematic. Idealism can cause illusions if you tune out the imperfect realities of everyday life. You may be attracted to people who need rescuing and may lend a helping hand to those who ultimately take advantage of you. You may avoid dealing with problems, hoping that if you close your eyes for long enough, they will disappear or some higher power will take care of them. If you are a woman, you should be particularly careful of attracting men who need help or, alternatively, living in the fantasy that Prince Charming will save you.

These scenarios may cause you to go into escapist mode, retreating from others, or to expect people to rescue you from your own follies. Strong physical and psychic sensitivities make it imperative to be careful with drugs and alcohol. Discrimination is a must with this conjunction. Without ideals, nothing can be accomplished. Yet ideals must be balanced with realistic assessments if they are to be achieved.

Sun Sextile or Trine Neptune ☉ ✷ / △ ♆

Personal drive and idealism work together. You possess good taste and refinement. Creative imagination and talents for the arts, decorating, or design are likely. Whether or not you pursue these talents, you appreciate beauty, and you love music, art, literature, or theater.

You are psychically sensitive to your environment. You feel what goes on around you and are in turn affected by your surroundings, although not as dramatically as those with the conjunction. Paying deliberate attention to your environment helps you sort out which feelings are yours and which are products of your immediate circumstances. If you develop inner listening, intuition helps in making decisions that you can rely on. Spending time in meditation or contemplation helps you develop and listen to your inner voice.

You are sensitive, compassionate, and romantic. You look for the good in people and derive enjoyment from doing good deeds and helping others. You want to be the best person you can possibly be and live in the best world possible.

Even with a favorable aspect, you must still be careful regarding idealism. Like those with the conjunction, you can be a visionary or subject to illusions or both. Looking for the beauty in life gives you the capacity to create beauty and to help others. It also gives you the tendency to recoil from and avoid what is not so beautiful. This may lead to the tendency to ignore problems in the hope that they will resolve themselves on their own.

Sun Square or Opposite Neptune ☉ □ / ☍ ♆

This combination makes you a romantic idealist, sensitive, compassionate, and artistically creative. You may be a visionary. Yet these aspects must be handled with care. The sense of identity provided by the Sun can become easily confused when it makes harsh aspects to Neptune. It is difficult to see yourself as others see you. You may underestimate your abilities or overestimate them, and therefore not necessarily see yourself as you are. It is also difficult to see people and situations as they are, being more likely to overly exaggerate the positive or the negative.

You search for beauty in life. This beauty may be expressed as talent in art, music, theater, or writing, or in decorating or design. Or you may simply enjoy beautiful surroundings and appreciate creative arts as healthy escapism.

Like all other aspects between the Sun and Neptune, the square and opposition convey psychic attunement. You feel the undercurrents of the moods and vibrations of people and places and may know things before they happen. It is difficult for you to distinguish your own feelings from those of your surroundings. This psychic attunement creates mystical leanings and the longing to connect with a higher power. Spending time alone each day in meditation and contemplation helps you distinguish between yourself and your surroundings, rejuvenate yourself, and connect with that higher power.

You long for a heavenly existence where everyone is kind and wonderful. Being idealistic, you look for the best in people and prefer seeing their virtues to their flaws. You compassionately lend a helping hand to those in need. It is possible for idealism to create illusions because in looking for what is beautiful, you tune out what is not so beautiful. This has the potential of creating blind spots. You may avoid dealing with problems, hoping they will go away by themselves. You may lend a helping hand to, or get involved with, people who take advantage of you. If you are a woman, you may attract men who have problems dealing with life.

The disparity between the ideal and life as it is can be tremendously disappointing. This may lead to retreating from people, to looking for others to rescue you from situations of your own making, or to falling into problems with drugs or alcohol so as not to have to face problems. Learning discrimination is a must. While it may seem unkind to you, it is much better for you to hold back from doing things for others until you have known them long enough to assess their true character.

JOYCE SAYS:

Traits to treasure: The sensitivity and compassion with which you treat people.
To transform: Develop discrimination so that you avoid unrealistic expectations that lead to disappointment.

SUN AND PLUTO

All aspects between the Sun and Pluto combine the ego and sense of identity with inner drive or compulsion, the power of the will, and the urges to transform or destroy. They give a profound understanding of the world and the instinctive ability to see through people and situations.

Sun Conjunct Pluto ☉ ♂ ♇

The conjunction of the Sun and Pluto fuses the sense of identity with the power of will, giving you an exceptionally strong will and a deep desire for accomplishment. You seek to know and understand. Incredible instincts and powers of observation provide the ability to pierce through situations, ideas, and people's facades to get to the heart of any matter. Your assessments are generally accurate, but not particularly sympathetic, as you have little tolerance for weakness in yourself or in others.

All-or-nothing best describes your personality. You have extreme likes and dislikes, and when you want something, nothing else will do. Your determination, perseverance, and willingness to stand up for what you believe are awe-inspiring. You achieve what you set out to accomplish.

Strong desires can be a double-edged sword. These desires stem from deep within and are such a propelling force that you are unlikely to question them. Because of this, they can take on a life of their own. You can sacrifice your own well-being for the sake of their accomplishment or become ruthless and dictatorial in their pursuit. While you have strong a capacity to understand people and human nature, it is difficult for you to see another's point of view when it counters your desires or deeply held beliefs. This leads to power struggles that can pit you against others and ultimately stand in the way of your accomplishments.

This planetary combination necessitates cultivating detachment. While you will never be completely detached, you can learn to harness your energy to properly use your power in accomplishing your goals.

Sun Sextile or Trine Pluto ☉ ✶ / △ ♇

The sextile and trine between the Sun and Pluto are not as intense or forceful as the conjunction, square, or opposition. The more natural combination of ego and sense of identity with inner drive make the effects less dramatic. You naturally harness and utilize your power and inner drive without experiencing inner turmoil. You are strong-willed compared to the average person. Though you desire to accomplish your aims, you are less driven and controlling than people with the conjunction, square, or opposition. Because of this, you create less tension around you and less resistance from others. Strong powers of observation, your good instincts in judging people and situations, and an innate sense of timing help bring people over to your side. The combination of all these qualities enhances the ability to accomplish chosen aims.

Sun Square or Opposite Pluto ☉ □ / ☍ ♇

The square and opposition have many similar characteristics to the conjunction, but instead of the energy fusing together, conflict exists between the sense of identity and inner drive. This conflict may be internal, or it may manifest in dealing with others.

Your nature is delving and researching. You seek to know, understand, get to the bottom of situations, and recognize people's underlying motivations. Your will is mighty, your likes and dislikes intense, and your presence powerful. Intense desires stemming from unconscious motivations propel you to go after what you want.

Your determination and perseverance make things happen. Fearlessly standing up for principles, you brook no interference from anyone. However, carried to the extreme, these are exactly the qualities that cause problems. You may be overly suspicious of other people's motivations, particularly when they disagree with you. You can become far too forceful and domineering in order to get what you want. You are so sure that you are right that you may become willful and arrogant and refuse to pay attention to others. This then creates resistance from people and gets you into power struggles that stand in the way of accomplishing your aims.

It is essential to examine your own motivations and how you handle situations. Desires stemming from deep within your psyche propel you to act obsessively. You may willingly sacrifice yourself to your aims, whether they are for a job, a relationship, or an ideal, without stopping to analyze why you want what you do or whether it is good for you. It is easier for you to try to control the environment than it is to control yourself.

Like those with the conjunction, it is necessary to cultivate as much detachment as possible. The planetary combination of the Sun and Pluto gives you tremendous power for unbelievable accomplishments or unfathomable self-destruction.

JOYCE SAYS:

Traits to treasure: How your strong will and desires propel you to accomplishment.

To transform: Avoid becoming obsessive and self-destructive in the pursuit of your aims.

Chapter 17

ASPECTS OF THE MOON

T he Moon represents emotions and feelings as well as the ways we mother, nurture, and take care of others and ourselves. All aspects from the Moon to other planets affect our feelings and how we emotionally respond to situations.

MOON AND MERCURY

All aspects between the Moon and Mercury combine the emotions with the intellect and subconscious responses with conscious thinking.

Moon Conjunct Mercury ☽ ☌ ☿

This conjunction unites feelings and intellect and the subconscious mind and the conscious mind. It provides good memory and strong intuition. Feelings are on the surface so that you can talk about them.

Thoughts and feelings function as one. This makes objectivity difficult. Emotions color your thinking, and thinking colors your feelings. The sign in which this conjunction occurs indicates whether thinking or feeling predominates. If this conjunction occurs in an air sign, you are less comfortable with feelings than with thoughts, and you attempt to rationalize your feelings to comply with logic. This may lead to denial of feelings. If this conjunction occurs in a water sign, feelings predominate, making rational analysis difficult, and feelings may obliterate objective assessments. This conjunction makes it essential to recognize where prejudices lie so that you may consciously compensate in the other direction.

Moon Sextile or Trine Mercury ☽ ✳ / △ ☿

The mind and the emotions are in harmony as are the subconscious mind and the conscious thought process. You are adept at communicating thoughts and feelings, as you are comfortable with both how you think and how you feel. You have facile memory and good recall. You instinctively pay attention to how other people think and feel, which helps in personal relationships and heightens debating skills. The elements that these celestial bodies fall in indicate how you think and what you pay attention to. In fire signs, thinking and feeling are more outgoing and inspirational; in earth signs, more practical; in air signs, more rational; in water signs, more feeling-oriented.

Moon Square or Opposite Mercury ☽ □ / ☌ ☿

Logic and feelings pull against one another. When something feels right, it may not be logical; but when it is logical, it does not necessarily feel right. At times your emotions prevail over rational judgment, and at other times rational judgment discounts feelings, which may lead to indecisiveness. It is important to consider both emotional needs and logical considerations without making one more important than the other one. In some instances, feelings are more important; in others, logic; and in some instances, a balance between the two is what is needed.

You are friendly, outgoing, and enjoy communicating with people, but it might be difficult to censor yourself. You may say the first thing that comes into your mind without thinking or inappropriately blurt out feelings. Discrimination in communication is a must.

JOYCE SAYS:
Traits to treasure: How your good memory and strong intuition help in decision-making.
To transform: Balance thoughts and feelings without letting either one predominate.

MOON AND VENUS

The Moon and Venus are the feminine celestial bodies in the horoscope. Together they represent mothering, nurturing, love, harmony, art, beauty, social instincts, charm, and the urge for personal connection.

Moon Conjunct Venus   ☽ ☌ ♀

This conjunction bestows charm and grace, a sympathetic nature, and a pleasing personality. You are loving, mothering, and nurturing. Taking care of those you care for comes naturally. The senses are strong. Beauty is important, elegance esteemed, and a fine home cherished. And being loved and appreciated is paramount.

The sign in which this conjunction takes place describes what you consider mothering and loving, how you give of yourself, and your emotional and relational needs. For instance, if the Moon and Venus fall in Aries, encouraging self-sufficiency is considered loving. If the Moon and Venus are in Cancer, taking care of loved ones is seen in traditional ways of being comforting and protecting.

Aspects from the Moon and Venus to other planets affect how you relate to others and your capacity for love and emotional expression. With favorable aspects, you are comfortable with your feminine side. You enjoy socializing, give and receive love and support readily, and have particularly good relationships with women. With difficult aspects, relational problems with women are likely and abilities of socializing and giving and receiving love and support are impaired along the lines of the afflicted planet.

Moon Sextile or Trine Venus   ☽ ✳ / △ ♀

This planetary combination puts the feminine side of your nature in harmony. Feelings and social urges are in accord, making the expression of warmth, sympathy, and love natural. Good social instincts make it easy for you to get along with people, and you are helpful without being overbearing.

Unless there are contrary indications in the chart, you are attracted to healthy associations, romantic and family relationships are harmonious, and the opposite sex finds you appealing. Relationships with women are particularly favorable, and women are helpful to you.

The desire for the "good life" makes you tend toward overindulgence. Be particularly careful of overeating. The signs that the Moon and Venus fall in specifically describe what you consider the good life and the way you express feelings and your social urges. For instance, with Venus and the Moon in earth signs, the focus is on material comfort. With Venus and the Moon in water signs, the focus is on emotional comfort.

Moon Square or Opposite Venus   ☽ □ / ☍ ♀

With the Moon and Venus in tension aspect, emotional needs pull against relational ones and the way in which you nurture contrasts with the way you express love. You are sensitive and need comfort and assurance in order to feel loved. You are loving and nurturing and desirous of taking care of loved ones, but it may be difficult for you to express what you feel. You may keep your feelings in when you should let them out and let them out when it is better to keep them to yourself.

Relationships in general and with women in particular may go through ups and downs. The signs the Moon and Venus fall in define the specific problems. Since the Moon and Venus have about equal weight astrologically, the key to transforming this aspect is to consider both the Moon and Venus simultaneously rather than going back and forth to choose between them. For instance, if the Moon is in Scorpio and Venus is in Aquarius, you are intensely emotional, but your ideal of love is intellectual and detached. You may espouse the Aquarian ideals of love, such as the belief that lovers should be free to have other friendships. Yet, the emotional jealousy and possessiveness of the Scorpio shows through. This mixed message gets in the way relationally unless you are willing to be honest about the contradictions. You need passion and intensity as well as mental chemistry for a successful relationship. When you are willing to be honest about this with yourself, you can communicate it clearly to your paramour.

The needs of the signs that the Moon and Venus fall in must be considered and balanced to obtain harmony. If the Moon and Venus make aspects to the outer planets, these planets must also be considered.

JOYCE SAYS:
Traits to treasure: Your sensitivity and the capacity for nurturing.
To transform: Blend emotional and relational wants and needs without making one more important than the other.

MOON AND MARS

The Moon is feminine and receptive. Mars is masculine and assertive. Aspects between the Moon and Mars combine how you feel and how you act. The interaction of these celestial bodies heightens emotions and courage.

Moon Conjunct Mars ☽ ♂ ♂

This combination of how you feel and how you act conveys strong, intense feelings that prompt actions. On the positive side, you have a fighting spirit. Leadership ability stems from daring and risk taking. You bravely stand up for your family or causes that you believe in.

On the negative side, the fighting spirit may be carried too far, with common sense and reason thrown out the window. Being impatient and easily feeling threatened can lead to losing your temper quickly. As a child, you may have thrown temper tantrums, and as an adult, controlling your temper reflects emotional maturity.

The manner in which your temper gets expressed depends upon whether this conjunction takes place in cardinal, fixed, or mutable signs. Cardinal signs, Aries, Cancer, Libra, and Capricorn explode more immediately. Fixed signs, Taurus, Leo, Scorpio, and Aquarius smolder inside; mutable signs, Gemini, Virgo, Sagittarius, and Pisces are verbally confrontational.

Moon Sextile or Trine Mars ☽ ⚹ / △ ♂

These aspects heighten ambition as subconscious feelings enhance personal drive. You have good energy. Strong emotions support your ability to take action. You stand up for your family and causes that you care about. While you are assertive and courageous, you are not necessarily overly aggressive. However, since all aspects between the Moon and Mars increase sensitivity, you tend to over-respond emotionally to upsetting circumstances.

The signs these planets fall in show how you assert yourself. In fire signs, you take direct actions; in earth signs, you expend energy in practical matters; in air signs, in intellectual matters; and in water signs, emotional ones.

Moon Square or Opposite Mars ☽ □ / ☍ ♂

Harsh aspects between the Moon and Mars make it difficult for you to control your temper. You may have a fighting spirit and stand up for what you believe in, albeit a bit too emotionally or aggressively, or emotions may drown out your ability to act. Self-control is needed to live up to your aspirations for leadership.

Extreme sensitivity can cause you to overreact to circumstances before you have thought about the consequences of your actions. Emotional crises result from being quick to feel insulted or taking things too personally. Because you are so readily hurt, it is hard for you to recognize that you can be insensitive to the feelings of others.

The manner in which you express yourself depends upon the signs that these celestial bodies fall in.

JOYCE SAYS:
Traits to treasure: Your fighting spirit and the way you protect those you love. To transform: Avoid unwarranted emotional outbursts or letting emotions get in the way of appropriate actions.

MOON AND JUPITER

Aspects between the Moon and Jupiter combine how one feels and emotionally responds to life with the urge to reach out and expand. These aspects enhance optimism, generosity, and the sense of being deserving.

Moon Conjunct Jupiter ☽ ♂ ♃

This conjunction conveys an optimistic, happy-go-lucky attitude toward life. You have a good sense of humor and are fun-loving. You easily express affection and tenderness to those you care about, and creating a happy home life is a priority. True enjoyment is derived from giving. Good will and a generous spirit endear you to others. The sign this conjunction falls in shows the manner in which your generosity unfolds. For instance, if in Taurus, you provide security, comfort, and possessions. If in Gemini, you are helpful with ideas.

As Jupiter expands whatever it touches, problems with this conjunction come from "too much." Extravagance and overindulgence are likely. You can overeat and gain weight easily. Overindulgence may take the form of overspending on yourself or being more generous with others than you can afford to be.

Moon Sextile or Trine Jupiter ☽ ＊ / △ ♃

You are good-natured, cheerful, and have a positive outlook on life and faith in the future. Like those with the conjunction, you express feelings and show affection easily, and creating a happy home life is a priority. Pleasure is derived from giving. You display kindness and generosity. Good will inspires the trust and cooperation of others and helps you attract material benefits. Relationships with women are particularly favorable.

Moon Square or Opposite Jupiter   ☽ □ / ☍ ♃

Difficult aspects between the Moon and Jupiter have many of the same positive qualities as the more favorable ones, but significantly expand tendencies toward overindulgence and extravagance.

Like all other aspects between the Moon and Jupiter, you are optimistic, have a positive attitude toward life, and have faith in the future. You are generous and this generosity makes you well-liked. Problems arise from too much of a good thing. You seek life's pleasures. Being overly optimistic may lead you to expect the best regardless of circumstances. Because you are generous, you expect the world to be generous to you. This may lead to spending money extravagantly and then expecting others to bail you out if you run into problems. It may also lead to overeating and overdrinking—again, too much of a good thing. Learning moderation is a must.

JOYCE SAYS:
Traits to treasure: Your generosity and good will toward people.
To transform: Avoid extravagant spending and overindulgence in food and drink.

MOON AND SATURN

Aspects between the Moon and Saturn heighten conservatism and traditional values. They convey practicality, feelings of emotional responsibility, reserve in expressing feelings, and maturity beyond one's years.

Moon Conjunct Saturn   ☽ ☌ ♄

With this conjunction, it is very likely that you came into this world as a mature human being. You have been serious, hard working, and responsible from an early age. As an adult, you have common sense, face life realistically, and take your duties seriously. Others know they can count on you. The problem is that you may be better at taking care of other people and situations than you are at taking care of your own needs.

Emotionally, life is not easy. Either you did not receive adequate nurturing as a child or, due to family circumstances, a great deal was expected of

you from an early age. This leads to being somewhat shy and overly responsible and self-protective. There is a tendency to fear the worst in situations.
Lack of self-confidence makes you doubt your capabilities until you prove
yourself. Believing that people care for you because of what you do for them
rather than for yourself makes you more likely to do things for people than
to express feelings. You may hide behind work and forego enjoyment. A sense
of being overburdened and feeling as if you get stuck with responsibility can
develop even though the responsibilities may be of your own making.

Being sensitive to rejection makes it difficult to feel loved and accepted
and to show emotional vulnerability. You are cautious with people until
they prove themselves trustworthy. While this seems like good common
sense, holding people at a distance may make you appear cold, even to loved
ones. You tend toward depression, as you feel thwarted easily.

As a child, self-protectiveness helped you survive emotionally, but as
an adult, it may create emotional isolation. Separating the past from the
present is essential with this conjunction.

Moon Sextile or Trine Saturn   ☽ ✳ / △ ♄

You are practical, cautious, and conservative, have common sense, and look at
situations realistically. You take responsibilities seriously and work industriously,
but you are not overwhelmed by it all or easily depressed. Family and friends
rely on you and being needed gives you comfort. Even though the aspect
between the Moon and Saturn is favorable, you are reserved, and expressing
yourself emotionally may be difficult. This makes it easier to do something
for those you care about than it is to show feelings. All this may lead to willingness to take on more responsibility than is reasonable. Recognizing what
you are responsible for and what you are not is a must. Otherwise you end up
feeling taken advantage of, particularly by those close to you.

Moon Square or Opposite Saturn   ☽ □ / ☍ ♄

Like those with the conjunction, it is as if you were born mature. You have
always been serious, hard-working, and responsible. You possess common
sense, take duties seriously, and face life realistically. The problem is that
realistic may equate with pessimistic. Others know they can count on you,
but you may be better at taking care of other people and situations than
you are at honoring your own needs.

Emotionally, life is not easy for you. Either you did not receive adequate nurturing during childhood or, due to family circumstances, much was expected of you from an early age. Perhaps you were criticized for not performing well enough. As an adult, this leads you to expect a great deal from yourself, but also to lack confidence in your capabilities and feel the need to prove yourself. This may lead to taking on too much responsibility, but feeling as if you have no choice. You may believe, consciously or unconsciously, that people care about you for what you do rather than for who you are, and that it is your job to "fix" situations. This makes it difficult to admit to having emotional needs, perhaps even to yourself.

Your sensitivity to rejection makes you extremely cautious with people, even those you are close to, which can lead to feeling lonely and unsupported and possibly depressed. There is a tendency to feel as if others prevent you from expressing feelings without recognizing that your hesitation stems from fears deeper within your psyche. In trying to protect yourself, you can build a wall that keeps others out and leads to emotional isolation. Separating what was needed to insure emotional survival in the past from what is appropriate emotional expression in the present is a must.

JOYCE SAYS:
Traits to treasure: Your reliability, maturity, and common sense.
To transform: Risk expressing your feelings, and avoid taking care of other people and situations better than you take care of yourself.

MOON AND URANUS

Aspects between the Moon and Uranus combine the emotions with the unconventional. They heighten emotional needs for freedom and autonomy and elevate the attraction to what is out of the ordinary.

Moon Conjunct Uranus   ☽ ☌ ♅

This conjunction unites the emotions with the urge for autonomy. You are a free spirit, independent, individualistic, and resourceful. You do not want to be pinned down or hemmed in. Freedom to do what you want when you want is imperative.

Originality and innovation come naturally. You perceive things differently than other people do and have little tolerance for convention or conformity. Craving excitement, you seek change and invention and refuse to be trapped by routine or the expectations of others.

Very likely, you learned to be independent early in life because of a changeable home environment where you could not depend upon those close to you. Now as an adult, stability feels confining. You may be emotionally changeable, impulsive, or unreliable, or you may have an unconscious attraction to people who are. This repeats early family patterns, which can create havoc in relationships.

The need for independence and autonomy and the attraction to unusual people are genuine urges. When they are healthy, you are inventive, have unusual friends, and are a proponent for social change. Yet, carried to the extreme, these needs result in overreacting to even the most reasonable expectations of others. In these instances, it is important to question whether you are truly responding to present situations or reacting to the unconscious belief that since you cannot trust others to be there for you, they have no right to expect you to be there for them.

Moon Sextile or Trine Uranus   ☽ ✶ / △ ♅

Emotional needs and freedom urges blend easily. You are independent and freedom-oriented and want to do things your own way. You come and go as you please, but you do so naturally and have no need to flaunt self-sufficiency. Because of this, you create no havoc around you and relationships do not suffer. You instill a sense of independence in your children without their feeling abandoned.

There is attraction to unique people, ideas, and situations. Being enterprising, you are alert to and seek new avenues of expression. The status quo is boring and uninteresting to you. Good instincts give you the ability to take risks that pay off.

Moon Square or Opposite Uranus   ☽ □ / ☍ ♅

The square and opposition have many of the same characteristics as the conjunction, only more extreme since the emotional urges and the freedom urges conflict with one another. You are independent and want the freedom to do what you want and to come and go as you please. Yet emotional urges pull you in one direction and self-sufficiency urges in another.

You may recognize these pulls within yourself, or you may attract people who play one side or the other. For instance, you may feel trapped when others want to get too close. Or you may believe you want emotional rapport but somehow attract people who need freedom, which creates chaos for you. Either way, emotional turmoil ensues. Very likely, the original source of this turmoil was an emotionally changeable home environment with adults who you could not count on when you were young. You learned to fend for yourself and either consciously still want to do so or unconsciously attract the same type of situations. As an adult, when you are hurt, your line of least resistance is to flaunt your independence and bolt rather than to work out problems. Learning not to overreact and to recognize and deal with situations as they are, rather than responding impulsively, is a necessity.

This is not to imply that your need for freedom and self-sufficiency should not be honored. The solution is finding the right way to honor these needs. It is natural for you to be attracted to unusual people, ideas, or circumstances. Your innovation and willingness to take risks need proper direction.

JOYCE SAYS:

Traits to treasure: Your inventiveness and free spirit.
To transform: Avoid behaving erratically when you feel emotionally boxed in.

MOON AND NEPTUNE

The Moon and Neptune are both sensitive celestial bodies. Their combination heightens intuition, imagination, psychic ability, spirituality, sympathy, and compassion. They also heighten the longing to live in an ideal, beautiful world.

Moon Conjunct Neptune ☽ ♂ ♆

This conjunction conveys imagination and creativity, intuition and psychic sensitivity, sympathy and compassion, and idealism and a romantic heart.

You are creative, imaginative, and sensitive to surroundings. Being in an aesthetically pleasing environment is essential to emotional well-being. You deeply enjoy music, art, or theater and appreciate simple beauties like the scent of flowers or the intricacies of falling snowflakes. Imagination can be creative or illusionary or both. Wanting life to be beautiful, there is a tendency to tune out what is not.

Your nature is romantic, idealistic, and spiritual. You are psychically attuned to what goes on around you, may know things before they happen, and are sensitive to the emotions of people you are with. This may make it difficult for you to distinguish your feelings from those of your companions. If not consciously aware of your sensitivity, you are at the mercy of fluctuating moods. Learning meditation helps you to stay in tune with yourself so that you are able to distinguish between inner moods and outer ones. Metaphysical studies help satisfy spiritual longings.

This conjunction conveys the desire to rescue or be rescued or both. Empathy is so strong that seeing someone in need is like a call for help. This leads to lending a helping hand irrespective of whether help has been requested. You look for the best in people and situations. This attitude is kind, generous, and sympathetic. However, if carried too far, it is overly idealistic and naive. Sympathy for the underdog, combined with an unwillingness to see people's faults, can put you in situations where the people you are trying to help take advantage of you. As a child, you may have had to care for a parent who had trouble facing reality, and as an adult, there is an attraction to people of the same ilk. As a parent, you may forever be trying to rescue your children. Developing discrimination about who to help is a must.

By the same token, you may avoid dealing with unpleasantness in your own life, hoping somehow that if you do not look, the situations will somehow clear up on their own. This leads to periodic crises when problems can no longer be avoided. Dealing with problems when they arise is a must, as is avoiding the use or drugs or alcohol as an escape mechanism.

Moon Sextile or Trine Neptune ☽ ⁎ / △ ♆

You are creative and artistic and have a rich imagination. This may lead to working in the arts or creative fields, or you may purely see and seek beauty in everyday life. You are psychically in tune with what goes on around you, and it is possible that you have impressions of what will happen in the future. Sensitivity may cause mood fluctuations depending upon your environment and your companions. Staying in touch with, and listening to, your inner voice helps you to distinguish between your moods and those of others. This inner voice also provides insight and intuition.

Even though the sextile and trine between the Moon and Neptune are favorable aspects, guarding against being overly idealistic is still a necessity. You long for a heaven-like existence where the world is good and people are kind. This may lead to naïvely trusting others or to avoiding dealing with your own problems, waiting for them to clear up on their own.

Moon Square or Opposite Neptune ☽ □ / ☍ ♆

Difficult aspects between the Moon and Neptune convey the same sensitivities as do the conjunction, trine, and sextile. You are psychically sensitive, compassionate, idealistic, creative, and have a romantic heart.

You possess creative imagination, and your nature is mystical. Talent in art, music, or theater may lead to career pursuits, or the arts may provide healthy escapes. Having everyday beauty in your life is essential. Beauty may take the form of an aesthetically pleasing environment or be experienced in simple pleasures such as looking at a landscape or listening to soft music.

You are so psychically attuned that your moods can fluctuate depending upon your environment and your companions. If unaware of your perceptions, it is difficult to distinguish between inner moods and outer ones. Being extremely intuitive, you may know things before they happen. Yet it is difficult to distinguish between daydreaming, fantasies, and intuitive perceptions. Meditation and metaphysical studies help you with these distinctions.

Like those with the conjunction, there is a desire to rescue or be rescued or both. Being overly idealistic and having empathy and compassion, you look for the best in people and situations. If you are a therapist, this helps you bring out the best in your patients. In the rest of life, this same idealism can be problematic. Seeing only the best in people means tuning out the worst. Seeing someone in need and offering help indiscriminately can lead to being taken advantage of. Very likely, as a child you cared for a parent who had trouble facing reality, and as an adult, you draw in similar people. As a parent, you may be unable to say no to your children, even when saying no is best for them. Learning discrimination is a must.

By the same token, in your own life, you may avoid dealing with problems until they are unavoidable crises. Then you long for someone to rescue you rather than facing situations on your own. Avoidance may come through simple denial of problems, or drugs or alcohol may provide escape mechanisms. Learning to deal with difficulties as they arise is a must, or your life will only remain calm between crises.

JOYCE SAYS:

Traits to treasure: Your compassion, sensitivity, and the willingness to lend a helping hand.

To transform: Be discriminating as to when to help others and when helping is inappropriate.

MOON AND PLUTO

Both the Moon and Pluto have to do with instinctive responses. The Moon represents the subconscious mind and early conditioning, and Pluto represents unconscious urgings and intensifies any planet it touches. Aspects between these celestial bodies intensify emotions and heighten the ability to pierce through surface appearances.

Moon Conjunct Pluto ☽ ☌ ♇

This conjunction unites the emotions and depths of the unconscious. It combines deep emotions with uncanny insights into human nature. You have strong feelings, intense likes and dislikes, and penetrating powers of observation. You notice what goes on around you and instinctively pierce through people, situations, and ideas to get to the heart of any matter.

Moderation is not for you in this life. Love and emotional fulfillment are very important, but also highly charged. You are either in love or not interested and have intense loyalties and deep commitments to whatever you care about. You give a lot and expect a lot in return. Caring so much can make you obsessive. Dramatically, you may feel as if your life will be over if your desires are not satisfied. When it comes to romance, strong sexual connections may be more important than harmony.

Your incredible insights into human nature can be lost when dealing with your own emotions. It is difficult for you to stand back and examine yourself and why you want what you do or even if what you want is good for you. Instead, much time can be spent agonizing over how to achieve your aims. When desires take over, you can make what you want more important than you are. Yet you tend not to talk about your feelings. You know your own vulnerability but are fearful of admitting it, even in significant emotional relationships. Instead, you are more likely try to coerce other people into doing things your way—for everybody's good and so that you will all be happy. This may set off significant resistance in others and create power struggles. Yet you are motivated by an intense desire to improve yourself and the world around you.

This conjunction conveys incredible power that can be very constructive or very destructive. With your astute powers of observation and deep understanding of human nature, you have the capacity to help others as well as yourself. Transformation comes from learning to control your own emotions rather than trying to manipulate everyone and everything else. Oddly enough, doing your best and then letting go of situations helps you achieve your aims far better than trying to control situations does.

Moon Sextile or Trine Pluto ☽ ✶ / △ ♇

Favorable aspects between the Moon and Pluto convey strong feelings and intense likes and dislikes but without the accompanying angst of the conjunction, square, or opposition. Because of this, you are not as driven by strong feelings. Love and emotional fulfillment are important to you. You have strong loyalties and deep commitments to whoever and whatever you care about, you are protective of those you love, and you try to help them live up to their potential. Your emotions are intense, but less so than those with the conjunction, square, or opposition. This gives you a better ability to control your emotions and be sensitive to the feelings of others.

Astute powers of observation help you perceive the truth underlying the motivations of people, the appearance of situations, or the meaning of ideas. Motivated by a desire to transform situations and yourself, you quietly exert courage and perseverance in overcoming obstacles. However, like all those with aspects between the Moon and Pluto, you are still capable of manipulating situations to your own end. You just do it in such a way as to make you more likely to get away with it.

Moon Square or Opposite Pluto ☽ □ / ☍ ♇

Like all aspects between the Moon and Pluto, your feelings are deep; you have strong likes and dislikes and penetrating powers of observations. You notice what goes on around you and instinctively understand people, situations, and ideas. Because of this, you may believe that you are always right, yet fear that, like the seer Cassandra in the *Odyssey*, no one will listen to you.

Love and emotional fulfillment are important but also highly charged, as all-or-nothing best describes you when it comes to whatever you care about. You give your best to everything you commit to and expect a lot in return. Caring so much makes you both obsessive and extremely sensitive. Whatever you want takes on a life-or-death urgency. This can wreak havoc in personal and professional relationships if you allow yourself to be overly sensitive to slights and to feel rejected readily. In romance, jealousy is easily aroused, and every little disagreement may be seen as a threat to the relationship. As a parent, you may overwhelm your children with protectiveness. When emotionally triggered, you may find yourself at the mercy of strong feelings and compelled to act irrationally. Fear of admitting vulnerability makes it difficult for you to be open even with those you are closest to. Instead, you may try to manipulate situations and coerce people into doing what you would like. All of this creates power struggles that get in the way of intimacy. You may end up actually being alone or feeling alone when what you really want are deep emotional connections.

It is important for you to examine why you want what you do, whether you have made appropriate choices, and whether the way you are going about attaining your aims gives you results you want. You will never be completely detached in this life, but the urge to transform makes it necessary for you to cultivate some detachment and to recognize when strong emotions get in the way of better judgment. Learning to express feelings appropriately goes a long way toward achieving emotional aims.

JOYCE SAYS:
Traits to treasure: Your deep feelings for, and strong commitments to, the people you love.
To transform: Avoid getting into emotional power struggles or behaving irrationally based upon emotional compulsions.

Chapter 18

ASPECTS OF MERCURY

Mercury represents the conscious mind and intellect. All aspects to Mercury influence how we think, communicate, and learn, as well as the type of information we pay attention to.

MERCURY AND VENUS

Aspects between Mercury and Venus combine the conscious mind and intellect with love, beauty, and sociability. Since Mercury and Venus are both closer to the Sun than is the earth, the only major aspects possible between them are the conjunction and the sextile.

Mercury Conjunct Venus   ☿ ♂ ♀

The conjunction unites intellect with sociability, love, and beauty. This gives charm, wit, refinement, and good taste. You look for the beauty in life, in surroundings, in art, or in literature. Unless contrary aspects exist, you keep relationships harmonious and avoid conflict by doing and saying the "right things." The sign this conjunction falls in determines what you believe to be the right things. If in a direct sign like Sagittarius, you consider them to be straightforwardness and telling the truth. If in a more diplomatic sign like Libra, you consider them to be harmony and socially appropriateness.

As this conjunction in essence combines the head and heart, it is important romantically to have a mate whom you consider your intellectual equal.

The head and heart functioning as one make it difficult for you to be either completely objective or completely romantic in relationships. The sign the conjunction falls in determines if your head or heart is stronger or if they are equal. In water signs, emotions hold sway. In earth signs, pragmatism wins. In fire signs, inspiration takes hold. In air signs, logic triumphs.

Mercury Sextile Venus   ☿ ✱ ♀

This sextile favorably links logic and sociability. You are charming and gracious, friendly and congenial, refined and easygoing. Being cooperative, you get along with people easily.

You communicate well, and interesting conversations are a must in all relationships. You are able to express likes and dislikes without offending people. Your comfort in talking about relational needs goes a long way toward getting them fulfilled.

JOYCE SAYS:
Traits to treasure: Your charm and sociability.
To transform: Keep the heart and head balanced.

MERCURY AND MARS

Aspects between Mercury and Mars combine how we think and communicate with how we act and go after what we want. Mercury represents decision-making, Mars, energy and assertiveness. The combination of these two planets heightens straightforward honesty and mental courage.

Mercury Conjunct Mars   ☿ ♂ ♂

Abundant mental energy gives you a sharp mind. You learn fast, think independently, and have keen powers of observation. You make decisions quickly and act decisively based on those decisions. You speak honestly and directly in a straightforward manner. The sign in which this conjunction takes place describes the particular manner in which you express yourself.

You have a need for mental stimulation, and you relish intellectual competition. Yet you can be mentally restless and impatient. Particularly if the conjunction is in cardinal or mutable signs, you get bored easily and there is a tendency to jump to conclusions before examining all the information.

Your directness, combined with your rush to get your point across, may make you more combative than you recognize and may make the difference between being verbally assertive and aggressive hard to discern. It is important to consider what you say before you speak, and to let others have their say.

Mercury Sextile or Trine Mars ☿ ✶ / △ ♂

An active and alert mind provides a sharp intellect, good powers of observation, and the ability to learn easily and think independently. Your speech is quick, and you have the courage to speak your mind. Spoken and written communications have the potential to be forceful and dramatic. Very likely, you enjoy a heated discussion and are a good debater. Even though this is a favorable aspect, you should take care to think before you speak and to beware of being overly assertive.

Mercury Square or Opposite Mars ☿ □ / ☍ ♂

Like all aspects between Mercury and Mars, you have a sharp mind, learn quickly, and think independently. You make decisions quickly and act on those decisions. The problem is that decisions may be made too quickly, before you have all the facts. Particularly if these aspects fall in cardinal or mutable signs, impatience can get in the way of gathering all the information necessary to form conclusions.

You speak honestly and directly. You say what you mean and mean what you say. On the positive side, you are truthful. On the negative side, diplomacy may feel like dishonesty, and a sharp tongue and lack of tact can lead to conflict. Anger is easily triggered, and you can perceive conflict where none exists. Having strong convictions, you may feel attacked when people do not agree with you.

To be most effective, it is important to listen to other people and to differentiate between assertiveness needed to get a point across and aggressiveness that leads to conflict.

JOYCE SAYS:
Traits to treasure: Your quick mind and sharp intellect.
To transform: Avoid getting involved in unnecessary conflict.

MERCURY AND JUPITER

Mercury is considered the "lower mind" focusing on day-to-day ideas, Jupiter, the "higher mind" focusing on ethics and belief systems. Combinations between Mercury and Jupiter expand thinking and communicating, making ideas bigger and thinking optimistic. Mercury also rules short-distance travel, and Jupiter, long distance.

Mercury Conjunct Jupiter   ☿ ♂ ♃

This conjunction makes you mentally upbeat, outgoing, and friendly. Intelligent and mentally curious, interests may lie in higher education, philosophy, foreign or domestic travel, or other cultures. Or your curiosity may be more about friends and neighbors. The sign this conjunction falls in describes precisely what you are interested in and how your mind works. However, whatever the sign, ideas spark your interest and learning is lifelong.

Communication skills in writing and speaking are excellent, and you have confidence in these abilities. You think big. Positive thinking helps you to perceive opportunities that others may overlook, and enthusiasm that you display for your ideas convinces others of their merit. This makes you good at sales, whether you are selling a product or championing an ideal.

The Mercury-Jupiter combination tends toward exaggeration and overlooking details. While in general you are honest, it is important that optimism does not cause you to exaggerate possibilities and, though with the best of intentions, to promise more than is possible to deliver.

Mercury Sextile or Trine Jupiter   ☿ ✶ / △ ♃

You enjoy learning, are intelligent, and have good powers of observation. Your mind is curious and expansive, and you go on learning throughout life. Interests may lie at lofty heights, such as in higher education, philosophy, belief systems, foreign travel, or other cultures, or you may purely be more curious than most about friends, neighbors, and local travel. Outgoing and friendly, you put people at ease.

Faith in the future heightens positive thinking and optimism. You see the glass as half full, not half empty. You are good at planning and organizing and excel at expressing ideas in writing or speaking. Being confident in these abilities, imparting information becomes a true joy. These qualities make it easy for you to persuade people to your line of thinking.

Mercury Square or Opposite Jupiter ☿ □ / ☍ ♃

Like all other aspects between Mercury and Jupiter, your mind is curious and expansive. You are innately intelligent and enjoy learning.

You are a big-picture person. You think positively and optimistically and see the best in situations. However, this can cause a lack of discrimination and, perhaps, common sense. You may overlook details or ignore telltale signs that the picture is not as rosy as you would like to believe. You are bright, but you may expect too much for too little and not put in the time and energy necessary to complete studies or projects. Developing discipline is a must. Too many ideas can cause you to be scattered; grandiose plans are not necessarily realistic, and you tend to underestimate how long tasks will take. Being overly self-confident can lead to promising more than is possible to deliver.

JOYCE SAYS:
Traits to treasure: Your positive thinking and the ability to see the big picture.
To transform: Avoid ideas that are too grandiose to ever come to fruition.

MERCURY AND SATURN

Combinations of Mercury and Saturn bring together thinking, communicating, and learning with discipline, work, structure, and possibly inhibitions. They convey an organized and analytical mind that thinks practically.

Mercury Conjunct Saturn ☿ ☌ ♄

This conjunction conveys mental maturity at an early age. Your thinking is serious, slow, and careful. Before drawing conclusions, you methodically gather all the information necessary to make up your mind. This gives you organizational talents and planning abilities, and you excel at putting facts and information together.

Your ideas tend to be traditional and conservative, and you approach new ideas cautiously, wanting to see proof of their workability. In speaking and writing, you communicate clearly and concisely.

Yet it is possible for fear and negative thinking to impede success. While you are intelligent, at an early age (or perhaps still) it is likely that you lacked confidence in your intellectual abilities. Fears about being smart enough can cause you to underestimate your mental prowess. In studies, you may over-learn to make sure that you know enough, or you may completely avoid intellectually challenging situations.

It is your nature to look for what can go wrong. This helps to plan ahead and avoid pitfalls. However, it can also cause you to be overly critical of yourself and others. This can lead to problems with self-esteem and difficulty in getting along with people. The tendency to see the glass as half empty rather than half full can lead to unnecessary worry, negative thinking, and possibly depression. By seeing what is wrong with a situation at the expense of seeing what is right, you may miss opportunities and view life as more difficult than it needs to be. However, because you are rational and pragmatic, it is possible to overcome these inclinations. The important distinction is between realism and pessimism.

Mercury Sextile or Trine Saturn   ☿ ✶ / △ ♄

This planetary combination gives you a serious mind and steady judgment. You have a good memory, are mentally patient, concentrate easily, and are studious. Mental discipline gives you the capacity to excel in learning and in putting together facts and information. You plan methodically and have good organizational and administrative skills. In speaking and writing, you communicate clearly and concisely, although wasting no extra words, somewhat tersely.

Thinking is traditional and conservative, and acceptance of new ideas comes slowly. Before you believe anything, you want to see proof of its workability. This makes you somewhat of a skeptic but not beyond convincing.

Mercury Square or Opposite Saturn   ☿ □ / ☍ ♄

Like all Mercury-Saturn aspects, you possess a serious and disciplined mind. You plan carefully, organize efficiently, and excel at putting together facts and information. Your ideas are traditional and conservative, and you approach new ideas cautiously, wanting to see proof of their workability.

Yet like the conjunction, it is possible for fear and negative thinking to impede success. While you are intelligent, you may lack confidence in your intellectual abilities. Possibly when you were young, shyness got in the way of fitting in at school, or no one in your family listened to you. This caused difficulties in speaking up that generalized into fears about intellectual endeavors.

It takes you time to put your thoughts together. As an adult, you may underestimate your mental abilities. In studies, you may over-learn to make sure you know enough, or you may completely avoid intellectually challenging situations. When you are uncomfortable, you have difficulty expressing ideas, only to later feel that no one listens to you or that your ideas are unappreciated. When comfortable in situations, you can be argumentative when others disagree with you, as disagreements can trigger old wounds. It is important to distinguish the present from the past. You develop confidence by becoming an expert in your field and hence becoming the voice of authority.

This planetary combination conveys critical thinking. You see what can go wrong in situations, which helps you to plan ahead and avoid pitfalls that others would miss. However, critical thinking can become negative and lead to excessive worry. This accentuates self-esteem issues and creates problems in getting along with others. It can also lead to depression. It is important to distinguish between realistic problem-solving and pessimistic fears.

JOYCE SAYS:
Traits to treasure: Your ability to think critically and solve problems.
To transform: Avoid letting pragmatism turn into pessimism.

MERCURY AND URANUS

Aspects between Mercury and Uranus bring together thinking, communicating, and learning with originality, inventiveness, and rebellion. They convey an original, inventive mind.

Mercury Conjunct Uranus ☿ ☌ ♅

Your thinking is independent and individualistic. You quickly grasp new concepts, as your interests lie in cutting-edge ideas rather than traditional ones. You have a brilliant mind, but the unwillingness to learn anything other than what directly interests you may cause difficulties in educational settings.

You easily come up with progressive ideas and are particularly adept in science, technology, computers, or social engineering. In an environment that values originality, you excel and thrive. Problems arise in more traditional environments. Your ideas may be so ahead of their time that others fail to comprehend their merit, and having little patience for those you consider intellectual inferiors, you refuse to attempt convincing them.

In all situations, you speak your mind straightforwardly and directly. This makes you honest and forthright and also gives you a sharp tongue. Because of this, you excel at taking difficult stands and fighting for causes. But when dealing with people, it can be difficult to comprehend that not everyone wants to hear the truth, or your version of it. Your behavior can be arrogant and offensive, and seeing yourself as the instrument of truth, you typically do not care. This can wreak havoc in relationships, where you blame others for not understanding you. A little diplomacy would go a long way in gaining understanding from others and acceptance of your ideas.

Mercury Sextile or Trine Uranus   ☿ ✳ / △ ♅

You are a highly intelligent, individualistic thinker, open to new ideas and unbound by tradition or other people's beliefs. Your interests lie in what is out of the ordinary, and you naturally come up with inventive ideas. You are particularly adept when it comes to science and technology, but also perceive societal trends.

You speak your mind straightforwardly and honestly, but do so in such a manner as to not offend people. In fact, your ability to communicate your ideas and convince people of their merit makes it possible for you to become a trendsetter.

Mercury Square or Opposite Uranus   ☿ □ / ☍ ♅

You think independently and individualistically, and abhor so-called conventional wisdom that touts the status quo. Your interests lie in progressive ideas that are out of the ordinary. Your mind is quick and brilliant, but not always clearly focused. Your unwillingness to study anything that does not interest you and your penchant for jumping from one topic to the next can cause difficulties in traditional educational settings.

From an early age, you have been a rebel mentally, one whose thinking no one could influence. You speak your mind in a straightforward, direct manner, and refuse to censor yourself. This makes you honest and forthright, but also brusque and tactless. You are a free thinker. But you are also opinionated, can refuse to listen to another's point of view when it contradicts your own, and can flaunt your dislike of authority.

In environments where you can be straightforward and direct, you thrive. You easily come up with inventive ideas, particularly in science or technology, but also in societal trends. Like those with the conjunction, you excel at taking difficult stands and fighting for causes. You are ahead of your time and you have little tolerance for those you consider intellectual inferiors. In situations where your ideas are not understood, you are likely to behave arrogantly and openly take pleasure in defying superiors. Your need for freedom of expression can get in the way of all relationships. Learning a bit of empathy as well as diplomacy would go a long way toward helping you get along with others and gain acceptance of your ideas.

JOYCE SAYS:
Traits to treasure: The original and inventive way your mind works.
To transform: Avoid intellectual arrogance or telling off those in authority.

MERCURY AND NEPTUNE

Aspects between Mercury and Neptune combine the conscious mind with the unconscious or superconscious mind, thinking and reasoning with intuition or psychic ability, and logic with beauty.

Mercury Conjunct Neptune   ☿ ♂ ♆

The conscious and superconscious minds work together. You are creative, imaginative, and intuitive, perhaps psychic. These qualities can make you a dreamer or a visionary. Very likely, you are drawn to mysticism, spirituality, or psychic phenomena, seek "higher consciousness," and look for beauty.

A subliminal awareness of your environment exists. This gives you the ability to sense things before they happen or to receive unspoken messages from people around you. If not consciously aware of these abilities, there can be difficulty distinguishing between what actually goes on and what you intuit. If aware, you have good instincts in dealing with people, knowing just what to say to bring them over to your point of view.

You excel at the use of imagination. This may take the form of creating images in your mind's eye of what you want to accomplish and using those images to propel you forward. It may be talent in writing poetry, fiction, fantasy, romance novels, or music, in photography, drawing, or painting, or in acting.

The positive side of imagination is creativity. The negative side is escapism or deception. It is possible for you to put off dealing with problems, hoping that if you close your eyes long enough they will go away. And while you excel at selling other people on your ideas, being naïve and trusting, you are also easily sold. Developing discrimination is a must.

Mercury Sextile or Trine Neptune   ☿ ✱ / △ ♆

The conscious and superconscious minds support one another. Reasoning and intuition work together. You are creative, imaginative, and intuitive, maybe psychic. There is an appreciation of beauty, and you may seek higher consciousness through mysticism, spirituality, or psychic phenomena.

A vivid imagination conveys talent in writing poetry, fiction, or music, in photography, drawing, or painting, or in acting. Imagination can also help with goal achievement. You have the ability to create images of what you want in your mind's eye and to use those images to propel you forward.

Very likely, you are subliminally attuned to your environment and receive unspoken messages from people, and possibly sense things before they happen. This gives you good instincts in dealing with people. No matter what your profession, you excel at selling others on your ideas.

Mercury Square or Opposite Neptune   ☿ □ / ☍ ♆

All aspects between Mercury and Neptune bring the conscious mind and logic together with the superconscious, intuition, or psychic ability. The square or opposition make harnessing this energy more difficult. You are creative, imaginative, and intuitive, and likely psychic.

Like all those with aspects between Mercury and Neptune, your vivid imagination gives you ability in writing poetry, fiction, romance novels, or music, in taking beautiful photographs, or in acting convincingly. In fact, harsh aspects may make you even more creative.

Mysticism, spirituality, and psychic phenomena are of interest to you, and personal experience in these domains is likely. You feel what goes on around you, receive unspoken messages from people, and sense things before they happen. Particularly in youth, it is difficult to distinguish between what people actually say and do and what you intuit. Your environment strongly affects you, so it is important to work to consciously identify the energies that come from your environment and those that stem from within.

To some degree it may be easier to live in your imagination than in the real world. You tend toward absentmindedness or being mentally disorganized and can have difficulty communicating in practical rather than creative arenas. It is easy to be naïve and overly trusting. Wanting the world to be nicer than it is can lead to avoiding problems until they become crises that can no longer be avoided. Developing discrimination is a must, and particular care is needed in signing documents.

JOYCE SAYS:
Traits to treasure: Your creative imagination and psychic abilities.
To transform: Make sure your perceptions are not overly idealistic.

MERCURY AND PLUTO

Aspects between Mercury and Pluto combine thinking, communicating, and learning with inner drive, compulsion, the power of will, and the urge to transform or destroy. Mercury represents the conscious mind, and Pluto, unconscious urges.

Mercury Conjunct Pluto ☿ ☌ ♇

Your mind is delving, penetrating, and researching. You have the ability to ferret out secrets, see through people, and get to the bottom of situations, somehow comprehending fundamental motivations and underlying meanings. Your instinctive judgments are accurate, but not particularly charitable.

Delving in mental pursuits, when you study a topic, you want to know all about it. You question everything, wanting to uncover the truth, even when the truth is uncomfortable. Because of this, you excel in fields involving research, investigation, analysis, psychology, and possibly the occult. Being somewhat obsessive leads to deeper, more insightful conclusions than others reach. However, once you form opinions, you can become obstinate and refuse to listen to contrary evidence.

You are secretive by nature and keep many thoughts to yourself. In communicating with people, it is your nature to say exactly what you think or to remain silent. There is little patience for those whom you deem intellectual inferiors. When arguing, you relish striking at an opponent's weak points, and the strike may get personal. This can result in power struggles or unnecessary conflict, or others may fear saying anything at all. Yet you are capable of subtlety. Saying what it takes to manipulate situations rather than browbeating people makes you far more persuasive in bringing them over to your side.

Mercury Sextile or Trine Pluto ☿ ⚹ / △ ♇

Your mind is analytical, delving, probing, and researching. Penetrating insights give you the ability to recognize environmental undercurrents, fundamental motivations of people, and underlying meanings of situations.

You have mental discipline and good comprehension. In studying a topic, the ability to quickly hone in on its core meaning exists. This helps you in fields involving research, investigation, psychology, and possibly the occult.

You are a persuasive communicator and can easily manipulate situations. The ability to recognize other people's motivations helps you to know exactly what to say to bring them over to your point of view.

Mercury Square or Opposite Pluto ☿ □ / ☍ ♇

You have such a delving, penetrating mind that your thoughts border on being obsessive. In the desire to know and understand, you are likely to read every book on a topic that interests you. Your search is to discover the truth, the underlying meaning, or the core, and you have the capacity to reach insightful conclusions. Because of this, you excel in fields involving research, investigation, analysis, psychology, the occult, and possibly spying.

However, once you make up your mind, being so sure that you are right, you can obstinately stick to conclusions despite evidence to the contrary.

In communicating with people, you say exactly what you think or nothing at all. It is possible to take people disagreeing with you as a personal affront. And while you might protest to the contrary, a part of you relishes intellectual combat. In arguments, it is all too easy to go for the jugular, particularly if you are hurt or lack respect for your opponent. This can create power struggles in which others end up blocking your aims as a way of getting even. In significant relationships, rifts become difficult to heal. You are far more persuasive when you tone down your communications and allow others to have their say.

JOYCE SAYS:

Traits to treasure: Your penetrating mind that sees through people and situations.

To transform: Tone down the way you talk to people to avoid power struggles.

Chapter 19

ASPECTS OF VENUS

Venus represents the principles of attraction and harmony. It is the planet of relationships, love, affection, and sociability. All aspects to Venus affect the ability to get along with others.

VENUS AND MARS

Venus is the planet of relationships, socialization, and femininity; Mars of individuality, assertion, and masculinity. Both represent sex, Venus as the power of attraction, and Mars as the pursuer. All aspects between them affect the balance between getting along with others and being true to oneself as well as sexual chemistry.

Venus Conjunct Mars ♀ ☌ ♂

This aspect conveys sex appeal, charm, and passion. You love life and want to make the most of it. You easily attract the opposite sex, and emotional and sexual involvements are intense. You may combine love and sex, love and lust, or sex and lust. The sign these planets fall in more specifically describe your love life and desires and determine whether Venus or Mars predominates.

You give a lot to those you care about and expect a lot in return. You need both freedom and closeness. If relationships get too close, you can feel smothered. If they get distant, you feel not cared for. A bit of conflict keeps things interesting as you can argue and make up, thereby maintaining the balance between the closeness and distance. This, however, may lead to stormy romances and difficult familial relationships, particularly if Venus and Mars fall in one of the feistier signs. You do best with a sexy, attractive mate.

Venus Sextile or Trine Mars   ♀ ✳ / △ ♂

You have sex appeal and magnetism and easily attract and get along with members of the opposite sex. You are affectionate, congenial, and faithful, yet express yourself dramatically. You get along equally well with men and women. Unless there are contrary indications, your love life is harmonious, and you derive great pleasure from sexual and emotional relationships. As Venus and Mars balance one another, you are able to balance sociability and grace with being honest and true to yourself.

Venus Square or Opposite Mars   ♀ □ / ♂ ♂

You are sexy, magnetic, and amorous. Emotional and sexual involvements are intense, but not necessarily easy. Romantic choices are made impulsively, and it is difficult to discern between sexual chemistry and love.

As Venus represents the urge to merge, and Mars the urge to go it alone, you have an internal conflict between closeness and autonomy. When relationships get close, you want more distance. When they are distant, you want more closeness. Your feelings are more easily hurt than is obvious, and you are quick to anger toward loved ones. This can lead to love-hate relationships. Conflict keeps liaisons exciting, and either you or your partner may be jealous or possessive. While you are personally sensitive, you are not always as sensitive to others. Balancing your needs with those of a significant other is a must.

JOYCE SAYS:
Traits to treasure: Your sex appeal and magnetism.
To transform: Deal with freedom-closeness issues openly rather than through conflict.

VENUS AND JUPITER

Venus is the planet of love and sociability, Jupiter, the planet of opportunity and expansion. The ancients called Venus "the lesser benefic" and Jupiter "the greater benefic." Combinations of these two planets represent luck and abundance, as well as love of luxury and comfort.

Venus Conjunct Jupiter   ♀ ☌ ♃

Your charming, warm, cheerful nature easily attracts people. You think positively, are outgoing and friendly, and generally popular. The conjunction of Venus and Jupiter conveys good luck with people and money. You are generous with others, and they are generous with you. Social and romantic opportunities are abundant, and you attract generous and wealthy associates and romantic partners, as well as good fortune in your own finances. Luck in making investments or in games of chance is likely.

You enjoy a good time, and others have a good time in your company. However, the potential for indulgence and extravagance exists. You can easily eat too much, or drink too much, or spend beyond your means on yourself or others. Developing discipline is important so as not to throw away your good fortune.

Venus Sextile or Trine Jupiter   ♀ ⚹ / △ ♃

You have good luck in attracting people and wealth. Social and romantic opportunities are numerous, and you attract generous and wealthy associates and romantic partners. Good fortune in your own finances may come through marriage or partnership or luck with investments or games of chance.

Personally, you are generous, optimistic, outgoing, and fun to be around. You like people and enjoy a good time, and others enjoy themselves in your company. In essence, the sextile or trine between Venus and Jupiter makes life easy and enjoyable (unless there are other planetary combinations to the contrary). This enhances the possibility of indulgence and extravagance and makes it easy for you to become lazy, as enough good comes your way without effort. Yet, with a little effort you can parlay your advantages into more good fortune.

Venus Square or Opposite Jupiter   ♀ □ / ⚹ ♃

Even difficult aspects between Venus and Jupiter bring luck, and you can attract people and wealth. You enjoy a good time, and social and romantic opportunities are numerous. Personally, you are generous, optimistic, and fun to be around.

However, extravagance in spending and overindulgence in food or drink are likely, and while lucky, you expect to be luckier than you turn out to be. No matter how good things are, you may expect them to be better. Believing that you should have everything you want can cause you to live beyond your means and then expect others to bail you out when the going gets tough. Being optimistic can cause you to promise more than you deliver. And while you attract people easily, you may be a better friend in good times than you are in bad times. Developing responsibility is a must.

JOYCE SAYS:
Traits to treasure: Your cheerfulness, generosity, and friendly nature.
To transform: Avoid spending more than you can afford or overindulging in food or drink.

VENUS AND SATURN

Venus is the planet of love and sociability, Saturn, of discipline and responsibility or barriers and restrictions. All aspects between Venus and Saturn combine love and duty. Relationships are taken seriously.

Venus Conjunct Saturn   ♀ ♂ ♄

This conjunction conveys seriousness toward associations. It unites relationships with responsibility. You are reliable and trustworthy in romance, friendship, and business. You are cautious and reserved as well. As stability and security are important relational components, it takes time for you to get to know and trust people. Very likely, you were mature at an early age, which may have made it easier to get along with older people than those your own age when young.

One danger with this conjunction is fear of rejection, which makes it possible to perceive rejection where none exists. In unfamiliar social settings, easily feeling excluded may lead you to remove yourself, thereby creating the separation that you fear. In ongoing relationships, fear that significant others do not love you or appreciate you enough may exist. To compensate, since love and duty go together, you may do everything you can for romantic partners or loved ones, even at the expense of your own needs. Believing that you are loved for what you do rather than who you are may make you want to become indispensable. You can avoid discussing relational problems due to the fear that merely bringing them up will more likely to lead to being abandoned than a mutually agreeable solution.

It is important to recognize the difference between your fears and actual situations. It takes courage to break through barriers and deal honestly with fears surrounding love and acceptance. If you overemphasize responsibility, you end up feeling overburdened and resentful. Eventually, you start calculating who did what for whom. If you feel safe, or no longer care, you become unwilling to do one iota more than your share. Or you may behave coldly as a way of getting even. If discussing relational differences is avoided out of fear of abandonment, resolving them becomes impossible, and behaving coldly may actually cause the abandonment you seek to avoid. Self-protectiveness can keep love out rather than protect you from being hurt.

Venus Sextile or Trine Saturn   ♀ ✳ / △ ♄

You are cautious and reserved in romance and social settings. It takes time to get to know people and to make commitments. Relationships are taken seriously, and you are loyal, steadfast, and reliable in friendship, romance, and business. You go out of your way to behave responsibly, but are better at balancing duties to others with your own well-being than are those with the conjunction, square, or opposition. A select few close friends are preferred to having lots of people around. In all likelihood, you were mature at an early age, and get along well with older people, and it is possible to benefit through partnership with older people.

Venus Square or Opposite Saturn   ♀ □ / ☍ ♄

Relationships are coupled with responsibility. You are reliable and trustworthy in all associations, take relational responsibilities seriously, and are cautious, reserved, and possibly shy. It takes time for you to get to know and trust people. Very likely, you were mature at an early age, making it difficult to fit in with your peers and easier for you to get along with older people.

Others lean on you because of your reliability. You are likely to have fears about rejection and lack of acceptance and to have difficulty in expressing true feelings. Because of this, you can perceive rejection where none exists, and isolate yourself so as to avoid disappointment. There is fear, conscious or unconscious, of not being loved or appreciated either at all or enough. This makes you overly sensitive to perceived slights and to feeling left out. To compensate, you may make yourself indispensable to loved ones, even at the expense of your own needs. While this may seem like good character, sacrificing personal happiness for duty can leave you feeling overburdened and resentful.

Resolving relational problems is difficult, particularly when they involve your doing too much, as it is hard for you to believe that talking about situations actually makes them better. You find it difficult to trust that people love or appreciate you for yourself rather than what you do for them, so you are afraid of bringing up problems. Ultimately, this may cause you to either withdraw or become cold, particularly when feeling unappreciated. Very likely, you learned to be self-protective in your formative years when you had no control over relationships. As an adult, it is important to recognize the difference between your fears and actual situations. Self-protectiveness can keep others at bay rather than protect you from being hurt. Courage is needed to break through your fears surrounding love and acceptance.

JOYCE SAYS:
Traits to treasure: The way you take care of people you love.
To transform: Avoid letting fear of being rejected get in the way of intimacy.

VENUS AND URANUS

Venus is the planet of love and sociability, Uranus, of freedom, independence, excitement, and revolution. Autonomy and individuality become important relational components when Venus and Uranus aspect one another.

Venus Conjunct Uranus   ♀ ♂ ♅

This conjunction conveys charm and magnetism. You are friendly, outgoing, and interesting. There is a love of social activity. On a casual level, you easily get along with a wide variety of people, but are most attracted to those who are out of the ordinary.

When it comes to love, you seek thrills and excitement. You are attractive to the opposite sex, fall in love quickly, and perhaps fall out of love just as quickly. Stable, routine relationships are boring to you. You do not want a relationship to restrict you. When in love, you want to come and go as you please, and you balk at expectations. If a romance becomes dull or becomes demanding, you can bail out quickly.

You are direct and honest and do not purposely hurt other people. Yet, being self-willed, your unthinking behavior can have just that effect. Your line of least resistance is to be so involved with your own wants that you overlook the needs of others, or blame them for having needs at all. A lasting relationship requires some tempering of your independence, but it also requires finding a mate who is also independent and individualistic and understands your need for autonomy as well as companionship.

Venus Sextile or Trine Uranus   ♀ ✶ / △ ♅

You have a zest for life, are magnetic and fun-loving, and possess charm and sex appeal. This makes it easy to attract people in friendship and in romance. You enjoy the company of a wide variety of people and are at home in varied social settings—in fact, the more varied, the better. You are most attracted to people who are unusual or out of the ordinary in some way. You balance autonomy and self-sufficiency with understanding of the needs of others. Love and sociability, and freedom and independence go hand-in-hand. You give loved ones the freedom they need, and you receive it in return.

Venus Square or Opposite Uranus   ♀ □ / ☍ ♅

You are attractive, magnetic, and charming, particularly to the opposite sex. Friendly and outgoing, you get along easily with a wide variety of people as long as the relationships remain casual.

In all relationships, you are most attracted to people who are out of the ordinary. When it comes to love, you desire exhilarating experiences. You seek thrills, adventure, and excitement, typically at the expense of stability. Love at first sight is likely, although it may be gone by second glance. You can change your mind for no apparent reason. And you can believe that as long as you are honest with your lover you should be able to do whatever you want. You can see even the most reasonable requests as demands and balk at authority.

If you are not consciously aware of your needs for freedom and independence, you may believe that you want stability but somehow attract lovers who want autonomy. It may be you who bails out when another person seems needy, or you may attract lovers who run when you want commitment. It is important to be truthful with yourself about your needs. Since lasting relationships for you require more freedom than for most, finding a mate who understands this is primary, as is learning to balance your needs with those of others.

JOYCE SAYS:

Traits to treasure: Your magnetic charm and honesty.
To transform: Avoid balking at even the most reasonable relational requests.

VENUS AND NEPTUNE

Venus is the planet of love and sociability; Neptune, of spirituality, compassion, imagination, and illusions. Aspects between them heighten creative imagination and romantic ideals and convey a caring, empathetic, compassionate nature.

Venus Conjunct Neptune ♀ ♂ ♆

You are compassionate, idealistic, and creative and possess gentleness and grace. You appreciate the arts, and long for beauty in life. A vivid imagination makes it likely that you have talents in art, music, theater, or photography, as well as in decorating or design.

You have an idealistic attitude toward life and seek spiritual understanding. Idealism leads you to look for what is good in people, and strong sympathies make you desirous of aiding those you come in contact with. Intuition helps you see people's potential, and if you are in a helping profession, you can help them to reach it. In romantic matters, these traits can be problematic.

A romantic by nature, you are most attracted to creative, artistic, or spiritual people, or those in need. You long for the ideal romance; when it comes to love, you either put your lover on a pedestal and ignore all faults and flaws, or stay by yourself because no one meets your standards. If your lover is on a pedestal, you do everything you can to please him or her. However, because you feel loved when needed, there is a tendency to attract needy people who for some reason need rescuing or have difficulties facing the realities of day-to-day life or have drug or alcohol problems. Disappointments occur when you discover your lover is less than perfect. The opposite scenario may also exist, where you are the one who wants to be rescued, again by the ideal lover. If you are disappointed often enough, you can become demanding in relationships or choose to be alone.

It is important to recognize that all human beings have faults and flaws as well as strong points. Another may deceive you, but it is also possible for you to deceive yourself. True acceptance means being willing to see a total person. Longing for the ideal relationship may be a longing for a spiritual connection that is best fulfilled through meditation, contemplation, or spiritual pursuits.

Venus Sextile or Trine Neptune   ♀ ✶ / △ ♆

You are compassionate, idealistic, and creative. You have a romantic soul and love of beauty, and possibly talents in art, music, theater, photography, decorating, or design.

There is an idealistic attitude toward life and a seeking of spiritual understanding. You look for the good in people and enjoy helping others, particularly those less fortunate. Intuition helps you to see other people's potential and to encourage them to achieve it.

Your gentleness of spirit and grace attract members of the opposite sex. Romantically, you are an idealist and long for the perfect connection. Even though the sextile and trine are favorable aspects, the potential to overidealize loved ones, ignore their flaws, or attract needy mates exists. Recognizing the difference between a person's potential and what he or she is really like is essential for lasting romance.

Venus Square or Opposite Neptune ♀ □ / ♂ ♆

Like those with all other aspects between Venus and Neptune, you are compassionate, idealistic, and creative, appreciate the arts, and long for beauty in life. A vivid imagination and creative eye make talent in the arts possible, particularly music, art, theater, photography, or decorating and design.

You are idealistic and have strong sympathies, particularly for the underdog. While you are kind and compassionate, you are not a good judge of character. Preferring to see only what is good in people leads you to overlook the faults and flaws of others. While this is true in all relationships, it is particularly true in romance, where you may prefer ideals or fantasies to dealing with real people.

The people you are attracted to are creative, artistic, spiritual, and those with escapist tendencies. Feeling loved when you are needed leads to attracting needy people and perhaps bestowing devotion unwisely. Believing that you must help another if you can makes it difficult to say no to others and can set up situations in which you are taken advantage of. Extreme disappointment sets in when you recognize the discrepancy between your ideals and actual situations. At this point, you may double your rescue efforts or you may withdraw. If disappointed often enough, you may choose to be alone rather than risk further disappointment. Retreating into drugs and alcohol is also possible to avoid facing disappointment. Or you may fluctuate between being the rescuer and the one who seeks to be rescued.

It is important to recognize that all human beings, including you, have faults and flaws as well as strong points. It is not possible to be all things to another or have another be all things to you. Recognizing someone's weak points early goes a long way toward true acceptance of the entire person. The longing you have for the ideal relationship may be a longing for a God or some spiritual connection that is best fulfilled through meditation, contemplation, or spiritual studies.

JOYCE SAYS:
Traits to treasure: Your loving concern for those you come into contact with.
To transform: Recognize that no one lives up to a Prince or Princess Charming image.

VENUS AND PLUTO

Venus represents love, sociability, and self worth in relationships; Pluto, inner drive or compulsion, the power of will, and the urges to transform or destroy. Aspects between them heighten emotional depth and intensity and the destructive or transformational power of love.

Venus Conjunct Pluto   ♀ ♂ ♇

You possess deep feelings, passion, and intensity. A natural psychologist, when not emotionally involved, you are an observant judge of character who can instinctively pierce through people's facades with stunning accuracy. In love or in friendship, you have strong likes and dislikes, are extremely loyal, and prefer spending time with a few close intimates to being surrounded by many acquaintances.

You are magnetically attractive to the opposite sex, but may not notice. For you, love is based on the mysterious chemistry of attraction rather than logical or even romantic reasons for getting to know someone. The chemistry is either there or it is not. You are either in love or not interested. Sexual passions run high, and there is longing for relational depth and intensity, and a mate who you give everything to and get everything from. Love can become like an addiction, with passions overruling all reason. You can be possessive and so can your lover. Power struggles are likely, as each of you, perhaps unconsciously, tries to enforce your will so as to get what you want from one another.

Moderation and detachment in romance are not completely possible for you in this lifetime, but they are important traits to cultivate. Your perceptions of people are so accurate when you are not romantically involved that you find it hard to believe that you can ever make a mistake. This causes you to push to get what you want from situations, rather than reevaluate them. Recognizing and dealing with your inner compulsions is the only way to find the transforming power of love that you seek.

Venus Sextile or Trine Pluto   ♀ ✳ / △ ♇

Love and sociability combine with depth perception, passion, and intensity. You seek deep meaningful relationships, preferring few close associations to numerous casual ones. You are typically a good judge of character, as an instinctive understanding of people helps you pierce through facades and recognize underlying motivations.

Your emotional nature is intense; your sex drive, high. You easily attract members of the opposite sex, but are not flirtatious. When it comes to romance, you seek a deep, committed relationship. You can be jealous and possessive, but are not as fanatical as those with the conjunction, square, or opposition. You are more likely to behave subtly, and perhaps manipulatively, in going after what you want than you are to get into overt power struggles. Yet while you can be demanding, you have the capacity to express your feelings in such a way as to allow others to gratify them. Love has a transformational power.

Venus Square or Opposite Pluto   ♀ □ / ♂ ♇

This planetary combination conveys passion, intensity, and depth perception. Moderation is not for you in relationships. You have intense likes and dislikes about all people; and when not emotionally involved, you have the ability to pierce through facades and see the true person. Your judgments are usually accurate, although not charitable.

The opposite sex finds you magnetically attractive, but you pay little attention unless the chemistry is right. In affairs of the heart, you are in love or not interested. Emotionally, you can be fanatical, as only deep, intense encounters are satisfying. You may not care whether or not you are happy romantically, because when you feel strongly, you are sure this is "the one." Strong sexual chemistry is typically the deciding factor, and lust may be mistaken for love. Yet, despite this, you are strong-willed and likely to choose a strong-willed partner. This leads to power struggles and emotional highs and lows. Every disagreement may feel like a threat to your survival.

You are so sure you have made the right romantic choice that it is difficult to reevaluate situations. Love can become an addiction. In fact, you would rather feel bad than feel nothing. Yet at some point, trying to coerce your paramour into doing what you want (because you are sure it is best for both of you) becomes exhausting. You may give up and be alone, or you may unconsciously push your partner away in order to get a rest. While you seek love to be transforming, what most needs transforming is the power of your unconscious urges.

JOYCE SAYS:
Traits to treasure: Your deep feelings and intense loyalties.
To transform: Avoid letting love turn into an addiction.

Chapter 20

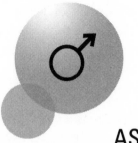

ASPECTS OF MARS

Mars represents the propensity for action. It is the planet of drive, initiative, and courage, as well as the planet of anger, temper, and sex. All aspects to Mars affect how energy is expended.

MARS AND JUPITER

Mars is the planet of action, Jupiter of expansion and opportunity. Aspects between them reflect the propensity for "lucky" actions and opportunities that come through assertion.

Mars Conjunct Jupiter ♂ ♂ ♃

The propensity for action unites with opportunity. This is a lucky planetary combination giving you an abundance of energy, optimism, enthusiasm, and self-confidence. You know how to enjoy life and are likely to be open and generous. Charm draws people to you.

Going after what you want comes naturally. You are self-confident and fully expect situations to turn out well. They usually do because of your good instincts as to when to take action. You courageously stand up for your beliefs but should watch the tendency to be overzealous in doing so.

You probably have athletic ability, along with competitive drive. A quest for travel, adventure, and excitement may also exist, with a curiosity for what is around the next corner. The sign this conjunction falls in more fully describes what you consider to be adventure and what type of goals you are likely to pursue.

Mars Sextile or Trine Jupiter ♂ ✳ / △ ♃

You have abundant energy, enthusiasm, optimism, and self-confidence. Good instincts as to when to take action bring you luck, so that you are generally successful in your pursuits. The willingness to translate your beliefs into practice and to stand up for what you believe in gives you leadership abilities. You are competitive, but still get along well with people. And easily accomplishing your aims fosters openness and generosity in helping others.

Athletic ability is likely, and a quest for travel and excitement may exist. You do not want to miss life's adventures.

Mars Square or Opposite Jupiter ♂ □ / ☍ ♃

This planetary combination provides plenty of energy, optimism, and enthusiasm. You have a restless temperament and are drawn to travel, excitement, and adventure. This gives you somewhat of a roaming quality. There is an expectation of the good life, an enjoyment of the best of everything, and perhaps a roguish charm.

You self-confidently expect success in your endeavors but may expect it to come too easily. Because of this, you do not necessarily put in the effort that it takes to make success happen. If these planets are in cardinal or mutable signs, finishing what you start can be difficult. You can tend to be extravagant and promise more than you deliver (with the best of intentions). Cultivating discipline and setting tangible goals that are achievable would allow you to make the most of your talents.

JOYCE SAYS:
Traits to treasure: Your abundant energy, enthusiasm, and openness to life. To transform: Put in the effort it takes to achieve results.

MARS AND SATURN

Mars represents drive, action, anger, and courage; Saturn, discipline, rules, limits, barriers, and fears. Aspects between Mars and Saturn combine action with either discipline or barriers, produce a Spartan attitude toward life, and provide the capacity for purposeful behavior and the ambition to be in authority.

Mars Conjunct Saturn   ♂ ♂ ♄

This combination gives you good organizational ability and the propensity for sound action. However, as Mars and Saturn are completely opposite energies, the conjunction can manifest in opposing ways. If Saturn harnesses Mars' energy, you are hard-working, ambitious, and disciplined. If Saturn inhibits Mars' energy, inertia takes over and the fear of failure makes it difficult for you to act at all. If Saturn alternatively harnesses and inhibits Mars, you go back and forth between being disciplined and inert. Whatever the case, your life is full of responsibilities and challenges that make hard work a necessity. The desire for authority provides motivation for accomplishment, and when you act, you do so with resourcefulness and endurance.

The expression of anger is a potential problem. You may be disciplined in its expression. However, particularly if you were severely disciplined when young, you may hold in anger when you should let it out, or you may blow up inappropriately after anger has turned into smoldering resentment. Recognizing the difference between anger and resentment is essential. Self-discipline gives you the capacity to strategically express anger if you can avoid becoming self-righteous.

The sign this conjunction falls in gives more specific information as to how you are likely to handle this energy. Since Saturn is the outer planet, it dominates Mars. However, if the conjunction falls in an aggressive sign such as Aries, assertive action is more likely than if it falls in a more laid-back sign such as Pisces.

Mars Sextile or Trine Saturn   ♂ ✶ / △ ♄

Favorable aspects between Mars and Saturn allow you to harness and direct your energy. This gives the capacity for serious, purposeful action. You are naturally organized and disciplined, set appropriate priorities, and go about achieving them in an efficient manner. Actions are cautious and well thought out. Assertion is balanced with practicality, and you excel at follow-through and long-term planning. Hard work poses no threat, and responsibilities no burden.

Mars Square or Opposite Saturn   ♂ □ / ☍ ♄

You are ambitious, desirous of authority, and have the capacity for hard work. Yet personal drive and responsibility issues conflict with one another.

This may manifest as trouble with authority figures, either outwardly or inwardly. If outwardly, you have direct conflict with people in authority. If inwardly, fear may cause you to give in to situations inappropriately and to build up resentment. You may also bounce back and forth between the two depending upon how safe you feel in situations. The same issues arise any time it is appropriate to standup for yourself.

You may have a problem with appropriate timing, as you may wait when you should act and then act when you should wait. This is partially caused by fears of inadequacy about your ability to meet standards, live up to responsibilities, or be successful. It is your nature to see obstacles. You may handle this either by working diligently to overcome obstacles and achieve success, or by giving up before you get started in order to avoid failure. Or, you may bounce back and forth between the two.

It is important to realistically assess responsibilities. One way that you make life harder than it needs to be is by assuming responsibilities that are not yours and then feeling put-upon by them.

JOYCE SAYS:

Traits to treasure: Your discipline, responsibility, and capacity for hard work. To transform: Avoid bogging yourself down with too much responsibility or letting fear of failure inhibit your capacity for success.

MARS AND URANUS

Mars represents drive, action, anger, and courage; Uranus represents freedom, independence, originality, change, and revolution. The combination of Mars and Uranus puts two feisty planets together. Individuality, autonomy, self-sufficiency, and independence are highlighted, and an attraction to unique or unusual circumstances is likely.

Mars Conjunct Uranus   ♂ ☌ ♅

This conjunction conveys ups and downs in life, many of your own making. You are independent and individualistic and live life by your own set of rules. You brook no interference from others. Having a unique perspective, you are frequently ahead of your times or see opportunities that others miss. You are attracted to circumstances that are out of the ordinary, possibly dangerous. In ordinary circumstances, you enjoy testing the limits and take pleasure in being disruptive. The needs for excitement and to challenge the status quo are driving forces.

You exhibit courage in standing up for your beliefs, but willfulness and bullheadedness are also possible. If this conjunction falls in cardinal or mutable signs, you are quick to lose your temper, particularly if you believe someone is trying to restrict your freedom. If in fixed signs, you lose your temper less quickly and have more perseverance, but you may make sudden changes.

This is an accident-prone aspect and conveys tremendous nervous energy. Sitting still is not one of your strong points. You excel in dangerous situations (provided you are not too reckless) or in situations where it is possible to achieve results on your own. Situations are more difficult when the cooperation of other people is necessary. It is important to learn to think before you act if you want results as well as action.

Mars Sextile or Trine Uranus   ♂ ⚹ / △ ♅

You are independent, individualistic, and go your own way but have no need to flaunt these characteristics. You naturally do your own thing, seeing possibilities that others would miss. The needs for excitement and change are satisfied by involvement in original, inventive endeavors. Abundant energy, creative drive, enthusiasm, and resourcefulness combine to give a can-do attitude toward life. You possess courage and will fight when necessary, but do not continually look to disrupt circumstances. You are somewhat ahead of your times, but typically have the capacity to enroll others in your ideals. If Mars is in a fixed sign, you finish what you start. If Mars is in a mutable or cardinal sign, you may be more interested the idea of a venture or beginning it than you are in seeing it through.

Mars Square or Opposite Uranus   ♂ □ / ☍ ♅

The square or opposition, like the conjunction, brings ups and downs in life, many of your own making. You are independent, individualistic, and self-willed, living by your own set of rules and brooking no interference from others. You have a unique perspective and are capable of seeing opportunities that others miss. However, the need for excitement can cause you to make snap judgments and behave recklessly, particularly if Mars and Uranus are in cardinal or mutable signs. The craving for excitement exists if these planets are in fixed signs, but your behavior is not as impulsive. You have the courage of your convictions and stand up for your beliefs, but are also willful and headstrong. Independence is flaunted, and overreaction to anything that seems to stand in its way is precipitous. This can cause conflict when none is needed. You may cause conflict yourself or you may attract others that cause it. Either way, conflict provides a break in routine and adds excitement and adventure, however unhealthy that may be.

You have tremendous nervous energy and a tendency to be accident prone, and since you lose your temper easily, the possibility of violence exists. It is important to learn to think before you act. You are original and inventive and will always need excitement and adventure. However, it is your Achilles heel to dislike being pushed around, and that can get in your way. Tempering your recklessness is necessary in order to achieve positive results from your actions.

JOYCE SAYS:

Traits to treasure: The courage and resourcefulness you display in taking action.

To transform: Avoid behaving disruptively to prove that no one can push you around.

MARS AND NEPTUNE

Mars represents drive, action, anger, and courage; Neptune, idealism, imagination, spirituality, compassion, and illusion. Aspects between them heighten creativity and idealistic action.

Mars Conjunct Neptune ♂ ☌ ♆

The best of this conjunction comes when working in creative or helping fields. Your imagination is strong and your nature, sensitive. You are a romantic at heart, creative and idealistic, and enjoy helping others, particularly those less fortunate. While you may not realize it, others can find you magnetic and glamorous. This, along with your creativity, helps in fields of entertainment or those that require selling your ideas.

Being highly imaginative, you see potentials beyond the visions of most. It is possible for you to achieve your lofty goals, but you may also choose unrealistic goals or take impractical actions in trying to achieve them.

Lack of physical energy and vitality are possible. Typically, you avoid conflict but are also capable of unconsciously starting conflict and then blaming it on others. You may act based on unconscious motivations or with subterfuge and secrecy. If you are an actor, these qualities help you blend seamlessly into your part. In everyday existence, you may lament that life is harder than it is supposed to be and seek to escape from responsibilities. This makes it important for you to avoid drugs and alcohol. It is also important to develop discrimination so as to balance ideals with everyday possibilities.

If you are a woman, you should be particularly careful when it comes to romance. You want to fall in love with the ideal, perfect person. This leads you to overlooking faults in those you love, or to having trouble finding anyone good enough to become involved with. It may be hard for you to accept that human beings are all imperfect. Over-idealism is more likely to lead to disappointment than fulfillment.

Mars Sextile or Trine Neptune   ♂ ⚹ / △ ♆

This planetary combination enhances imagination, creativity, and perhaps artistic abilities. You are idealistic and romantic, and your actions are sympathetic. You enjoy of being of service to or helping others, particularly those in need.

This planetary combination does not convey strong physical energy, but intuition and strategic ability heighten the capacity for action. If you tune in, intuitively you know when to act and when to wait. You dislike conflict, and therefore try to act in ways that promote harmony. This gives you the capacity to quietly achieve your aims.

Mars Square or Opposite Neptune   ♂ □ / ☍ ♆

This planetary combination bestows creativity and imagination. You are idealistic and romantic, and possibly glamorous and magnetic, and yet are easily discouraged. It is difficult for you to decipher when to act and when to wait, or to know precisely what actions to take in order to attain the best results. Your ideals are high, but so is your naivete, and your actions may resemble Don Quixote's fighting windmills.

Actions may be propelled by motives that are hidden from others and perhaps even unknown to yourself. There is a tendency to trust the wrong people and be taken advantage of, to be self-deceptive, or perhaps to deceive others. You abhor disagreements and typically avoid them. Yet you may also unconsciously start conflict and blame it on others. Since you see yourself as a nice person with good intentions, when it comes to disagreements, you hold yourself as the wronged party without examining situations to see your own input. This makes it difficult for you to learn from mistakes.

This planetary combination works best when working in creative or helping fields. While you will always be idealistic, it is important to face the reality that everyday life is not ideal. Otherwise, you get discouraged easily and want to escape from responsibilities. It is wise for you to avoid the use of drugs or alcohol. It is also important to develop discrimination in order to recognize the difference between fantasies and possibilities.

If you are a woman, be careful of seeking the ideal, perfect mate. This leads you to overlook faults in lovers, or to have difficulty finding anyone good enough to become involved with. Over-idealism typically leads to disappointment.

JOYCE SAYS:

Traits to treasure: The imagination and vision that allows you to see possibilities.

To transform: Beware of acting naively or falling into escapist behavior.

MARS AND PLUTO

Mars represents action, anger, and courage; Pluto, inner drive or compulsion, the power of will, and the urges to transform or destroy. Aspects between them combine drive and action with desire. This heightens willpower, drive, intensity, and the desire nature.

Mars Conjunct Pluto ♂ ☌ ♇

This conjunction gives tremendous power for constructive or destructive action. It heightens ambitions, desires, sex drive, and the willingness to stand up for principles. Personally, you want what you want and nothing else will do since your desires stem from deep inside your psyche. Hardworking, perseverant, and typically fearless, you put tremendous energy into pursuing goals. No task is too difficult once you decide upon it. And you courageously stand up for your principles and for people close to you, seeing this as a point of honor.

You thrive on competition and push to overcome your limits. Problems can arise if you become too pushy with others. The desire to get your way can lead to acting overly aggressive. Very likely, you do this because of certainty that you are right. However, these actions can cause power struggles where people are either with you or against you. Ultimately, power struggles can get in the way of accomplishing goals. This makes it of the utmost importance that you learn to listen to and respect the rights of others. Developing some detachment and learning to step back and reevaluate your goals and the means by which you go about achieving them is important, particularly if Mars and Pluto are in fixed signs. Difficult as it is for you to realize, compromise is not the same thing as selling out your principles.

Mars Sextile or Trine Pluto   ♂ ✳ / △ ♇

This planetary combination heightens your ambitions and intensifies your desires, but makes constructive action easier than with the conjunction, square, or opposition. You have endurance, willpower, and courage. Enjoyment is derived from challenges and overcoming limits.

You put a great deal of energy into achieving goals. Steadfast and self-confident; you excel at decisive action and instinctively know what to do to make things happen. While you want your way, you typically have the ability to get it without offending others. You will fight if you have to, but are good at molding (or manipulating) situations in such a way that conflict is not usually necessary.

Mars Square or Opposite Pluto   ♂ □ / ☍ ♇

This planetary combination intensifies your desire nature and heightens your ambitions. Like the conjunction, you want what you want and nothing else will do. Desires stem from deep within the psyche. You have incredible endurance, willpower, and courage, and a strong sex drive. You may use your personal power constructively or destructively. You willingly stand up for your rights, those of the people you care for, and for your principles.

You push to overcome personal limits and limits imposed by the environment. No one is going to tell you what to do or how to do it. You thrive on competition, playing to win, but whether you realize it or not, you enjoy conflict. If Mars and Pluto are in cardinal or mutable signs, you can lose your temper all too easily. If in fixed signs, you anger quickly but smolder inside, building up resentment before you finally blow up.

You are so sure that you are right and that what you want is best that you can be overly forceful and aggressive in pursuing your aims. Disagreement from others, even reasonably expressed, can be seen as an attack that must be fought off. You may even become abusive when feeling threatened or thwarted. Power struggles that get in the way of achieving your aims are likely.

Learning to control your energy without suppressing it is a necessity. The possibility of accomplishing a great deal exists when you stop wasting energy in conflict and appropriately direct it toward achievement.

JOYCE SAYS:

Traits to treasure: Your tremendous drive for achieving whatever you set out to do.

To transform: Avoid getting into conflict that interferes with achieving your aims.

Chapter 21

ASPECTS OF JUPITER AND SATURN

Jupiter is the planet of opportunity and abundance. It has to do with good fortune and the ability to reach out, grow, and learn from experience. It also has to do with values and beliefs. Aspects from the inner planets to Jupiter heighten optimism, generosity, and good luck, as well as extravagance and indulgence. Jupiter is in a sign for one year, so aspects between Jupiter and the outer planets occur around the same time for people born close together.

JUPITER AND SATURN

Jupiter and Saturn have opposite natures. Jupiter represents expansion, Saturn, contraction; Jupiter, abundance, Saturn, limitation; Jupiter, optimism, Saturn, pessimism. Jupiter emphasizes philosophical concepts while Saturn has to do with the world as it is. Aspects between Jupiter and Saturn combine the urges to reach out and grow with those of self-preservation. They also combine ideas and beliefs with the realities of everyday life.

Jupiter Conjunct Saturn   ♃ ☌ ♄

This conjunction occurs approximately every twenty years. It brings together the principles of expansion and contraction. You may naturally unite philosophical concepts and the way the things actually work, or you may need to find practical ways to express ideals so that they can work in the real world. It is important to consider ethical implications as well as practical realities in decision-making processes. At best, you display adept organizational skills and create structures that enhance opportunities. When Jupiter and Saturn are proficiently balanced, your instincts tell you when to move forward and when to wait, when to be optimistic and when to reevaluate, when to enjoy yourself and when to crank up effort. If Jupiter and Saturn are out of balance, there can be difficulty discerning among these alternatives. The sign this conjunction falls in and aspects between it and inner planets in the chart indicate how you are likely to integrate these energies. Your task is to find a balance between them.

Jupiter Sextile or Trine Saturn   ♃ ✳ / △ ♄

With Jupiter and Saturn in favorable aspect to one another, the principles of expansion and contraction are naturally combined, as are philosophical beliefs and work in the real world. You have good timing, set realistic goals, and know when to move forward and when to set limits. Idealism and practicality work together, and you have the capacity to be optimistic in the face of obstacles. How ambitious you actually are depends upon how the aspects these planets form with inner planets. A bit of tension is more likely to enhance ambition than too much ease.

Jupiter Square or Opposite Saturn   ♃ □ / ☍ ♄

The square or opposition pits the urge for expansion against the urge for contraction. You may have difficulty discerning when to move forward and when to wait. It is difficult for you to reconcile philosophical or ethical considerations with real life practicalities. You may fluctuate between optimism and pessimism. When overly optimistic, you may enter into situations without enough forethought and end up with more work and responsibility than you anticipate. When overly cautious or pessimistic, you can be so exacting that you miss opportunities. Aspects between Jupiter and Saturn and your inner planets clarify how you are likely to integrate these energies. If Saturn is stronger than Jupiter, you lean toward seeing problems. If Jupiter is stronger than Saturn, you lean toward seeing opportunities.

JOYCE SAYS:

Traits to treasure: Your capacity to combine ideals with practicalities.
To transform: Make sure that opportunities for growth and expansion are balanced with practical methods of achieving them.

JUPITER AND URANUS

These planets are idealistic. Aspects between Jupiter and Uranus combine philosophy, luck, and expansion with freedom, originality, and break-throughs. Both of these planets give the impetus to move forward. Together they change the status quo.

Jupiter Conjunct Uranus   ♃ ☌ ♅

The conjunction of these planets heightens the values of freedom and inde-pendence. Your belief system is liberal and forward-thinking. Intellectually curious, you prefer unusual ideas to more traditional concepts. If the con-junction forms aspects with inner planets, you excel at seeing new possi-bilities and stand up for progressive views that are ahead of your time. If the aspects are favorable, you have incredibly good luck.

Dislike of routine, desire for freedom, and craving for excitement can push you to take risks. You enjoy the unexpected and want life to be an adventure. This adventure may be a personal one, or you may crusade to make changes in the society you live in. You have a generous spirit that gives freely to others, but you rebel against any type of restriction.

Jupiter Sextile or Trine Uranus   ♃ ✳ / △ ♅

Favorable aspects between Jupiter and Uranus convey good luck in life. Particularly if these planets also form favorable aspects to the inner plan-ets, you instinctively to know how and when to take risks that pay off.

Your beliefs are liberal and independent and your thinking original and inventive. Learning is a lifelong process, and you are tolerant of other people's beliefs. You greatly value freedom and independence, but have no need to wave these qualities under anyone's nose (unless these planets afflict per-sonal ones).

Jupiter Square or Opposite Uranus   ♃ □ / ☍ ♅

Your beliefs are liberal, forward thinking, and very likely at odds with pre-vailing social attitudes. You stand for freedom and independence, and are attracted to what is new and out of the ordinary. There is a desire to change the status quo.

If these planets receive aspects to inner planets (particularly unfavorable ones), you dislike routine, desire freedom, and crave excitement. You are a natural rebel and refuse to be told what to do or how to do it. With the courage of your convictions, you stand up for what you believe in, and would rather go your own way than compromise. You may take actions purely for their shock value.

Problems arise because you naively believe that because you are right, you will prevail, and you expect to be luckier than you turn out to be. If you want to succeed, carefully considering the likely results of your actions rather than jumping into situations is a must. And learning to be tolerant of other people's points of view goes a long way toward warding off relational difficulties.

JOYCE SAYS:

Traits to treasure: Your adventurous spirit that gives you the ability to see new possibilities.

To transform: Avoid thumbing your nose at the status quo purely for the sake of doing so.

JUPITER AND NEPTUNE

Both planets are idealistic. Jupiter represents religion and belief systems; Neptune, talking to God directly. Jupiter rules generosity and abundance; Neptune, compassion and universal caring. Jupiter has to do with excesses, and Neptune, escapism.

All aspects between these two planets increase an interest in the spiritual or mystical and heighten caring and compassion, particularly toward those less fortunate.

Jupiter Conjunct Neptune ♃ ☌ ♆

The conjunction of Jupiter and Neptune unites religion or belief systems and spiritual ideals. Your beliefs are idealistic, compassionate, and spiritual. They embody high ideals that envision the world as it is possible to be. If these planets receive aspects from inner planets, idealistic and spiritual beliefs guide your life. There is a need to believe in something greater in order to feel fulfilled. You display caring and compassion in dealing with people and look for the good in situations.

A fertile imagination makes it possible for you to be artistically creative, a visionary, or an escapist. Sensitivities may lead you to act on behalf of those in need or to avoid looking at what is unpleasant. If Jupiter and Neptune afflict the inner planets, overcoming a rose-colored-glasses approach to life is essential. Particular discernment is needed in joining religious or spiritual groups and in recognizing that not everyone else's motives are as idealistic as yours. Also, it is important to be careful that escapism does not turn into overspending or problems with drugs or alcohol.

Jupiter Sextile or Trine Neptune   ♃ ✶ / △ ♆

Your philosophical and spiritual beliefs support one another. Your beliefs are idealistic, compassionate, and spiritually oriented. They embody high ideals for world possibilities. If these planets form aspects to inner planets, you integrate these beliefs into daily life. You look for the good in situations, are sensitive to the needs of others, and are caring and compassionate in dealing with people, particularly those less fortunate. You have a strong imagination and may be artistically creative.

If aspects between Jupiter and Neptune and the inner planets are difficult, you must be careful of an overly idealistic approach to life. If aspects between Jupiter and Neptune and the inner planets are favorable, you can more easily exercise caring and compassion with good judgment, but still have to beware of being overly idealistic. Discernment is needed to see situations as they are rather than as you would like them to be.

Jupiter Square or Opposite Neptune   ♃ □ / ☍ ♆

Religious and spiritual beliefs are extremely idealistic. You may long for a heavenly existence or cosmic unity that is beyond what is possible on earth. If Jupiter and Neptune receive difficult aspects from inner planets, expectancies are overly idealistic.

Like all those with aspects between Jupiter and Neptune, you are caring and compassionate and need some form of spiritual belief system in order to feel whole. However, in searching for the ideal, you may overlook everyday realities. You may be too trusting, expect too much from people and situations, and, with the best of intentions, promise more than you deliver. The disparity between life as it is and life as it is supposed to be can be difficult to reconcile. It is important to balance ideals with reality.

JOYCE SAYS:

Traits to treasure: Your capacity for high ideals that envision what is possible.

To transform: Recognize when high ideals are workable and when they are not.

JUPITER AND PLUTO

Both Jupiter and Pluto relate to riches. This combination of planets combines belief systems with depth perception, opportunity with power, and the urge to learn or grow with the urge to transform or destroy.

Jupiter Conjunct Pluto ♃ ♂ ♇

Your beliefs are deep and penetrating. You like to get to the bottom of ideas, philosophical constructs, or religious teachings. This planetary combination brings good fortune in accumulating financial resources.

If these planets form aspects to your inner planets, you have deeply held convictions that you want others to share, and you are strongly ambitious and desirous of success and power. If Jupiter and Pluto receive favorable aspects, you succeed in convincing others of the validity of your beliefs, gain leadership positions easily, and are lucky in accumulating large sums of money. If Jupiter and Pluto receive difficult aspects, pushing too hard to get others to agree with you creates resistance and power struggles that get in the way of achieving aims. Internally, you may alternate from feeling powerful to feeling powerless.

Jupiter Sextile or Trine Pluto ♃ ✳ / △ ♇

There is a desire to get to the bottom of ideas, philosophical constructs, or religious teachings. Your urge to grow and change and your desire for power and riches support one another. This is a lucky planetary combination. The houses that these planets fall in show where you derive that luck. If these planets receive aspects from inner planets, you are ambitious. Favorable aspects give you good organizational abilities. Self-confidence and significant faith in your beliefs help in attaining leadership positions.

Jupiter Square or Opposite Pluto   ♃ □ / ☍ ♇

There is conflict between personal beliefs or societal beliefs and your drive for power. If these planets receive aspects from inner planets, you may overstep your reach in trying to achieve goals, or upon achieving goals, wonder if that is all there is. The possibility of fluctuating between self-confidence and self-doubt exists.

If aspects with inner planets are difficult, you may be dogmatic or arrogant about your beliefs and get into power struggles with those who disagree with you. It is also possible to get into power struggles with those you perceive as standing in your way to success. Being so sure that you have the right answer makes compromise difficult. Yet power struggles of your own making impede your aims. Learning how to share power and get along with others is essential.

JOYCE SAYS:

Traits to treasure: Your abilities to see opportunities that lead to good fortune. To transform: Avoid becoming so dogmatic about your beliefs that you create unnecessary power struggles.

SATURN

Saturn is the planet of duty and responsibility. It represents the status quo, practicality, the work ethic, and also restrictions and inhibitions. Aspects from the inner planets to Saturn heighten personal discipline and responsibility and possibly fears and inhibitions. Aspects between Saturn and the outer planets are generational and occur for all people in the same age range.

SATURN AND URANUS

Saturn is in a sign for two and a half years, Uranus for seven. Aspects between these two planets occur for everyone in the same age range. They represent the pulls between tradition and inventiveness, the status quo and breakthrough, duty and freedom.

Saturn Conjunct Uranus   ♄ ☌ ♅

This aspect occurs approximately every forty-five years. It occurred in 1942 and 1988. This conjunction unites responsibility and freedom, the status quo with the urge for change. This generation has the task of making pragmatic changes in the social structure. To do so, as an individual, it is necessary to balance these forces within yourself. At best, Saturn and Uranus unite the best of the past with what is possible for the future. Practicality combines with originality and responsibility with individuality. At worst, these principles fight one another. On a societal level, this creates conflict between the past and the future. On a personal level, it creates conflict between caution and change and increases the likelihood of problems with authority. It can seem difficult to live up to traditional expectations and be true to yourself. The entire chart shows how you are likely to handle this conjunction.

Saturn Sextile or Trine Uranus   ♄ ✶ / △ ♅

Your generation is a bridge between the past and the future. Favorable aspects between Saturn and Uranus make it possible to make pragmatic changes in the social structure harmoniously. Instead of fighting one another, the past and the future somehow blend together. As an individual, you embody this blend. You balance responsibility with freedom, practicality with originality, and duty with autonomy. You can take the best of the past and combine it with what is needed for the future. Since Saturn and Uranus are both outer planets, their aspects with inner planets more specifically reflect how you utilize this energy.

Saturn Square or Opposite Uranus   ♄ □ / ☍ ♅

All aspects between Saturn and Uranus have to do with making changes in the social structure. Difficult aspects indicate conflict in doing so for your generation. The square and opposition pit the status quo against the future and inertia against change. For you as an individual, a conflict exists between conformity and personal freedom and traditional expectations and individual liberty. Depending upon the makeup of your entire chart, you may preserve the status quo, revolt against authority, or alternate back and forth between the two. Your challenge is to find a way to be both free and responsible at the same time.

JOYCE SAYS:

Traits to treasure: Your concern for both personal freedom and individual responsibility.

To transform: Avoid either getting stuck in the past or, alternatively, too readily throwing away tradition purely for the sake of change.

SATURN AND NEPTUNE

Saturn is in a sign for two and a half years, Neptune for fourteen years. Aspects between these two planets are generational and occur simultaneously for everyone in the same age range. Saturn represents the realities of everyday life—practicality, the work ethic, and responsibilities. Neptune represents spirituality, psychic ability, compassion, and escapism. Saturn has to do with the outer world; Neptune, the inner world. Aspects between Saturn and Neptune combine materialism with spirituality and practicality with idealism.

Saturn Conjunct Neptune ♄ ☌ ♆

This conjunction occurs approximately every thirty-five years. It occurred in 1953 and 1989. It combines the practical considerations with spirituality. It may unite the realities of everyday living with the ideals of the way life should be, or self-preservation can conflict with compassion, and practicality with dreams and visions. If Saturn and Neptune work together, the likelihood of making your dreams come true exists. If Saturn and Neptune pull against one another, too much practicality may obliterate possibilities, or overly idealistic dreams may override practical considerations necessary for accomplishment. Aspects between Saturn and Neptune and inner planets in your chart indicate more specifically how this conjunction affects you.

Saturn Sextile or Trine Neptune ♄ ⚹ / △ ♆

These aspects make it possible to move toward a higher purpose by balancing practical considerations with compassion or spiritual ideals. Intuition and pragmatism work together. Those in your age range balance the realities of day-to-day life with aesthetic, spiritual, or idealistic pursuits. If Saturn and Neptune are in favorable aspects to your inner planets, you have the capacity to act in such a way that more easily makes your dreams come true.

Saturn Square or Opposite Neptune   ♄ □ / ☍ ♆

These aspects pit practicality against idealism for those in your age range. The responsibilities and demands of everyday life conflict with dreams and ideals. You may feel as if you can do what is needed or you can do what is ideal, but not both. The longing for a kinder, gentler world may engender unrealistic goals. Practicality can turn into pessimism that thwarts your dreams, or self-preservation instincts can kill off compassion. Or you can bounce back and forth between being overly idealistic and overly cautious. It is essential to balance these two planets, particularly if they aspect personal planets, in order to have both dreams and ideals and to achieve them.

JOYCE SAYS:

Traits to treasure: Your concern for both ideals and practical realities.
To transform: Avoid letting dreams obliterate practicalities or practicalities obliterate dreams.

SATURN AND PLUTO

Saturn is in a sign for two and a half years, Pluto anywhere from twelve to thirty-two. Aspects between them are generational and occur simultaneously for everyone in a certain age range. Saturn represents the outer world, authority, the status quo, and responsibility. Pluto represents mass consciousness and transformation as well as the inner world, unconscious urges, desires, and personal power. Aspects between Saturn and Pluto combine urges for power and authority and have to do with outer achievements and inner drives.

Saturn Conjunct Pluto   ♄ ☌ ♇

This conjunction occurred in 1947, 1982, and 1983. It unites authority with power and control, and deep inner desires with the urge for outer achievement. People your age have strong ambitions for status and power. If this conjunction receives aspects from inner planets, you possess the determination needed to achieve your desires, and willingly put in the time, effort, and energy it takes to do so. Hard work does not threaten you.

This conjunct may cause inner struggles, particularly if it receives difficult aspects from personal planets. There can be resistance to change, fear of scarcity, or overreaction to perceived threats. You may see the world as a cold, hard place that you need to control in order to be safe. This makes it imperative that you do not use extreme measures in pursuing your goals. This conjunction portends great power for "good or evil." The house that Saturn and Pluto fall in depicts your greatest ambitions and possibly your greatest fears.

Saturn Sextile or Trine Pluto   ♄ ⚹ / △ ♇

These aspects make it possible for people in your age group to make societal changes in an orderly fashion. If Saturn or Pluto receive positive aspects from inner planets, desires and ambitions support one another, self-expression is positively controlled, and you respond well to pressure. This makes you well-organized, a skilled strategist, and a disciplined worker. You have the ability to attain power and control without necessarily antagonizing other people.

Saturn Square or Opposite Pluto   ♄ □ / ☍ ♇

These aspects pit power and control against one another in your age group. Inner urges can conflict with outer authority. Strong desires and ambitions exist. If these planets receive aspects from your inner planets, you are determined to achieve selected goals. Heavy responsibilities are likely, and life has a way of presenting you with obstacles that you must work hard to overcome. You may also create your own difficulties. Problems with authority may arise, as you refuse to be told what to do or how to do it. You may resist change, even when change is for the better. And in your determination to achieve goals, it is possible to become cold and calculating and ignore the needs of others. These aspects make it essential to balance power and control urges with the needs and rights of others.

JOYCE SAYS:
Traits to treasure: Your ambition and incredible drive to accomplish what you want.
To transform: Avoid becoming Machiavellian in pursuing your goals.

Chapter 22

ASPECTS OF URANUS, NEPTUNE, AND PLUTO

Uranus represents individuality, independence, originality, and freedom, as well as sudden change and disruption. Uranus also rules science and has to do with the intellect. It is the planet associated with revolution. Aspects from the inner planets to Uranus heighten self-sufficiency and possibly erratic behavior. Aspects between Uranus and the outer planets are generational and affect everyone within the same age group.

URANUS AND NEPTUNE

Uranus is in a sign for seven years, Neptune for fourteen. Aspects between them are generational and have to do with the Zeitgeist. They combine originality and creativity, individuality and compassion, and science and spirituality.

Uranus Conjunct Neptune ♅ ☌ ♆

This conjunction occurs approximately every 170 years, the last one in the early 1990s in Capricorn. A conjunction of these planets combines idealism and innovation, and intellect and intuition. Your generation was born to make fundamental changes in the world, combining the compassion it takes to help humanity with the urges for scientific and intellectual advancement. Ideally, your generation helps those less fortunate by showing them how to help themselves. Aspects to this conjunction in your chart show how you integrate this energy.

Uranus Sextile or Trine Neptune ⛢ ⁎ / △ ♆

Your generation was born at a time when spiritual ideals and scientific ones supported each other, and you embody this combination. Scientific breakthroughs can occur based upon intuition, and it is possible to blend individual needs with compassion for others. How this planetary combination affects you individually depends upon the houses these planets fall in and the aspects they receive from other planets.

Uranus Square or Opposite Neptune ⛢ □ / ☍ ♆

This configuration pushes for reform or revolution. Your generation was born at a time when individuality and idealism confronted one another. There may be conflict between spiritual ideals and intellectual ones. The influence of this planetary combination depends upon the houses that Uranus and Neptune fall in and the aspects they receive from other planets. It is possible for your definition of doing what is right or ideal to conflict with your need for individuality. This leads to thinking that you can either live up to what you believe a good person would do or that you can be true to yourself rather than looking for ways to satisfy both ideals.

JOYCE SAYS:
Traits to treasure: Your generation's ability to combine individuality with compassion and intellect with intuition.
To transform: Avoid acting without concern for others or letting the needs of the collective override personal needs.

URANUS AND PLUTO

Uranus is in a sign for seven years, Pluto for twelve to thirty-two. Aspects between them apply to a generation of people. They have to do with the Zeitgeist in which they occur and how those born in a particular generation affect the times they live in. Both planets have to do with change; Uranus in a revolutionary way, Pluto as a transformational influence.

Uranus Conjunct Pluto   ♅ ☌ ♇

This revolutionary conjunction occurs approximately every 115 years, the last time being in the 1960s in Virgo. Your generation places a high value on freedom and individuality and has the role of transforming society. Born at the beginning of the computer era, this generation has produced many entrepreneurs in science and technology, and their start-up companies have revolutionized the workplace.

How this conjunction affects you depends upon the house that it falls in and the aspects it receives from other planets. If its aspects are from inner planets, you are entrepreneurial, a law unto yourself, and abhor the status quo.

Uranus Sextile or Trine Pluto   ♅ ⚹ / △ ♇

Your generation instinctively knows how to progress on social, scientific, and humanitarian issues in order to transform society. For you individually, particularly if these two planets favorably relate to your inner planets, freedom and independence urges easily combine with the urge for personal power.

Uranus Square or Opposite Pluto   ♅ □ / ☍ ♇

Your generation shakes up the society into which you were born. Social and political upheavals are common in your lifetime, and your generation supports what other generations consider extreme doctrines. These two planets in difficult aspects put the urges for freedom and independence in conflict with the urges for power and control.

If Uranus or Pluto receive aspects from your personal planets, it is possible for you to be involved with the events of the times. If either Uranus or Pluto receives squares or oppositions to your personal planets, you seek freedom and power. You are likely to be combative in your fight for justice and lack the ability to compromise. There is a need to guard against excessive self-will and intolerance of another's point of view.

JOYCE SAYS:

Traits to treasure: Your generation's abilities to revolutionize and transform society.

To transform: Avoid getting caught up in excessive self-will or self-righteousness.

NEPTUNE

Neptune represents creativity, beauty, spirituality, and idealism on the positive side and fog, illusion, escapism, deception, and victimization on the negative side. Aspects from the inner planets to Neptune heighten idealism, creativity, and spirituality, as well as possibilities for naivete and escapism. Aspects between Neptune and the outer planets are generational and affect everyone in the same age range.

Neptune Sextile Pluto ♆ ✳ ♇

Aspects between Neptune and Pluto are generational. Pluto brings elements of death and rebirth, destruction and reform. Both these planets have to do with subconscious and unconscious urges. Neptune and Pluto have been traveling in and out of a sextile the since the 1940s. This planetary combination represents an opportunity for spiritual advancement and ideally the possibility of bringing about compassionate change.

JOYCE SAYS:
Traits to treasure: Your generation has the opportunity to be involved in idealistic transformation.

PLUTO

Pluto is the planet of death and rebirth. It has to do with inner drives and compulsions. Since it is the outermost planet (most of the time), all aspects to Pluto from others planets have been previously discussed.

ABOUT THE AUTHOR

J oyce Levine is "the astrologer's astrologer" and has been a professional in the field for more than thirty years. She is a member of the National Council for Geocosmic Research Executive Committee and has been a board member for the United Astrology Conference. Joyce Levine speaks and teaches regularly and has contributed to many astrological publications such as *Dell Horoscope, Horoscope Guide, American Astrology,* and media such as *The Boston Globe* and A&E's *The Unexplained.* She lives in Boston, Massachusetts.

You can get a free copy of your chart at the following web site addresses:

http://www.joycelevine.com
http://www.alabe.com